Encyclopedia of
Craft Projects
for the first time®

Encyclopedia of Craft Projects

for the first time®

Vanessa-Ann

Ann Benson

Rebecca Carter

Syndee Holt

Carol Scheffler

Linda Orton

A Main Street Book

Material in this collection adapted from the following:
Beading for the First Time © 2001 by Ann Benson
Polymer Clay for the First Time © 2000 by Chapelle Ltd.
Rubber Stamping for the First Time © 1999 by Chapelle Ltd.
Scrapbooking for the First Time © 1999 by Chapelle Ltd.
Soapmaking for the First Time © 2001 by Linda Orton
Candlemaking for the First Time © 2001 by Chapelle Ltd.

Library of Congress Cataloging-in-Publication Data Available

1 3 5 7 9 10 8 6 4 2

Main Street is an imprint of Sterling Publishing Co. Inc.

© 2002 by Sterling Publishing Co., Inc.
Published by Sterling Publishing Co., Inc.
387 Park Avenue South, New York, NY 10016
Distributed in Canada by Sterling Publishing
℅ Canadian Manda Group, One Atlantic Avenue, Suite 105
Toronto, Ontario, Canada M6K 3E7
Distributed in Australia by Capricorn Link (Australia) Pty Ltd.
P.O. Box 704, Windsor, NSW 2756, Australia
Printed in China
All rights reserved

Sterling ISBN 1-4027-0512-3

CONTENTS

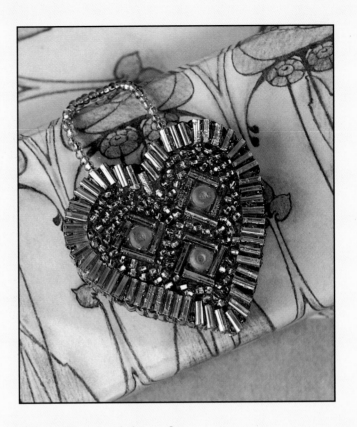

Polymer Clay for the First Time

Rubber Stamping for the First Time

Scrapbooking for the First Time

Soapmaking for the First Time

BEADING
for the first time®

Ann Benson

Beading for the first time

Introduction

The history of the use of beads as decorative accents dates back to pieces found that were used by people of ancient cultures. It spans thousands of years and not only connects every continent, but every civilization of the world.

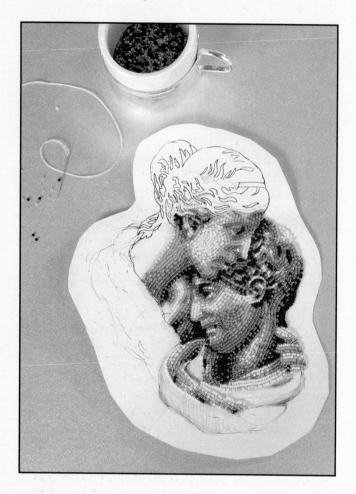

Beads have been in existence since at least 2500 B.C. Examples of beadwork from that era, found at the tombs of Ur, were created with thousands of tiny, fairly consistently sized lapis lazuli beads.

In Egypt, there is evidence that billions of small beads were made for the express purpose of beadwork. As early as 500 B.C., the netted technique, commonly called the "gourd stitch," was developed and used for beadwork, broad collars, funerary jewelry, and mummy nets.

Around 200 B.C., bead manufacturers developed the process of making drawn beads. This formula made possible the production of mass quantities of small, uniformly sized and shaped beads.

The evolution of modern beadwork has been directly influenced by the law of supply and demand. Initially, these drawn beads, known as "Indo-Pacific" beads, were used like currency for the purpose of goods exchange by European explorers who traveled to Africa and Asia.

Similarly, beads were introduced to the Western Hemisphere with the arrival of the European explorers sent to claim and colonize the North and South American continents.

It is assumed that in every case, the traders were successful in exchanging the beads by demonstrating to the native peoples how the beads could be incorporated into other textile arts, such as weaving.

Beads became widely available only after there was interest expressed in incorporating them into already practiced arts and crafts.

Beadwork has evolved over time to satisfy changing fashion trends and desires of the culture. In response to demands for more refined beads, smaller and more colorful beads became available. Subsequently, scale, patterns, and intricacy of workmanship have also changed.

Through various beading techniques and combination of bead types and colors, beadworkers have found the medium to be perfectly suited to artistic expression. Many say they experience a sense of calm and joy while working with the delicate pieces of glass.

Getting Started *What do I need to get started?*

Beads

Seed Beads: Most of us are familiar with these small beads that are often used in traditional Native American jewelry. They are round or oval in shape and have a centered hole.

Seed beads are made of glass that is heated to a molten state. Generally, the beads are colored when metals and other chemicals are infused into the molten mixture. The molten glass is extruded to form beads. When cooled, the beads are sorted for size, from 15/0 (very tiny) to 6/0 (the largest seed bead).

There are no standard packages for beads. Each company that sells beads to an individual consumer has its own put-up size. The following scale may help you determine the number of packages to purchase:

For size 14/0 seed beads:
    1 gram = approximately 200 beads
For size 11/0 seed beads:
    1 gram = approximately 120 beads

Delica Seed Beads: Delica seed beads are also quite small, corresponding roughly to 11/0 seed bead size. The beads are extruded to have a large hole and thin wall, and the shape is tubular. They are excellent for needle-weaving techniques such as the brick stitch on page 50 and the peyote stitch on page 53, because of their consistency in size and shape and because their large holes will accommodate several passes of thread (which is necessary in some weaving techniques). Delicas are readily available in a very wide range of colors and finishes.

Hex Seed Beads: Hex seed beads are six-sided extruded beads with very large holes and very thin walls. They are similar in size to delicas, but the range of colors and finishes is quite a bit more limited. They are also excellent for weaving and are not too difficult to find.

Three-cut Seed Beads: Three-cut seed beads come in two sizes, 12/0 and 9/0. They are literally cut after extrusion to form the flat shiny surfaces that give them a faceted look. The range of colors and finishes is extremely limited, but three-cuts are widely used nevertheless—they are favored on elegant evening clothes because of their extreme sparkle and shine. Note: The holes may be inconsistent, so buy more than you think you will need as a good percentage might be unusable.

Bugle Beads: Bugle beads are long narrow beads with a center hole running the length of the bead. They range from #1 (approximately 2 mm long) to 25 mm (roughly 1"). Occasionally, bugle beads can be found in even longer lengths, but availability is very inconsistent. The most popular sizes to work with are #2 (4 mm), #3 (6 mm), and #5 (12 mm). Generally, bugle beads are used to embellish a design mainly worked in seed beads. Bugle beads work especially well in hand- or loom-woven designs.

Fancy Glass Beads: Available in so many varieties, it is impossible to describe all of the fancy glass beads. Most bead stores and mail-order catalogs will have hundreds of different styles, and most of those styles will come in a range of colors and finishes. Some are merely one color of glass formed into a ball with a beading hole, while others may also incorporate precious metal foils or threads of colored glass.

Faceted Crystal Beads: These cut-crystal beads have a wonderful diamond-like fire when light-struck. They are made of fine quality glass (usually with a high lead content) and are shaped by a mechanized cutting process. They are extremely expensive but readily available.

Cut-crystal beads are available in many shapes and sizes, from 4 mm cone-shaped beads to 18 mm ovals. They are available in a good range of colors (mostly transparent).

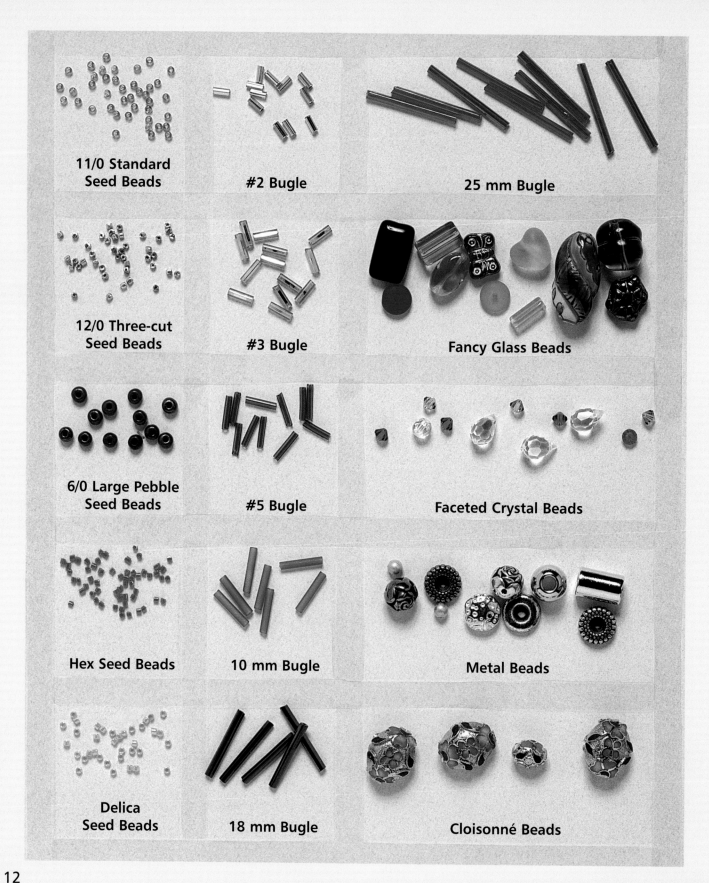

11/0 Standard Seed Beads

#2 Bugle

25 mm Bugle

12/0 Three-cut Seed Beads

#3 Bugle

Fancy Glass Beads

6/0 Large Pebble Seed Beads

#5 Bugle

Faceted Crystal Beads

Hex Seed Beads

10 mm Bugle

Metal Beads

Delica Seed Beads

18 mm Bugle

Cloisonné Beads

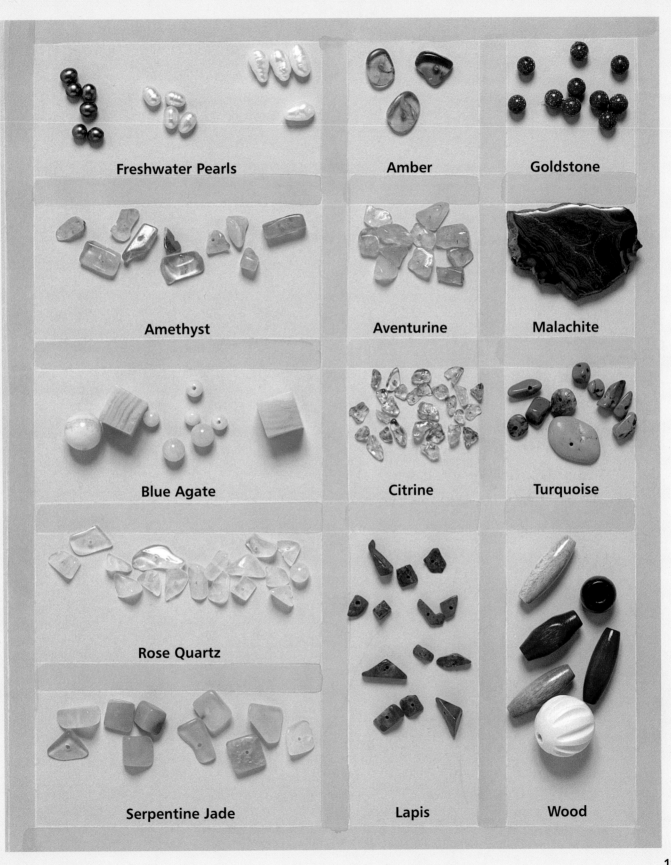

Freshwater Pearls

Amber

Goldstone

Amethyst

Aventurine

Malachite

Blue Agate

Citrine

Turquoise

Rose Quartz

Serpentine Jade

Lapis

Wood

13

Natural Beads: Natural beads offer a tremendous range of selection. Bone, wood, semiprecious stones—all are easy to find and the choices of color and shape are unlimited. Most bead suppliers carry natural beads (such as turquoise, amethyst, and citrine) in chips of varying grades and finished beads of assorted shapes and sizes.

Most carved beads are made from semiprecious stones; turquoise, amethyst, cinnabar, and some hard quartzes are frequently rendered into recognizable shapes and symbols for use in jewelry-making. Some of the harder semiprecious stones, for instance rose quartz or yellow topaz, are available in faceted shapes. Natural beads are useful in jewelry-making and for embellishing designs that are mainly worked in seed beads.

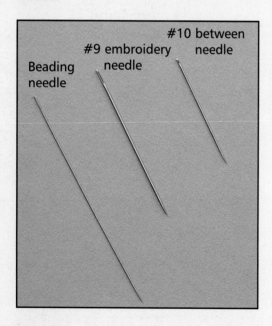

Needles

Needles are essential for almost every technique and project in this book. Make certain to have a good assortment of sharp needles on hand.

Beading needles are traditionally long and thin to accommodate many beads at one time. These needles are particularly useful when stringing strands of beads for bracelets, necklaces, and long fringes. Beading needles are also well suited to weaving on a loom as they can catch several beads at a time when making the return trip on the weft thread.

Traditional beading needles are not well suited for beading on surfaces or needle-weaving. The smaller #9 embroidery needle is ideal when working with seed beads size 11/0 or larger. For some finely drilled stones and pearls, a #10 between needle is recommended.

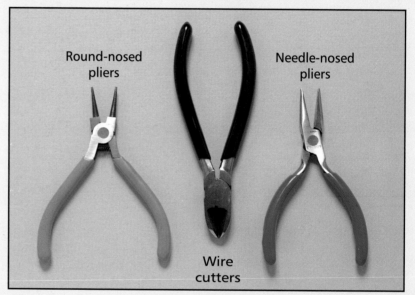

Tools

Several projects require the use of pliers and wire cutters. Round-nosed pliers are used mainly for forming loops in wire eye pins and head pins. Needle-nosed pliers are used for closing loops, flattening and closing crimps, and attaching rings. Wire cutters are used for trimming head pins, eye pins, and beading wire.

You do not have to make a special trip to the craft store to purchase these tools as they are commonly found in most hardware stores. As you become more involved in beading as a needleart, you may require more specialized tools for accomplishing the more difficult techniques. In such case, there are some very fine bead mail-order companies that can accommodate your needs.

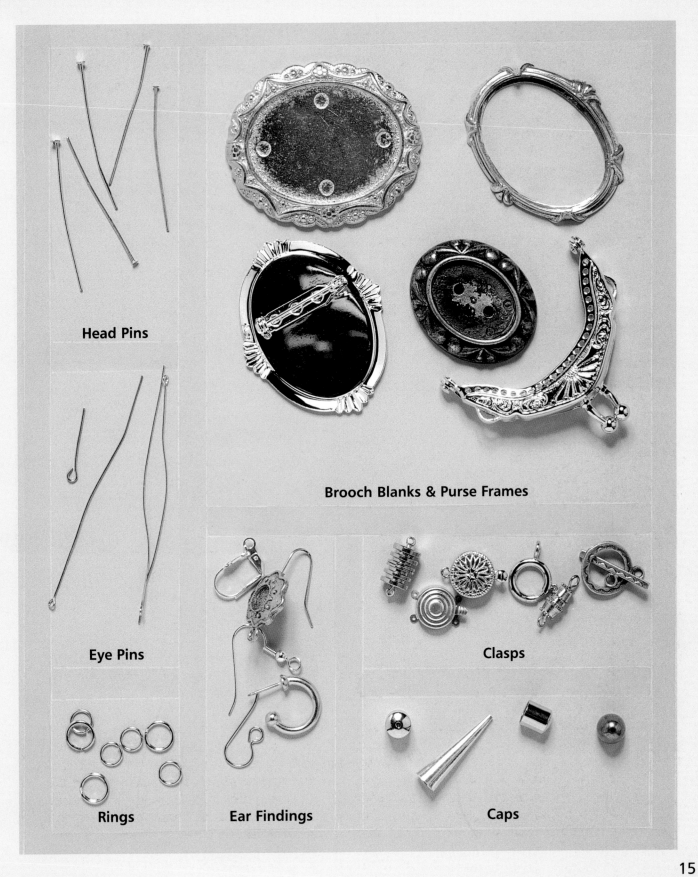

Head Pins

Brooch Blanks & Purse Frames

Eye Pins

Clasps

Rings

Ear Findings

Caps

Jewelry Components

It is easy to make beautiful beaded accessories using jewelry components, also known as "findings." Some strung beadwork (open ended strands, as opposed to continuous loops) will require a component—in most cases, a clasp. Here is an overview of the various sorts of components and their uses:

Head Pins: Head pins are used to attach beads to other types of components such as ear wires and necklace blanks. They are long rigid wires with one end flattened to prevent the bead from slipping off.

Eye Pins: Eye pins are similar to head pins but instead of a flattened end, there is a loop on one end to which a head pin might be attached.

Rings: Rings are often used to attach beads mounted on head pins or eye pins to another component. Rings are also used to form the end of a necklace to which a one-sided clasp such as a claw clasp has been attached. Rings allow free movement of a dropped head pin, which would otherwise be restricted in its movement to one direction.

Brooch Blanks: Brooch blanks are formed metal shapes (some with pin backs already attached) on which beadwork may be mounted. Some blanks that would ordinarily be used to hold a single large cabochon (an oval stone with a flat back, usually of a semiprecious stone such as turquoise or rose quartz) can be used for small pieces of beadwork.

Purse Frames: Purse frames are also made of formed metal and are available in a variety of finishes. These are a very effective type of closure for needle-woven bags.

Ear Findings: Ear findings are available in a wide assortment of styles and types, from simple wires to preformed ear studs with loops for attaching beads. Note: Clip-on earrings are easy to find for those who do not have pierced ears.

Clasps: Clasps are used to close bead strands. Most clasps are two-part metal units that open and close. There are many different types of clasps, some quite decorative; such clasps can become an element of design as opposed to a piece of hardware.

Caps: Caps are used to finish a string or multiple strings of beads. Caps are cylindrical or conical, made of metal, and contain an eye pin. The completed string(s) of beads is knotted onto the eye pin and covered with the cap. The remaining end of the eye pin is then attached to a clasp or ring.

Crimps: Crimps are small tubes of metal that are crushed with pliers or a specific crimping tool to hold wires or cords together. They are useful in attaching clasps to necklaces made of wire.

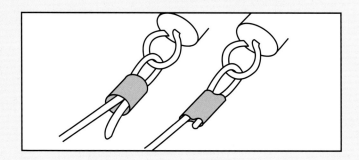

Necklace Blanks: Necklace blanks are generally found in most mail-order catalogs. These can be simple chains or rigid formed wire. Most have clasps already attached, so all you need to do is attach your beads using another component such as a bail or head pin.

Looms

Looms can be very helpful in weaving large (or long) pieces that might otherwise be cumbersome to handle. Good looms can be found in many different sizes and qualities. Some are adjustable to accommodate weaves several inches wide, while others are limited to 2"–3" of width.

All operate on basically the same principle—long or vertical threads (called warp) are placed on the loom and stretched tight. Beads are then attached to these warp threads, using a needle and thread in a horizontal direction, creating weft threads.

The manufacturer of your chosen loom will supply specific directions for attaching warp and finishing the ends of a loomed piece of beadwork. In most cases, the warp can be rolled up at the bottom end so the weave can be quite long. As the work progresses, roll the woven beadwork back and the reserve warp forward.

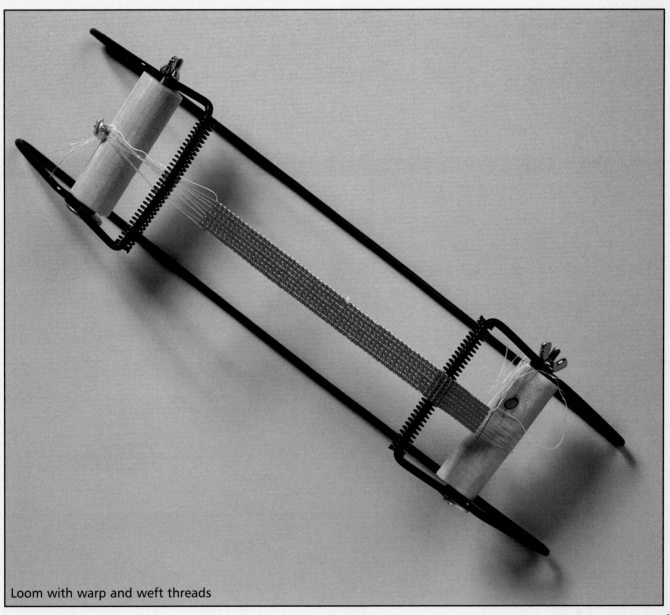

Loom with warp and weft threads

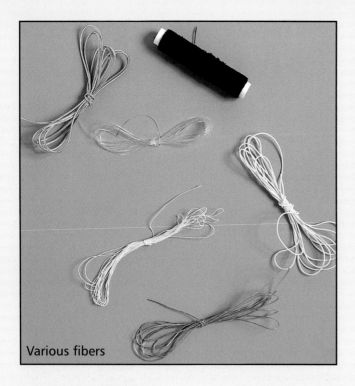

Various fibers

In many cases, the thread or cord will be stiff enough to slip through a bead's hole without the use of a needle. However, lighter weight fibers require the use of a needle. Choosing a needle can be tricky as the eye of the needle must accommodate the thread and still pass through the bead. Another option is to use tape to form a "shoelace" end.

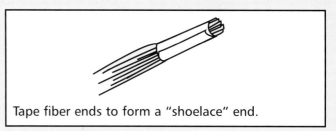

Tape fiber ends to form a "shoelace" end.

Choosing a Fiber

For stringing beads, almost any kind of flexible thread or cord can be used, providing the holes of the beads will accommodate the thread's diameter.

A fiber of an appropriate weight is essential for a nice presentation. For example, very heavy beads must be strung on a substantial fiber, such as elastic, heavy nylon, perle cotton, or multifilament rayon. Nylon monofilament, which is similar to fishing line, is also a good choice for projects with a good deal of weight.

When choosing a fiber, consider the drape of your project. For example, if you are working a necklace and want the necklace to move freely, light silk or nylon, perhaps doubled for strength, is a good choice. But if you want the necklace to take on a defined shape, or to curve predictably, you should use a lightweight twisted wire or nylon monofilament.

For beading on surfaces, needle-weaving, and weaving on a loom, ordinary sewing thread is used most often. A neutral or coordinating color looks best.

Length of Thread

Unless otherwise indicated, cut a 24"–30" length of thread to begin the project. Thread the needle. Slip beads on needle and work beading design, according to project instructions. Note: A longer thread tends to tangle, and a shorter thread necessitates frequent threadings.

Adding a New Length of Thread

When approximately 3" of thread remain unbeaded on the needle and the design is not yet complete, it is time to add a new thread.

Remove the needle from the old thread and cut a new 24"–30" length. Thread the needle, leaving a 5" tail. Tie the end of the old thread and the end of the new thread in a square knot, positioning the knot about 1" from the last bead.

Place a tiny dot of glue on the knot. Wipe off any excess glue and continue beading as if one continuous thread were being used. Note: The glue need not be dry before proceeding.

Allow the thread ends to protrude from the work until the new thread is well established within the design. Pull gently on the knotted ends and clip them close so that they disappear into the design.

Patterns for Beading

For stringing beads, follow individual project instructions for beading order. Many projects include full-color diagrams to help illustrate the written instructions.

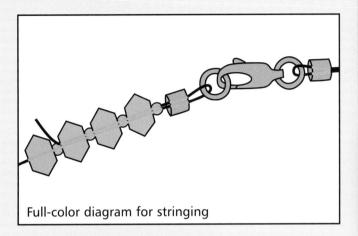

Full-color diagram for stringing

When beading on card stock, the best method for transferring a design is to photocopy it directly onto the card stock.

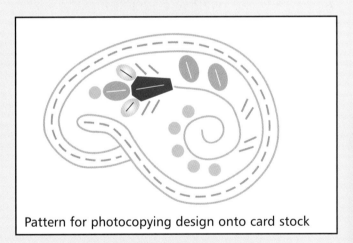

Pattern for photocopying design onto card stock

For beading on fabric, trace the design directly from this book, using a transfer pencil to draw your design onto paper first. Iron the traced design onto the fabric surface. Remember that the design must initially be reversed, or it will come out in mirror image. Another option is to use a light source from underneath. Place the fabric over the design and tape both to a window; trace the design that will emerge as the light shines through.

Beads can be placed to completely cover a design in a printed fabric, or to enhance the printed design.

Beads placed to cover design

An original design can also be sketched directly onto washable fabric using a #2 pencil, which will wash out after one or two launderings. If the sketched design is to be covered entirely in beads, you can use a fine-tipped permanent marker.

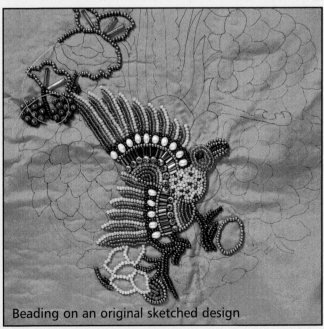

Beading on an original sketched design

The patterns and color keys provided for squared needle-weaving may remind you of counted cross-stitch patterns. One gridded oval represents one bead to be worked into the design. Each colored oval found on the pattern corresponds to a specific size and color of bead, identified on the key which accompanies the pattern.

The pattern is drawn to show vertical rows of beads. Each subsequent row is attached to the previous vertical row by a series of evenly spaced loops of thread. Note: The ideal pattern is to loop after every third bead. In some cases, where great strength is desired, you may want to loop more frequently.

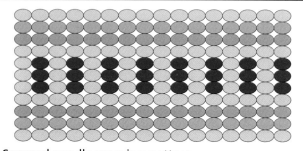
Squared needle-weaving pattern

The patterns and color keys provided for brick stitch needle-weaving and peyote stitch needle-weaving are similar to patterns for squared needle-weaving. However, these patterns are different in that they are drawn to show staggered rows of beads that create a diagonal effect when the design is woven.

The brick stitch causes beads to lie against one another

Brick stitch needle-weaving pattern

horizontally while the peyote stitch causes beads to lie vertically against one another.

For each weaving technique, the rows are initially somewhat unstable and may seem difficult to work. Be patient! After two or three rows, the weaving will be quite easy to handle.

Beading Tips

Spilled Beads: There is no use crying over spilled beads. Instead, put a new bag in your vacuum cleaner and vacuum them up. If only a few
beads spilled, wet the tip of your finger to pick them up.

Static Cling: A moistened paper towel reduces the static electricity that builds up around glass beads. Place the wet towel on your flat container while working.

Jumping Beads: If you store your beads in a plastic bag, they will probably try to jump out when you open it. Blow into the bag lightly and the moisture from your breath will settle the beads enough to pour them out.

Counting Beads: It is very tempting when weaving to loop away without recounting your beads after threading on a very long row—but you will only do this once. If you have to remove a row, first pull the needle off the thread. Then use the tip of the needle to gently pull the thread out of the beads.

Organization: Sort beads and place them in small containers with flat, small-lipped lids. A muffin tin also comes in handy as a useful organizer.

Removing Beads: If you accidentally sew on the wrong color or a misshapen bead, or if your work is puckering, remove the offending bead by breaking it off with needle-nosed pliers. Close your eyes and look away as the bead breaks.

How do I use glue to decorate an object with beads?

**What You
Need to
Get Started:**

<u>Beads:</u>
#2 and/or #3
 bugle beads:
 light green (300)
11/0 seed beads:
 light green (300)
6/0 seed beads:
 light green (6)

<u>Etc.:</u>
#9 embroidery
 needle
Jewelry glue
Thread: light green
Wooden blank:
 heart-shaped,
 1½"

Beads can be glued to most surfaces. Curved or shaped surfaces can present problems when using other beading techniques. However, there are lots of possibilities when beading with glue. This sparkling ornament is created by gluing beads onto all sides of a three-dimensional wooden blank.

Glued Heart Ornament

Here's How:
Note: You will need a clear-drying glue with a strong bond, but one that will allow you some working time. A thirty-minute dry time is ideal.

1. Select beads by comparing bugle beads to one side edge of wooden blank, and choosing size that most closely matches (but is not larger than) width of side edge.

2. Apply glue liberally onto side edge. Using tip of needle, set bugle beads into glue. Allow to dry.

3. Using needle and thread, string beads to desired length for ornament hanger.

4. Glue thread ends of hanger onto back side of wooden blank. Note: You will be working on this side first. Beads will cover thread ends.

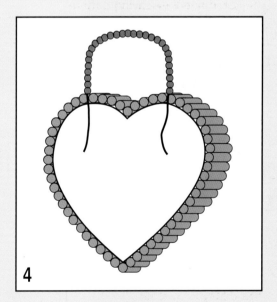

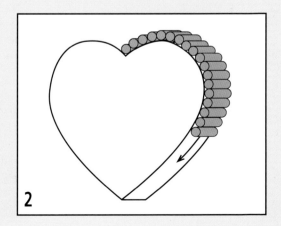

5. Form and glue border of #2 bugle beads around outside edge of back side, adjusting position of beads to accommodate shape.

6. Glue three units of four #3 bugle beads around one 6/0 bead. Fill and glue remaining areas with 11/0 seed beads. Allow to dry. Note: Seed beads look better when placed on their sides so holes are not visible, unless flat placement is part of design.

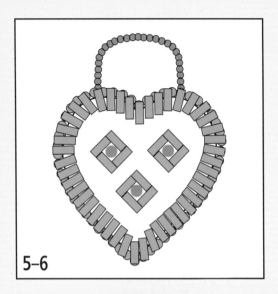

5–6

7. Repeat Steps 5–6 for top side of wooden blank.

Troubleshooting:

To ensure a good grip on the beads, allow the glue to seep into the bead's hole. Do not be afraid to bury the bead in glue. As it dries, the glue will shrink and become clear to reveal the bead.

Avoid glue buildup that may interfere with bead placement by keeping a wet paper towel nearby to clean the tip of your placement tool as needed.

Work in small sections so you can arrange the beads as desired before the glue dries.

When gluing beads on a multisurfaced object, allow each side to dry before going on to the next.

Once the glue dries you cannot go back and shift beads. So do not allow one slightly-out-of-place bead to bother you. Your design does not have to be perfectly symmetrical.

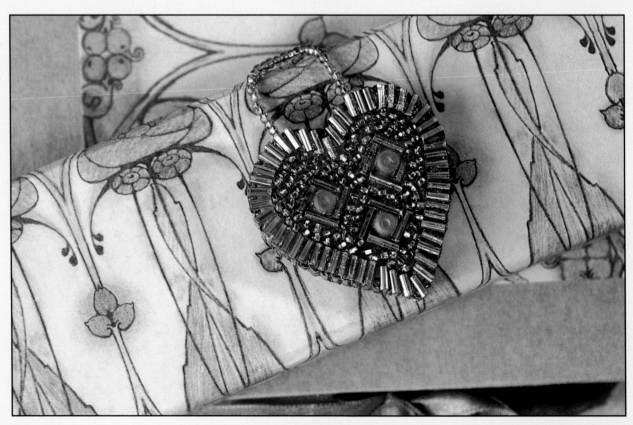

How do I string beads on wire?

Beaded wires can be twisted into three-dimensional shapes and used in a variety of ways. This design is made by stringing beads on wires to create three flowers and two leaf clusters, then twisting all wires together to form the napkin ring.

Beaded Wire Napkin Ring
Photograph on page 25.

Here's How:
1. Cut twenty-eight 12" lengths of wire.

2. For turquoise flower, slip lavender seed bead on seven wires to middle of length. Fold each wire. Slip blue lace agate bead on one doubled wire. Slip one turquoise squared tube on each remaining doubled wire. Twist remaining length of each wire starting beyond last bead. Position all beaded wires together and twist as one.

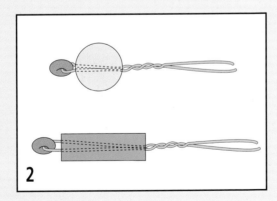

3. For amethyst flower, slip lavender seed bead on six wires to middle of length. Fold each wire. Slip rose quartz bead on one doubled wire. Slip one amethyst flat bead on each remaining doubled wire. Twist remaining length of each wire starting beyond last bead. Position all beaded wires together and twist as one.

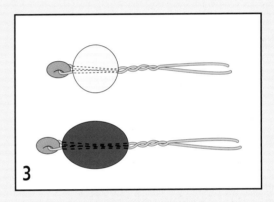

4. For flourite flower, slip three lavender seed beads, one flourite flat bead and three more lavender seed beads on five wires to middle of length. Fold each wire. Twist remaining length of each wire starting beyond last bead. Position all beaded wires together and twist as one.

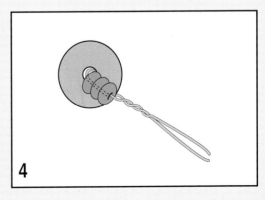

23

5. For light green leaf, slip one light green seed bead on wire to middle of length. Fold wire. Slip one light green seed bead on doubled wire. Separate wire ends. Slip eleven light green seed beads on each end of wire. Double wire ends again. Slip eight light green seed beads on doubled wire. Twist remaining length of each wire starting beyond last bead.

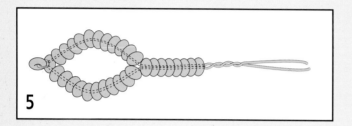

6. For medium green leaf, slip one medium green seed bead on wire to middle of length. Fold wire. Slip one medium green seed bead on doubled wire. Separate wire ends. Slip nine medium green seed beads on each end of wire. Double wire ends again. Slip six medium green seed beads on doubled wire. Twist remaining length of each wire starting beyond last bead. Repeat for second leaf.

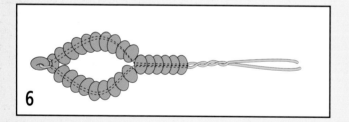

7. For dark green leaf, slip one dark green seed bead on wire to middle of length. Fold wire. Slip one dark green seed bead on doubled wire. Separate wire ends. Slip eight dark green seed beads on each end of wire. Double wire ends again. Slip three dark green seed beads on doubled wire. Twist remaining length of each wire starting beyond last bead. Repeat for second leaf.

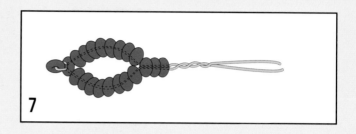

8. Position all leaf wires together, centering light green leaf between two medium green leaves and two dark green leaves, and twist as one.

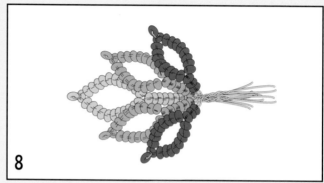

9. For fronds, slip one light green seed bead on wire to middle of length. Fold wire. Slip two light green, one medium green, one light green, two medium green, one dark green, one medium green, and twelve dark green seed beads on doubled wire. Twist remaining length of wire starting beyond last bead. Repeat for five fronds.

10. Position all frond wires together and twist as one.

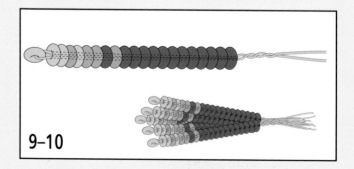

24

11. Position flowers, leaves, and fronds together and twist all wires uniformly to 4" length. Note: Make certain the twist is very tight at the 4" mark.

12. Cut entire twisted group of wires at 4" mark. Bend cut end back ½" to wrap around base of flower spray, forming a ring.

Design Tips:

Use lightweight wire, such as 34 gauge if it is available. Gold-finished wire is pretty enough to be left exposed as part of the design.

Plain metal wire looks dull and should be hidden with a covering of some sort. If you are creating flowers with wire, the twisted wire can be covered with floral tape.

Make certain any visible twisted section of wire has a uniform appearance.

Troubleshooting:

Wire will come off the roll in a spiral shape. Take care to avoid pulling too quickly on this spiral as it will kink. Kinks do not render the wire unusable, but do make it more difficult to position the beads properly if they fall within the design area.

How do I string beads on a head pin jewelry component?

Beads:
Glass bead: large
4 mm round
   beads:
   matte gold (2)

Etc.:
Head pin:
   gold-finished,
   .22-diameter,
   2"-long
Round-nosed
   pliers
Wire cutters
Wire necklace
   blank

It is easy to make beautiful beaded accessories using jewelry components, also known as "findings." This simple but elegant necklace is created using a preformed necklace blank, two gold beads, one large glass bead, and a head pin.

Rigid Wire Necklace

Here's How:

1. Slip beads on head pin, alternating one gold bead, large glass bead, and then second gold bead.

2. Using wire cutters, trim head pin to ³⁄₁₆" beyond last bead.

3. Using round-nosed pliers, form a loop in end of head pin. Slip loop on wire necklace blank and carefully close loop.

How do I string beads on multiple jewelry components?

What You Need to Get Started:

Beads:
4 mm round beads: gold-finished (2)
10 mm round beads: faux pearl (2)
18 mm teardrops: faux pearl (2)

Etc.:
Caps for 10 mm beads: filigree (2)
Ear wires: gold-finished (2)
Eye pins: gold-finished, 1½"-long (2)
Head pins: gold-finished, .22-diameter, 1½"-long (2)
6 mm rings: gold-finished (2)
Round-nosed pliers
Wire cutters

By combining head pin, eye pin, cap, ring, and ear wire components, you can quickly create these attractive earrings.

Faux Pearl Component Earrings

Here's How:

1. Slip teardrop bead and cap on head pin. Slip pearl bead and gold bead on eye pin.

2. Using wire cutters, trim head pin and eye pin to ⅜" beyond cap and gold bead.

3. Using round-nosed pliers, form a loop in end of head pin and eye pin. Slip loop of head pin and eye of eye pin on ring and carefully close each loop. Slip loop of eye pin on ear wire and carefully close loop.

4. Repeat Steps 1–3 for remaining earring.

(Spaces between beads are exaggerated to show stringing.)

Ear wire
Eye pin
4 mm round
10 mm round
6 mm ring
Cap
Head pin
Teardrop

1–3

How do I string beads on a needle and thread?

What You Need to Get Started:

Beads:
Assorted beads

Etc.:
Beading needle
Embroidery
   scissors
Jewelry glue
Thread, heavy-
   weight:
   off-white

Stringing beads on lighter weight fibers requires the use of a needle. Choosing a needle can be tricky as the eye of the needle must accommodate the thread and still pass through the bead. No clasp is needed to finish this necklace, making it one of the most basic, yet versatile designs in beading.

Continuous Loop Necklace

Here's How:
Note: Traditional beading needles, which are long and narrow, are excellent for stringing small beads, as they can pick up several beads at a time. Tapestry needles work particularly well when using a heavier weight fiber and larger beads.

1. Cut thread about 6" longer than desired length of necklace. Note: Remember that the finished necklace must be larger than your head—36" is a good length.

2. Thread needle. Slip beads on needle in desired pattern to 36" length.

3. Knot ends together. Apply dot of glue onto knot. Allow to dry.

4. Work excess thread back into bead strand. Loop thread around one bead. Apply dot of glue onto looped thread and pull taut. Repeat looping to secure beads if necessary. Trim excess thread.

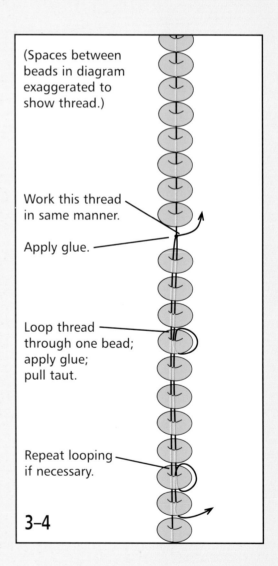

(Spaces between beads in diagram exaggerated to show thread.)

Work this thread in same manner.

Apply glue.

Loop thread through one bead; apply glue; pull taut.

Repeat looping if necessary.

3-4

Design Tips:

Round beads are quite well suited to this type of application, but odd-shaped beads may also be used. If you are using natural stone chips, try to sort them first to avoid using those that have jagged or sharp edges.

Space beads so that each can be shown to its best advantage. A good design method is to place one or several small beads between two larger beads. This is particularly effective when stringing some natural beads which tend to twist unattractively due to their irregular shape.

How do I string beads on elastic?

**What You
Need to
Get Started:**

Beads:
Assorted beads

Etc.:
Craft scissors
Elastic thread:
   clear
Jewelry glue

Elastic thread is available in a variety of weights and colors and should be used where a continuous loop of strung beads must fit closely. Clear elastic thread, which is easy to knot securely, is used to string these multicolored bracelets, which can be worn individually or in a group.

Simple Bracelet

Here's How:
Note: Elastic thread is stiff enough to slip through a bead's hole without the use of a needle.

1. Cut thread about 6" longer than desired length of bracelet. Note: The finished strand length should be your wrist measurement plus 1" before tying. If you are making the bracelet as a gift and do not know the wrist size, 6" is generally a good length when using elastic thread.

2. Slip beads on thread in desired pattern to desired length.

3. Tie two ends together in a simple knot. Apply dot of glue onto knot. Allow to dry.

4. Trim excess thread.

How do I incorporate knotting into stringing beads?

What You Need to Get Started:

<u>Beads:</u>
15 mm amber bead
4 mm glass beads with large holes (70)

<u>Etc.:</u>
Claw clasp: gold-finished
Embroidery scissors
Head pin: gold-finished, .22-diameter, 2"-long
Jewelry glue
Knotting tool
Needle-nosed pliers
Rayon thread, lightweight: gold
10 mm ring: gold-finished
Sewing needle
Tapestry needle
Wire cutters

Knotting allows you to space beads along a strand and to use a beautiful thread as part of your design.

Knotted Necklace with Amber Bead

Here's How:
1. Cut six 6' lengths of thread. Note: The knots will reduce the length dramatically.

2. Thread tapestry needle with all threads.

3. Slip one glass bead on needle and loosely tie a single knot. Place knotting tool inside loop of knot and gently slide knot close to bead. Continue beading and knotting to 22" length. Note: This is called the "knot sliding technique."

4. Knot clasp on one end of length. Knot ring on remaining end.

5. Using sewing needle, sew each thread end back into last few knots on both ends. Apply dot of glue on knots that hold clasp and ring.

6. Slip one glass bead and amber bead on head pin.

7. Using needle-nosed pliers, form loop in end of head pin. Slip loop through center glass bead on knotted strand.

8. Using wire cutters, trim head pin so it can be tucked back into hole of large bead.

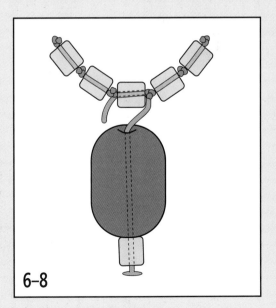

6–8

9. Using needle-nosed pliers, shape head pin and tuck it into hole of large bead.

Design Tips:

Minimize gaps by making certain the knot is made close to the bead.

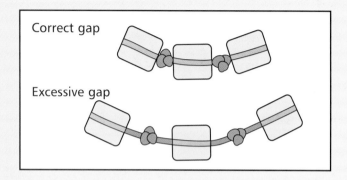

Correct gap

Excessive gap

A specific tool can be acquired to help the process of knotting. However there are several common household items that may be used instead, to avoid the cost of an expensive tool. A darning needle, a metal skewer, or the open end of a diaper pin can be used quite effectively.

Troubleshooting:

Avoid using wire or stiff fibers as they are not good choices for knotting.

If your fiber has been wound around a card, it may be kinked. Press out the kinks with a steam iron before knotting to avoid a very crooked strand.

In most cases, there will be a slight crookedness to the strand because the knots will not all be exactly the same size or tautness—this is normal. Steam from a clothing steamer can help to lessen the crookedness. Pull down slightly on the strand to straighten it, then apply steam.

How do I use pressure crimps to close a string of beads?

What You Need to Get Started:

Beads:
8 mm round beads with holes large enough to accommodate leather cord: silver (3)

Etc.:
Clasp: silver-finished
Craft scissors
Jewelry glue
Masking tape
Needle-nosed pliers
Pressure crimps: silver-finished (2)
6 mm rings: silver-finished, (2)
Thin leather cords: coordinating colors, 12"-long (3)

In this design, you will learn to attach pressure crimps. Crimps are used to finish the end of a cord such as leather or rattail so a clasp can be neatly attached. The two open sides of the crimp are flattened over the cord and pressed down tightly. The slight claw at the base of the crimp catches the cord and secures it.

Braided Leather Bracelet

Here's How:
1. Trim cord so ends are neat and unfrayed.

2. Apply dot of glue onto center of pressure crimp. Position three cords, making certain that ends line up. Allow glue to dry. Note: With this type of finding, glue is not absolutely necessary, but it will help to secure the leather even more firmly.

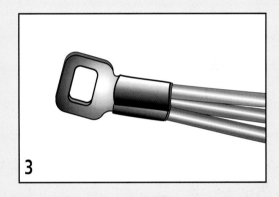
3

4. Tape crimped end of cords to work surface.

5. Braid cords to 3" length, making certain plaits are evenly spaced.

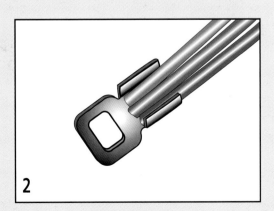
2

3. Using needle-nosed pliers, press one side of crimp down first, then remaining side, until cord is secured.

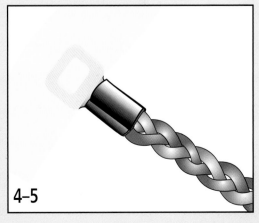
4–5

6. Slip one bead on each cord and work into braid, adjusting tautness of cord to accommodate beads. Braid cords again to 3" length.

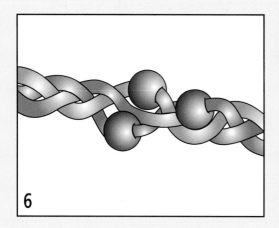

7. Wrap end of braid with small strip of masking tape. Trim cord so ends are even.

8. Repeat Steps 2–3 for cord ends.

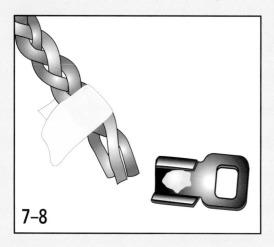

9. Remove tape.

10. Using needle-nosed pliers, attach rings and clasp at both ends.

Design Tips:
   Keep the plaits uniform when braiding the leather. Position the beads so the leather settles around them in an attractive manner.

   Try using brightly colored leather with large colored beads for a piece of jewelry that has a fun, youthful look.

How do I sew beads on card stock?

What You Need to Get Started:

Beads:
#2 bugle beads:
  lavender (7);
  red (10)
8 mm crystal:
  lavender
6 mm
  freshwater
  pearls: (2)
11/0 seed
  beads:
  light aqua
  (15);
  light blue
  (15);
  medium blue
  (15); metallic
  gold (250);
  red (350);
  rose (40)

Etc.:
Bath towel:
  thick, white
#10 between
  needle
Card stock:
  white
Craft scissors
Double-sided
  fusible
  webbing
#9 embroidery
  needle
Fabric for
  backing
Iron and ironing
  board
Jewelry glue
Paper: white
Pin back: gold-
  finished, 1¼"
Thread:
  coordinating
  color

In this project, you will sew beads onto ordinary card stock paper to create an extraordinary piece of jewelry. Card stock is the most desirable weight of paper for use as a beading surface because it is pliable, yet it will also withstand the repeated pull of a needle and thread.

Red Shoe Pin
Photograph on page 38.

Here's How:
1. Photocopy Red Shoe Pin Pattern on opposite page directly onto card stock.

2. Trim the card stock to ½" all around pattern edge, keeping corners somewhat rounded to avoid catching thread.

3. Cut one 30" length of thread and thread needle.

4. Place bugle bead on card stock directly over its photocopied symbol. Bring needle from back of card stock to front at one end of bugle bead. Slip bugle bead on needle and let it slide down thread until it rests on surface. Take needle from front of card stock to back, pulling until bead rests firmly against surface. Note: Bugle beads are almost always sewn on individually.

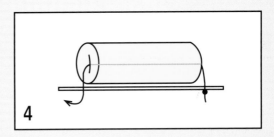

5. Place crystal on surface directly over its photocopied symbol so one cut facet lies flat against surface. Bring needle from back of card stock to front. Slip crystal on needle and let it slide down thread until it rests on surface. Take needle from front of card stock to back at other end of crystal.

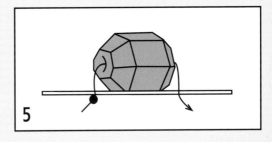

Red Shoe Pin Pattern & Key

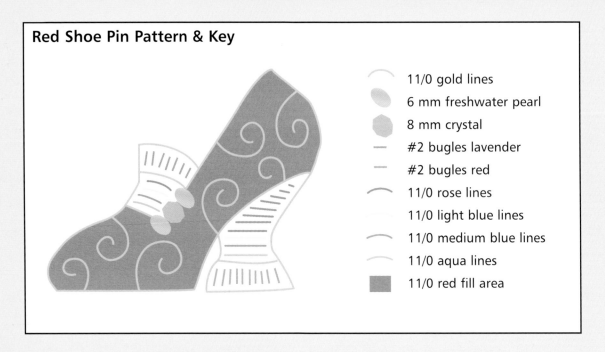

⌒ 11/0 gold lines

⬭ 6 mm freshwater pearl

⬡ 8 mm crystal

— #2 bugles lavender

— #2 bugles red

⌒ 11/0 rose lines

⌒ 11/0 light blue lines

⌒ 11/0 medium blue lines

⌒ 11/0 aqua lines

▨ 11/0 red fill area

6. Since freshwater pearls have extremely fine holes, use #10 between needle and check to see that pearl slips over needle before marking card stock surface for it. Place pearl on surface directly over its photocopied symbol so flatter side lies against surface. Bring needle from back of card stock to front. Slip pearl on needle and let it slide down thread until it rests on surface. Take needle from front of card stock to back at other end of pearl.

7. Sew lines of rose, light aqua, medium blue, and light blue seed beads onto card stock. For each color, bring needle from back of card stock to front at desired starting point. Slip several beads on needle. Lay line against surface and check to see that they comfortably fill desired space. Take needle from front of card stock to back. Secure line using couching technique: returning in direction of starting point, bring needle from back of card stock to front after three beads. Stitch over line, taking needle from front of card stock to back. Repeat for length of line.

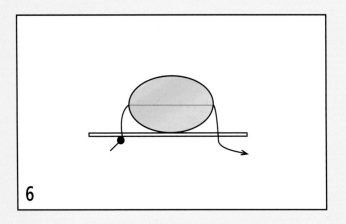

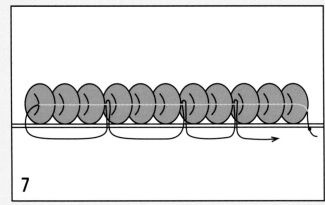

8. For curves and outlines, seed beads may be sewn on two at a time. Bring needle from back of card stock to front about two bead lengths ahead of desired starting point (A). Slip two metallic gold seed beads on needle and let them slide down thread until they rest on their sides on surface. Take needle from front of card stock to back to secure beads (B). Bring needle from back of card stock to front two bead lengths ahead of second bead in line (C). Slip two more beads on needle and let them slide to surface. Take needle from front of card stock to back in first hole made (A). Repeat for length of line.

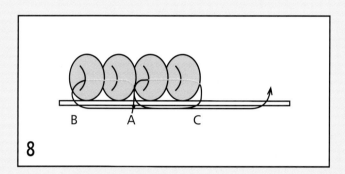

9. Strengthen metallic gold seed bead line with backtracking by bringing needle from back to front just beyond last bead in line and running thread back through all beads in line—run through only three beads at a time, particularly if line is curved. Tighten line until smooth and neat, but not puckering. Take needle from front to back and secure thread. Note: If beads being backtracked have very fine holes, use a #10 between needle.

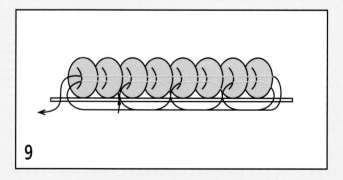

10. Repeat Step 7 with red seed beads to fill in red areas. For small areas and tight curves, sew seed beads onto card stock individually. Bring needle from back of card stock to front at desired starting point. Slip bead on needle and let it slide down thread until it rests on surface. Take needle from front to back through same hole or very close by to secure bead.

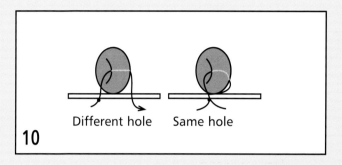

11. To finish back of surface-beaded project, layer and center in order, from bottom: bath towel, beaded card stock wrong side up, fusible webbing with paper removed, backing fabric right side up, and clean white paper. Press iron flat on white paper for five seconds. Shift iron and press for two more seconds to eliminate any steam holes. Allow to cool.

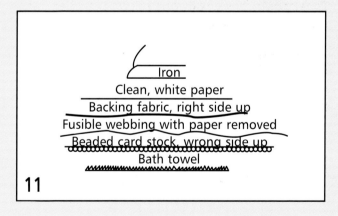

12. Trim excess fabric from edges of beaded project.

13. Apply thin line of diluted glue around trimmed edges to secure.

14. Glue pin back onto back of shoe. Sew through holes on pin back to front of beaded project and secure.

Design Tips:

Ordinary sewing thread is best for beading, and since it is available in a wide array of colors, you can coordinate the color of your thread to the color of your beads.

Each bead will vary a bit in terms of size, so you may not be able to exactly match the placement shown on the card. If you can, try selecting the bead to match the space. If you notice that there are many odd-shaped, flat, narrow, or wide beads, set them aside for possible use when filling in odd-shaped spaces.

Troubleshooting:

If you want to trace a design, a good way to do that is to use a light source from underneath. Place your card stock over the design and tape both to a window; trace the design that will emerge as the light shines through. You may also use a transfer pencil to draw your design first, then iron it onto the surface. Remember that the design must initially be reversed, or it will come out in mirror image.

When trimming excess fabric or paper from the beaded design, take care not to accidentally cut a long string of beads near the edge.

For additional threadings, refer to *Adding a New Length of Thread* on page 18.

How do I sew beads on fabric?

What You Need to Get Started:

Beads:
12 mm
   amethyst
   flat beads (2)
#2 bugle beads:
   light blue
   (38);
   light green
   (24)
4–5 mm
   freshwater
   pearls (20)
Light jade chips
   (4)
11/0 seed beads:
   medium green
   (106);
   pink (18);
   turquoise (4)
6/0 seed beads:
   light pink (16)
Turquoise chips
   (4)

Etc.:
#10 between
   needle
#9 embroidery
   needle
Embroidery
   transfer pencil
Purchased shirt
   with collar
Thread: white

Fabric is the most widely used surface for beadwork. The best fabrics to use are those that have a tight weave but also have some substance. This project is created using a purchased shirt and surface-beading techniques.

Collar Adornment
Photograph on page 41.

Here's How:

1. Using transfer pencil, trace Collar Adornment Pattern on opposite page onto white paper first. Iron design onto collar points. Note: Initially, reverse design or it will come out in mirror image.

2. Cut one 30" length of thread and thread needle.

3. Beginning with large lower flower, position turquoise chip on collar. Bring needle from back of collar to front and slip chip on needle, letting it slide down thread until it rests flat against collar. Slip one turquoise seed bead on needle and take needle back through hole in chip. Pull thread taut until seed bead acts as an anchor on surface of chip, forming flower center.

3

4. Sew nine pearls around turquoise chip to form flower.

5. Sew three light blue and three light green bugle beads on opposite sides of flower to form leaf clusters.

6. Repeat Step 3 for jade chip with medium green seed bead.

7. Work stems in medium green seed beads toward remaining flowers. Run backtracking thread through beads to stabilize curves.

8. Repeat Step 3 at stem indicated for amethyst flat bead with pink seed bead.

9. Sew thirteen light blue bugle beads around amethyst bead to form flower.

10. Sew three light green bugle beads on side of flower to form leaf clusters.

11. Repeat Step 6.

12. Repeat Step 7 for short stem.

13. Sew one pearl at stem indicated to form flower center.

14. Repeat Step 3 for six light pink 6/0 beads with pink seed beads around pearl to form flower.

15. Repeat Step 10.

16. Repeat Step 7 for two remaining stems.

17. Repeat Step 3 at stem indicated.

18. Repeat Step 3 for two light pink 6/0 beads with pink seed beads.

19. Repeat Step 5.

Design Tips:

Select a garment that has a pointed collar and is made of a tightly woven fabric. Knit fabrics are not suitable.

Choose any color of fabric that coordinates with the beads you have chosen.

A garment that has been beaded may be hand-washed and line-dried after beading.

If a very lightweight fabric such as silk, satin, or taffeta is used for beadwork, a backing such as cotton broadcloth or lightweight felt should be fused onto the fabric to stabilize it. Following manufacturer's instructions, use lightweight fusible web bing to adhere a backing onto project fabric before beading.

When using a hoop to stabilize fabrics, make certain that the entire area to be beaded fits within the hoop. Once beads are sewn onto the fabric, it cannot be shifted, as the beads will get in the way of the hoop.

Troubleshooting:

For additional threadings, refer to *Adding a New Length of Thread* on page 18.

Collar Adornment Pattern & Key

#2 bugles light blue
#2 bugles light green
11/0 medium green lines
4–5 mm freshwater pearl
6/0 light pink
12 mm amethyst
turquoise chip
light jade chip

How do I sew beads on needlepoint canvas?

Just as in regular needlepoint, where one stitch is formed over the intersection of two canvas threads, beads are sewn individually to the intersection of two canvas threads. The appearance of the finished work is quite similar to needlepoint because each bead is approximately the same size and shape as a traditional half-cross stitch.

Holly Heart Ornament

Here's How:

Note: Experienced needlepointers will notice that the thread is running in a different direction. In order to make the bead slant to the right, the thread must slant to the left. Additionally, the fine embroidery or between needle required will feel very tiny to a stitcher accustomed to the firm bulk of a tapestry needle.

1. Tape edges of needlepoint canvas.

2. Cut one 60" length of off-white thread. Double thread on needle and knot thread ends.

3. Following Holly Heart Ornament Pattern on page 44, work one horizontal row at a time for uniform appearance—from right in short backstitches or from left in long backstitches. Bring needle up from back of canvas (A). Slip one bead on needle and take needle to back of

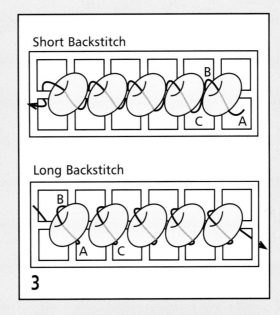

canvas (B). Bring needle from back of canvas (C). Secure thread by holding it against back of canvas and stitching over it with first few beads. Continue in this manner to end of horizontal row. Start next row and return in opposite direction using appropriate stitch. Note: Mark off each row on the graph after completion, as it will help you keep track of your place.

What You Need to Get Started:

Beads:
#2 bugle beads: silver-lined gold (50)
14/0 seed beads: cream (5); dark green (100); metallic gold (75); light green (75); medium green (100); medium pink (35); pale pink (6); red (40)

Etc.:
#10 between needle
Embroidery scissors
Felt for backing: dark green, 4" square
#18 interlock needlepoint canvas: 3" square
Jewelry glue
Masking tape
Satin ribbon, 1/8"-wide: red, 8"-long (2)
Steam iron and ironing board
Threads: dark green; off-white

4. Trim canvas to ¼" around design. Clip curves as shown and turn under. Using steam iron, press clipped edges flat so canvas does not show on beaded side of piece.

Pressed flat, trimmed, and clipped

4

5. Using pressed beadwork as template, cut two pieces of felt to size and shape. Trim one

piece of felt ⅛" all around for padding.

6. Sew one piece of ribbon to wrong side of beaded canvas at each curve of heart.

7. Sandwich padding felt between wrong side of beaded canvas and backing felt. Using needle and dark green thread, slip-stitch backing felt to beaded canvas, enclosing padding felt and ribbons ends.

8. Sew a row of bugle beads all around edge of heart-shaped ornament. When bugle beads are in place, backtrack through all the bugle beads to position

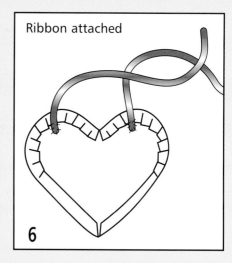

Ribbon attached

6

them more firmly. Bury excess thread in ornament and trim it close.

9. Tie ribbon ends in bow and trim as needed. Note: A dot of glue on the knot will help keep the bow intact when hanging it.

Design Tips:

Use 11/0 seed beads on 14-count canvas. Use 14/0 seed beads on 18-count canvas.

If possible, paint the design on the canvas before beading, following your stitching chart.

Troubleshooting:

Use interlock (single thread lock-weave) canvas or Penelope (double-threaded canvas). Mono (single thread overweave) canvas is too unstable for use with beads.

For additional threadings, refer to *Adding a New Length of Thread* on page 18.

Holly Heart Ornament Pattern & Key

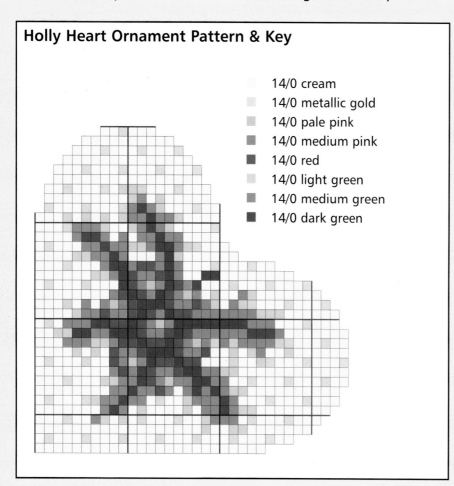

	14/0 cream
	14/0 metallic gold
	14/0 pale pink
	14/0 medium pink
	14/0 red
	14/0 light green
	14/0 medium green
	14/0 dark green

How do I weave a daisy chain using a needle?

This hand-weaving technique uses a single needle to create a pretty strand that looks as if it is made up of tiny flowers. When worked entirely in one color, it has a lacy look; when worked in multiple colors as in our anklet, the flowery look emerges.

Daisy Chain Anklet
Photograph on page 46.

Here's How:
Note: Each unit of the chain is composed of nine beads, eight "petals" of the same color in a circle around one "center" of a different color.

1. Cut one 24"–30" length of thread. Note: Additional lengths of thread can be added if necessary. The finished anklet length is 9¼".

2. Thread needle, allowing long thread end at beginning of weave. Note: You may tape the end of the beginning thread to a flat surface for stability.

3. Slip eight beads of first color on needle. Run needle back through first bead on thread as shown in diagram. Slip red bead on for "center." Then run needle through lower left bead of circle of eight.

4. Slip one bead of second color on needle. Run needle through lower right bead of first "flower." Slip one more bead on needle and run needle through first bead of second color. Slip six more beads on needle. Slip red bead on for "center." Then run needle through lower left bead of circle of eight.

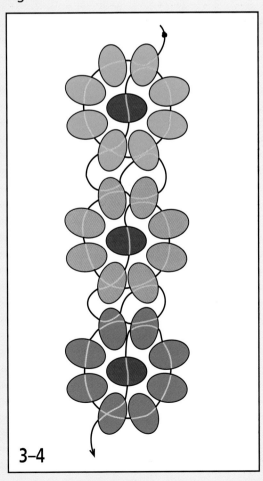

3–4

What You Need to Get Started:

Beads:
11/0 seed beads: light blue (32); gold (24); light green (32); medium green (24); lavender (32); orange (24); light pink (32); red (31); turquoise (24); yellow (24)

Etc.:
Claw clasp: silver-finished
Embroidery scissors
10 mm ring: silver-finished
Sewing needle
Thread: off-white

45

5. Repeat Step 4 for thirty-one flowers—each one a different color than previous.

6. Run thread through lower left bead of last flower.

7. Sew clasp on one end of length and ring on remaining end, running thread through adjacent beads three times.

8. Bury thread ends in weave by running each thread end back into last bead.

9. Trim excess thread, taking care to avoid cutting weave threads.

Troubleshooting:

For additional threadings, refer to *Adding a New Length of Thread* on page 18.

How do I create a beaded design using squared needle-weaving?

The technique used for basic needle-weaving is similar to that of crocheting. After the first row is worked, subsequent rows are looped into the first row in a predictable way. Unlike crochet, which is usually worked from written instructions, bead needle-weaving is worked from a gridded pattern. These candleholders are decorated with a needle-woven band of beads.

Wrapped Candleholder
Photograph on page 49.

Here's How:
Note: Bead amounts will depend on how long each band must be woven to wrap around the candleholder you choose.

1. Cut one 30" length of thread and thread needle, leaving 5" tail.

2. To keep design pattern beads from slipping off thread, create "stopper bead." Slip one bead on needle and let it slide down thread to 3" from end of thread. Loop thread back through bead and pull taut. Secure stopper bead to flat or slightly curved surface to stabilize thread. Note: The stopper bead will be removed after the first few rows.

3. Following Wrapped Candleholder Pattern on page 48, string beads for Row 1 from top to bottom. Skipping last bead, insert needle back through all beads. Note: The needle should emerge from the top bead of Row 1.

What You Need to Get Started:

Beads:
11/0 seed beads:
  dark blue;
  light blue;
  metallic gold;
  lavender

Etc.:
Candleholder
  with
  round shaft
Embroidery
  scissors
Sewing needle
Thread:
  off-white

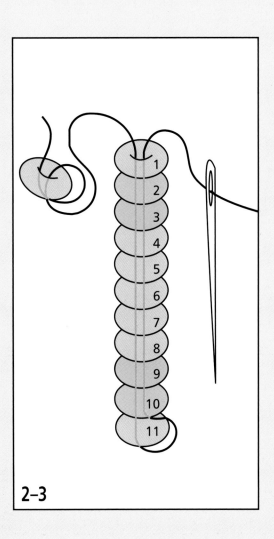

2–3

47

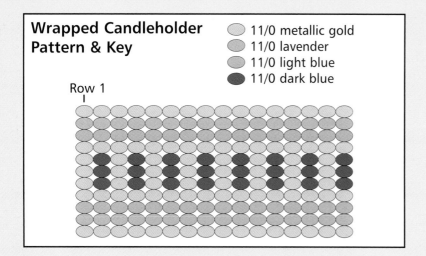

Wrapped Candleholder Pattern & Key

- ⬭ 11/0 metallic gold
- ⬭ 11/0 lavender
- ⬭ 11/0 light blue
- ⬭ 11/0 dark blue

Row 1

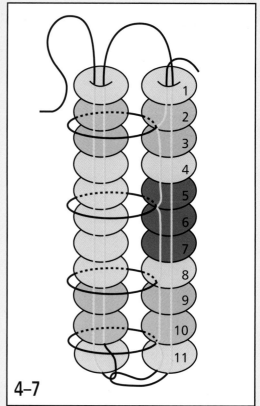

4-7

4. String beads for Row 2, from top to bottom. Insert needle into loop exposed at bottom of Row 1. Pull thread gently until entire second row is taut, but not tight, and beads rest against first row without puckering. Note: The work in needle-weaving always proceeds in the direction of the beadworker's dominant hand.

5. Insert needle into last bead of Row 2, and bring thread out until it is taut, but not tight. Loop thread around Row 1 so it is nestled between beads 11 and 10 of Row 1. Insert needle into beads 10 and 9 of Row 2, bringing needle out between beads 9 and 8 on Row 2. Again, thread should be taut, but not tight.

6. Loop thread around Row 1 so it is nestled between beads 9 and 8 of Row 1. Insert needle into next three beads on Row 2—beads 8, 7, and 6—bringing needle out between beads 6 and 5 on Row 2. Tighten thread again.

7. Loop it around Row 1 so it is nestled between beads 6 and 5 of Row 1. Insert needle into next three beads on Row 2—beads 5, 4, and 3—and repeat looping and inserting process until thread emerges from bead 1 of Row 2.

8. Repeat Steps 4–7 for all subsequent rows until band is long enough to wrap snugly around candleholder. Note: The weaving gets easier to handle as the design grows.

9. When about 3" of thread remains unbeaded on needle, it is time to add new thread. Remove needle from thread and cut new 30" length. Thread needle, leaving 5" tail. Note: A longer thread tends to tangle, and a shorter thread necessitates frequent threadings.

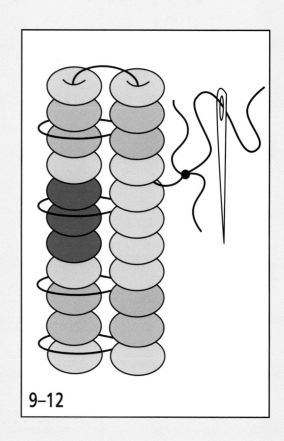

9–12

10. Tie a square knot so that knot lands 1" from where old thread emerges from beadwork.

11. Place tiny dot of glue on knot. Wipe off any excess glue. Note: The glue need not be dry before proceeding.

12. Continue beading as if one continuous thread were being used. Allow thread ends to protrude from work until new thread is well established within weave.

13. Pull gently on thread ends and clip them close so they disappear into woven design. Note: It might be necessary to use a smaller needle until the area of the knot has been passed.

14. Trim any excess threads that occur in body of weave.

15. Wrap length of woven band around candleholder, lining up beads of last row next to beads of Row 1.

16. Repeat Steps 4–7, treating last row as if it were Row 1 and Row 1 as if it were Row 2.

17. Bury excess thread in weave.

How do I create a beaded design using brick stitch needle-weaving?

What You Need to Get Started:

Beads:
11/0 seed beads:
  metallic bronze
  (80); dark
  metallic copper
  (80); metallic
  gold (80);
  metallic
  silver (80)

Etc.:
Embroidery
  scissors
Jewelry glue
Plastic barrette:
  tortoiseshell,
  5/8" x 3½"
Sewing needles (2)
Thread: medium
  brown

The brick stitch is a diagonal weaving technique worked in hand using two needles. All work progresses outward from a central foundation row. In this technique the beads lie horizontally against one another like alternating bricks. The resulting weave is strong and flexible, and can be used for many different purposes.

Brick Stitch Barrette

Here's How:
1. Cut one 24" length of thread, and thread each end onto a needle.

2. Following Brick Stitch Barrette Pattern on opposite page, slip first seed bead of foundation row on one needle and let it slide down thread to center. Slip second seed bead on one needle and weave second needle through opposite hole in bead. Pull thread taut, but not tight so beads rest against each other. Continue in this manner to form foundation row.

3. To minimize tangling, remove needle from thread end that will work rows above foundation row.

4. Working in opposite direction, slip one bead on remaining needle at a time and loop thread back into foundation row to end of second row. Note: Beginning with the second row, each row will have one less or one more bead than the previous row.

5. Returning in opposite direction, slip one bead on needle at a time, and loop thread back into second row to end of third row, forming diagonal weave.

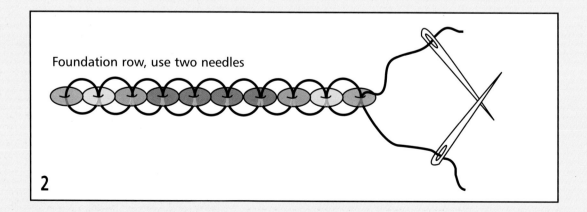

Foundation row, use two needles

2

6. Repeat Step 5 for remaining rows below foundation row. Remove needle from thread.

7. Rethread remaining thread onto needle. Rotate work piece 180° and repeat Steps 4–6 for rows above foundation row.

8. Bury excess threads in weave.

9. Apply glue onto back of woven piece. Center and place woven piece on barrette. Using paper towel, wipe any excess glue from edges of woven piece. Note: Do not be concerned about glue that may seep up through the weave as it will dry clear.

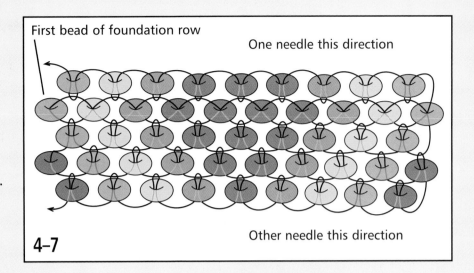

First bead of foundation row

One needle this direction

Other needle this direction

4–7

Design Tip:
    Delica beads also work particularly well when using the brick stitch.

Troubleshooting:
    For additional threadings, refer to *Adding a New Length of Thread* on page 18.

Brick Stitch Barrette Pattern & Key

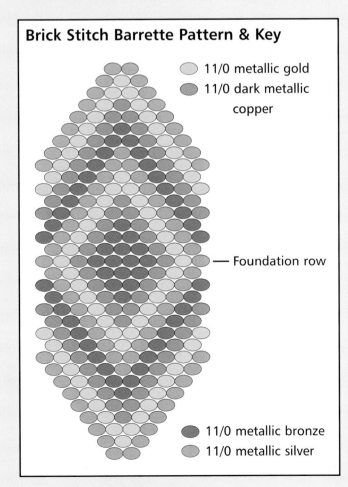

◯ 11/0 metallic gold

⬤ 11/0 dark metallic copper

— Foundation row

⬤ 11/0 metallic bronze

◯ 11/0 metallic silver

How do I create a beaded design using peyote stitch needle-weaving?

What You Need to Get Started:

Beads:
11/0 seed beads:
  powder blue
  (11); coral (12);
  metallic gold
  (250); lime
  green (11);
  orange (8);
  purple (450);
  rose (11);
  turquoise (11);
  lemon yellow
  (12)

Etc.:
Beading needle:
  small
Embroidery flosses:
  blue; coral; gold;
  lime green;
  turquoise
Embroidery
  scissors
Masking tape
Sewing needle:
  medium
Thread: off-white

The peyote stitch is a weaving technique worked in hand using a single needle. The weave causes the beads to lie vertically against one another in a staggered pattern. It is very flexible and can be used flat or adapted into three-dimensional shapes. It is easy and pleasurable to do and works up quickly.

Peyote Stitch Bookmark

Here's How:
Note: Unlike squared needle-weaving where the beads are in neat horizontal and vertical rows, the peyote stitch creates a diagonal effect. The beads that begin and end each row will not be directly above or below the beginning and ending beads of the adjacent rows. At first this may be somewhat confusing, but if you follow the pattern consistently, the weave will stabilize after a few rows.

1. Cut one 24" length of thread and thread needle.

2. Following Peyote Stitch Bookmark Pattern on opposite page, slip beads for top two rows and first bead of third row—beads 1–15—on beading needle at same time, leaving 3"–4" of thread at end. Note: Try to select beads with especially large holes for the top and bottom rows as they will accommodate the floss fringe.

3. Tape thread end onto flat surface for stability.

4. Run needle through bead 13, slip bead 16 on needle and run needle through bead 11. Continue in this manner to end of row.

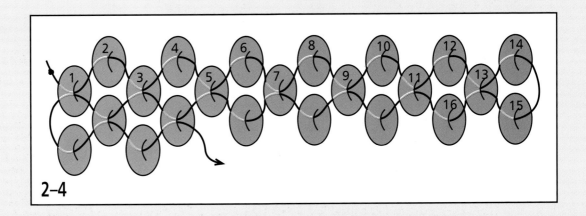

2–4

5. Turn work at end of row to be able to proceed with weave in direction of your dominant hand.

6. Continue working each individual bead between two beads of previous row.

7. When weave is complete, bury thread end within weave. Trim thread end.

8. Thread sewing needle with turquoise embroidery floss. Double floss and run through first bead in top row. Knot fringe close to bead and trim fringe length to 4". Repeat for remaining beads and floss in following order: blue, lime green, turquoise, gold, coral, and turquoise.

9. Rotate bookmark 180° and repeat Step 7 for fringe on bottom row.

Design Tips:

For this design, choose beads with particularly large holes, as you will be working a double strand of embroidery floss through the holes of the top and bottom rows to create a fringe.

The peyote stitch can be used to create very wide weaves for use in larger beaded items such as handbags, and can be worked around shapes such as tubes and cylinders.

Troubleshooting:

Take care when turning at the end of each row to keep the tension of your thread consistent so that the edge is neat.

For additional threadings, refer to *Adding a New Length of Thread* on page 18. Try to work it so the knot of the new thread lands in the center of a row to avoid a lumpy-looking edge.

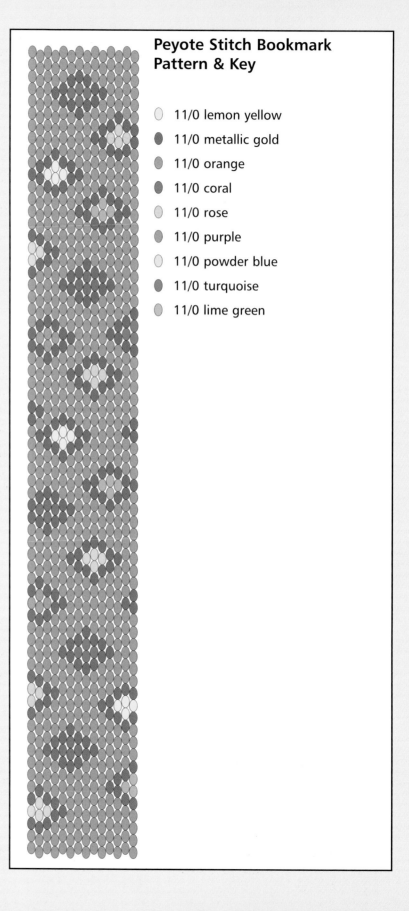

Peyote Stitch Bookmark Pattern & Key

- ○ 11/0 lemon yellow
- ● 11/0 metallic gold
- ● 11/0 orange
- ● 11/0 coral
- ○ 11/0 rose
- ● 11/0 purple
- ○ 11/0 powder blue
- ● 11/0 turquoise
- ● 11/0 lime green

How do I weave a beaded design using a loom?

Looms are excellent for weaving large (or long) beaded pieces that might otherwise be cumbersome to handle. Long vertical threads (called warp) are placed on the loom and stretched tight. Beads are then attached to these warp threads using a needle and thread in a horizontal direction.

Loom-woven Band
Photograph on page 57.

Here's How:
1. Following manufacturer's instructions, warp loom with ten warp threads. Note: In any loomed piece the warp will have one more thread than the number of beads across the width of the design.

2. Cut one 30" length of thread and thread needle. To start horizontal (or weft) thread, knot end of thread onto left outermost warp thread. Note: Make certain to knot the thread onto the right outermost warp thread if you are left handed.

3. Following Loom-woven Band Pattern on page 56, slip beads for top horizontal row on needle.

4. Pass beaded thread under warp threads, positioning beads and threads so one bead falls between two warp threads.

5. After beads are seated into warp, pass needle back through beads so weft thread goes over warp threads.

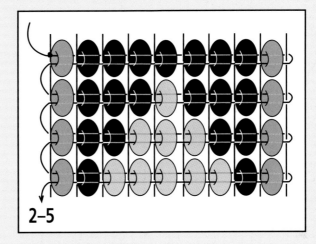

2–5

6. Repeat Steps 3–5 for remaining horizontal rows.

7. Bury any excess thread in weave.

8. To finish ends of band, separate warp threads into groups of two threads, beginning from each side of center weft bead. Note: Outermost warp threads will remain single.

9. Trim each group of threads as one for a clean edge. Thread #9 embroidery needle with these threads.

10. Slip twelve black and one of each remaining color (in order of rainbow) 11/0 seed beads on needle.

What You Need to Get Started:

Beads:
11/0 seed beads:
  black; light
  blue;
  medium blue;
  gold; light
  green;
  lime green;
  medium
  green;
  lavender;
  orange;
  pink;
  turquoise;
  yellow

Etc.:
Beading loom
Beading needle
Embroidery
  scissors
Thread:
  off-white

55

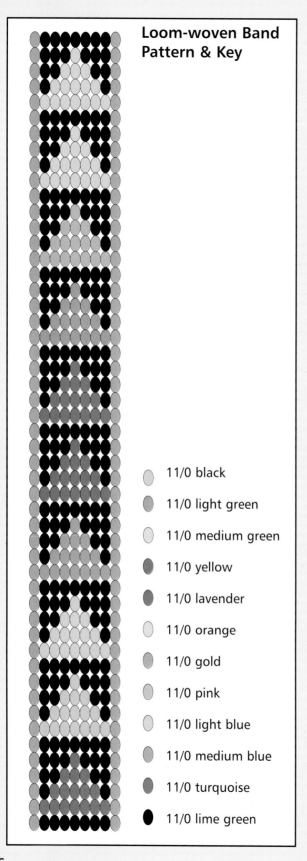

Loom-woven Band Pattern & Key

11. Knot threads, positioning beads very close to woven band. Note: It may be necessary to knot over the first knot one or more times to make certain that the beads are secure.

- 11/0 black
- 11/0 light green
- 11/0 medium green
- 11/0 yellow
- 11/0 lavender
- 11/0 orange
- 11/0 gold
- 11/0 pink
- 11/0 light blue
- 11/0 medium blue
- 11/0 turquoise
- 11/0 lime green

Alternate Design Patterns & Keys

- 11/0 yellow
- 11/0 orange
- 11/0 pink
- 11/0 purple
- 11/0 blue
- 11/0 green

- 11/0 cream
- 11/0 tan
- 11/0 gold
- 11/0 copper

- 11/0 yellow
- 11/0 red
- 11/0 purple
- 11/0 blue
- 11/0 teal
- 11/0 green

12. Apply small dot of glue on knot. Trim excess thread.

13. Repeat Step 10 for each remaining warp thread. Skipping last bead, insert needle back through all beads. Bury excess thread in weave.

Troubleshooting:

For additional threadings, refer to *Adding a New Length of Thread* on page 18.

How do I string beads to create lace?

What You Need to Get Started:

Beads:
11/0 seed beads:
   matte green;
   matte purple

Etc.:
Beading needle
Fabric scissors
Iron and ironing
   board
Linen: sage green
   (⅙ yard);
lavender
   (⅙ yard)
#2 pencil
Ruler
Sewing machine
Thread: sage
   green;
   lavender

"Lace" can be made with beads in a manner that is similar to the way lace is crocheted. Evenly spaced patterns of beads are worked in rounds or rows until a lacy look results.

Beaded Lace-edged Coasters
Photograph on page 61.

Here's How:
1. Cut two 5"-square pieces from each color of linen.

2. Place lavender fabric squares with right sides together. Sew all around edges with ½" seam allowance, leaving 2" open for turning. Trim seams, clip at corners, and turn right side out. Press edges flat and stitch opening closed to create coaster. Repeat for sage green fabric squares.

3. Mark back of each coaster in ½" intervals for working lace. Mark lavender coaster further by dividing each half inch into thirds.

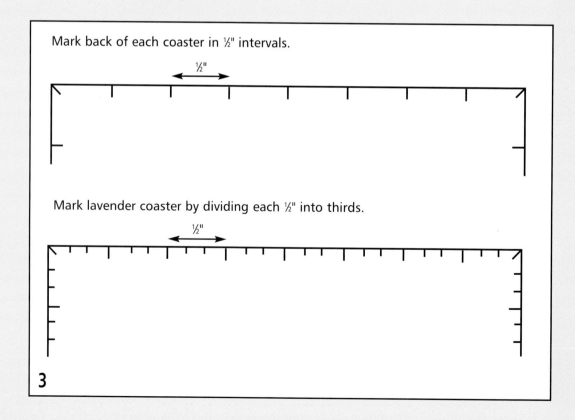

Mark back of each coaster in ½" intervals.

½"

Mark lavender coaster by dividing each ½" into thirds.

½"

3

4. Cut one 30" length of sage green thread and thread needle. For first round of beads on green coaster marked in ½" intervals, bring needle out at center mark on one side. Slip eleven beads on needle.

5. Insert needle into fabric at next mark, catching just enough fabric to be secure, and bring needle back through last bead on resulting loop.

6. Slip ten beads on needle.

7. Repeat Steps 5–6 at each interval all around coaster.

8. For second round on green coaster, bring needle out in fourth bead of first loop. Slip seven beads on needle.

9. Skip three beads on loop and run needle through eighth bead. Bring needle back through last bead on second round.

10. Slip six beads on needle and run needle through fourth bead on next loop. Bring needle back through last bead on second round.

11. Repeat Steps 9–10 from loop to loop all around coaster. Note: When looping around each corner, slip two additional beads on needle.

12. When beading is complete, run thread through beads into fabric and bury it in weave of fabric.

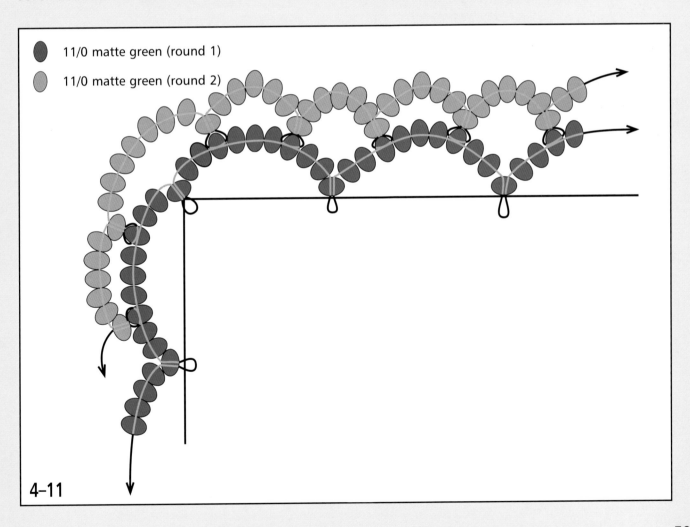

11/0 matte green (round 1)

11/0 matte green (round 2)

4–11

13. Cut one 30" length of lavender thread and thread needle. For first round of beads on lavender coaster, bring needle out at any mark on one side. Slip eight beads on needle.

14. Insert needle into fabric at next mark, catching just enough fabric to be secure, and bring needle back through last three beads on resulting loop.

15. Slip five beads on needle.

16. Repeat Steps 14–15 at each interval all around coaster. Note: When looping around each corner, slip two additional beads on needle, insert needle into fabric at corner, catching just enough fabric to be secure, and bring needle back through last four beads on resulting loop. Slip six beads on needle and work loop from corner to next side.

17. When first round is complete, secure thread and trim it close.

18. For second round on lavender coaster, thread needle. Bring needle out at one corner through six beads as indicated.

19. Slip six beads on needle.

20. Run needle through third bead again, looping last three beads on thread. Guide beads toward existing beadwork, taking up slack in thread and forming a "picot" or three-bead group.

21. Slip two beads on needle and run needle through indicated beads on next two loops.

22. Repeat Steps 19–21 from loop to loop all around coaster. Note: When looping around each corner, run needle through indicated beads to form a separate picot.

23. When beading is complete, run thread through beads into fabric and bury it in weave of fabric.

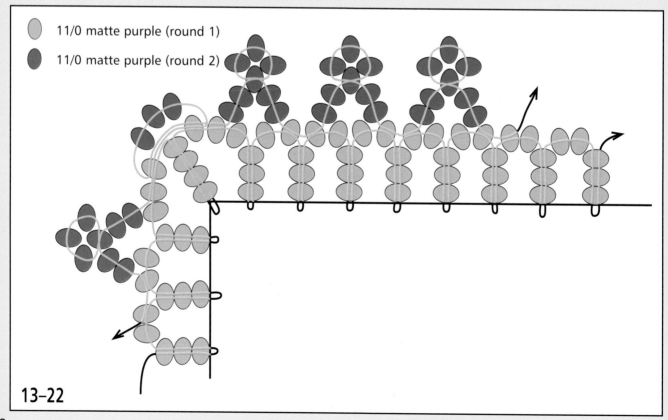

11/0 matte purple (round 1)

11/0 matte purple (round 2)

13–22

Design Tips:

The best choice for beading lace is 11/0 seed beads, largely because they have rounded edges which allow flexibility in the way the beads lie against each other.

Troubleshooting:

For additional threadings, refer to *Adding a New Length of Thread* on page 18.

How do I combine stringing with surface beading?

What You Need to Get Started:

Beads:
10 mm firepolish crystals: bronze (7)
4 mm round beads: matte gold (14)
11/0 seed beads: black (12); dark bronze (150); metallic gold (150); pewter (350)

Etc.:
Barrel clasp: gold-finished
Card stock
Craft scissors
Double-sided fusible webbing
Ear findings: matte gold-finished, celtic-type pattern (2)
#9 embroidery needle
Head pins: gold-finished, .22-diameter, 1¼"-long (2)
Lightweight leather for backing: black, 3" square
Round-nosed pliers
Wire cutters

This project demonstrates how surface beading on card stock can become an attractive pendant by adding on fringes for embellishment and strings of beads for a necklace. Simple component techniques are used for the matching earrings.

Celtic Knot Necklace & Earrings

Here's How:
1. Photocopy Celtic Knot Pattern directly onto card stock.

2. Trim the card stock to ½" all around pattern edge, keeping corners somewhat rounded to avoid catching thread.

3. Cut one 30" length of thread and thread needle.

4. Refer to Steps 8–9 on page 37. For curves and outlines, sew metallic gold and pewter 11/0 seed beads onto card stock. Run backtracking thread through beads.

5. Refer to Step 7 on page 36 and Step 10 on page 37. Fill in background areas with black and dark bronze 11/0 seed beads.

6. For one drop on pendant, bring needle to front surface at one dot. Slip beads of each drop on needle. Skipping last seed bead, run thread back through all beads. Repeat for each drop.

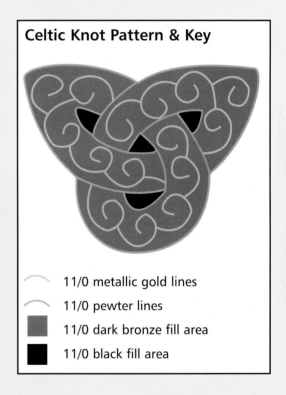

Celtic Knot Pattern & Key

⌣ 11/0 metallic gold lines
⌣ 11/0 pewter lines
▬ 11/0 dark bronze fill area
▬ 11/0 black fill area

7. For one necklace strand on pendant, bring needle out at either dot on top left edge. Slip four pewter seed beads, one matte gold round bead, one firepolish crystal, one matte gold round bead, and one dark bronze seed bead on needle. Slip pewter seed beads on needle to 7½" length.

8. Sew one part of clasp onto bead strand, looping thread back through

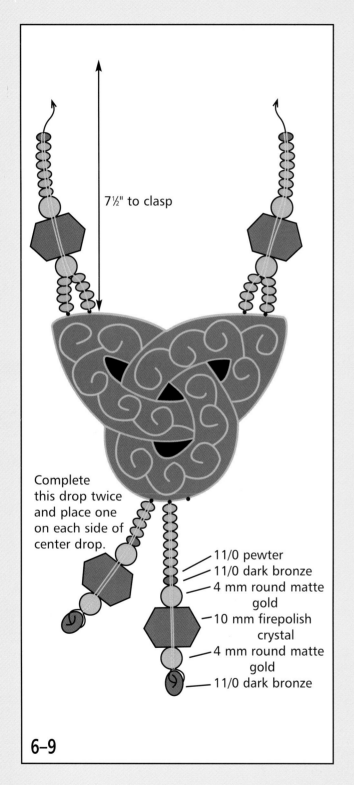

7½" to clasp

Complete
this drop twice
and place one
on each side of
center drop.

11/0 pewter
11/0 dark bronze
4 mm round matte
gold
10 mm firepolish
crystal
4 mm round matte
gold
11/0 dark bronze

6–9

last few beads until clasp is secure. Run thread back through all—except last four seed beads—on strand.

9. Add four more pewter 11/0 seed beads and take needle through remaining dot.

10. Bury thread in back of stitching and trim excess close to project.

11. Repeat Steps 6–9 for necklace strand on top right edge of pendant.

12. Refer to Steps 10–12 on page 37. To finish back of surface-beaded project, apply fusible webbing and leather.

13. To make earrings, slip beads for each drop on head pin. Using wire cutters, trim head pin to ⅜". Using round-nosed pliers, form an open loop. Slip loop of head pin on ear finding and carefully close loop.

Troubleshooting:

For additional threadings, refer to *Adding a New Length of Thread* on page 18.

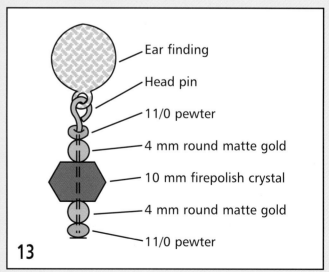

Ear finding
Head pin
11/0 pewter
4 mm round matte gold
10 mm firepolish crystal
4 mm round matte gold
11/0 pewter

13

How do I finish a beaded piece of needlepoint canvas?

This eyeglass case is worked in beaded needlepoint on #14 interlock needlepoint canvas with 11/0 seed beads. It is finished with coordinating fabric that adds to the elegant look of the beaded design.

Oriental Carpet Eyeglass Case
Photograph on page 67.

Here's How:
1. Refer to Steps 1–3 on page 43. Following Oriental Carpet Pattern on page 66, work from top row to bottom row. Note: The last row charted is the center row in the design.

2. Turn chart 180° and continue working design from center row—but not repeating center row.

3. Using steam iron, steam back of work and reshape it so it is squared. Note: Take care when handling glass beads that have been under the iron as they can be quite hot to the touch.

4. Trim canvas to ½" around design and clip corners.

5. Using pressed and trimmed beadwork as a template, cut two pieces from lining fabric and one from backing fabric.

6. Press canvas edges under finished beadwork. Press edges of remaining three pieces under to same size.

7. Stitch one lining piece onto back of beadwork, hiding raw edges.

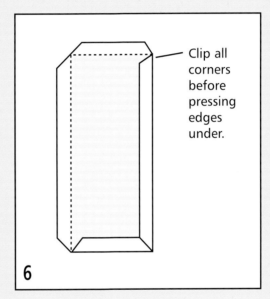

Clip all corners before pressing edges under.

6

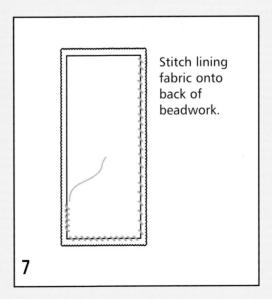

Stitch lining fabric onto back of beadwork.

7

What You Need to Get Started:

Beads:
11/0 seed beads:
  aqua (1000);
  dark blue (900);
  pale blue (300);
  light green (100);
  pink (1100);
  light purple (308);
  medium purple (280); red (240);
  yellow (960)

Etc.:
#9 embroidery needle
Fabric for lining and backing (1/8 yard each)
Fabric scissors
#14 interlock needlepoint canvas: 5" x 9"
Steam iron and ironing board
Thread: off-white

8. Stitch remaining lining and backing pieces so raw edges are together.

9. When both backing and beadwork have been lined, stitch them together, leaving one edge open to form eyeglass case.

Troubleshooting:

For additional threadings, refer to *Adding a New Length of Thread* on page 18.

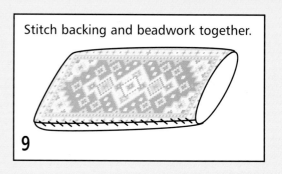

Stitch backing and beadwork together.

9

Oriental Carpet Pattern & Key

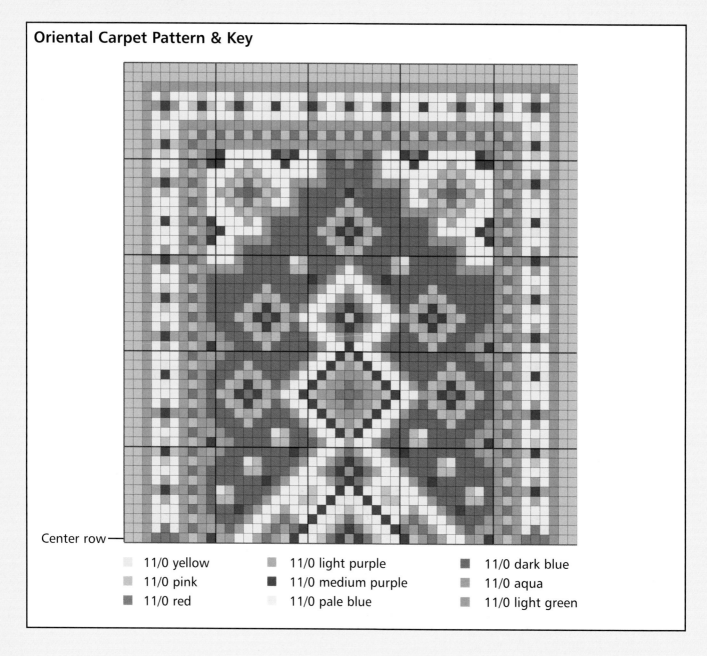

Center row

11/0 yellow	11/0 light purple	11/0 dark blue
11/0 pink	11/0 medium purple	11/0 aqua
11/0 red	11/0 pale blue	11/0 light green

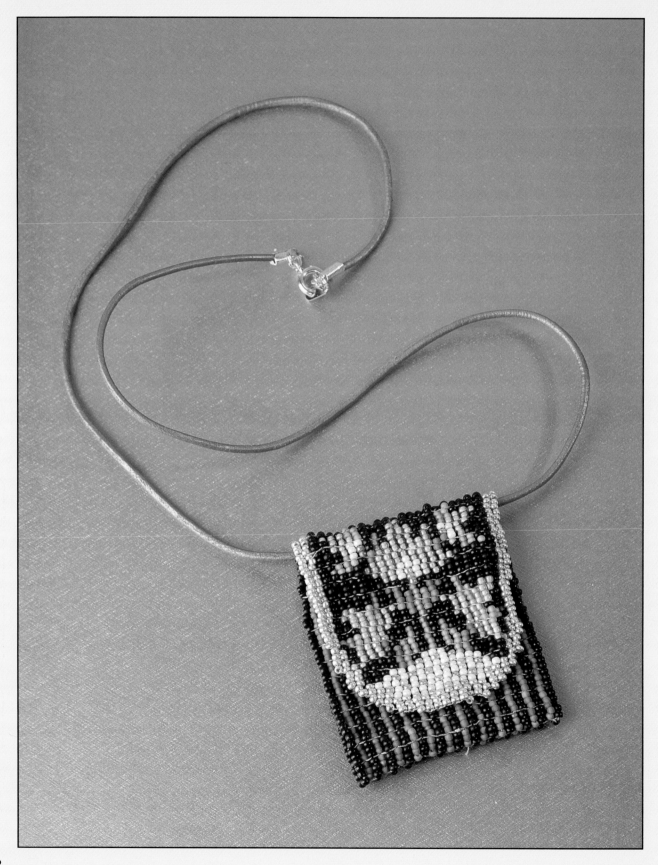

How do I join squared needle-weaving?

What You Need to Get Started:

Beads:
11/0 seed beads:
matte aqua (5 grams); black (5 grams); metallic gold (200); lime (60); lavender (75); light orange (30); purple (20); rose (50)

Etc.:
Clasp: gold-finished
Embroidery scissors
Jewelry glue
Leather cord: medium weight, 18"-long
Needle-nosed pliers
Pressure crimps: gold-finished (2)
6 mm rings: gold-finished (2)
Sewing needle
Thread: tan

This design is worked in needle-weaving. The leather strap is sewn onto the finished piece; pressure crimps and clasp are added to the ends of the leather.

Woven Bag Necklace

Here's How:
1. Refer to Steps 1–14 on pages 47–49. Following Woven Bag Necklace Pattern on opposite page, weave entire piece. Work the flap as charted, adding and decreasing beads in length as indicated. Note: The pattern is not shown in its entirety; the body of the bag is made of alternating vertical rows of black and matte aqua, each eighty-one beads long.

2. When entire piece has been woven, fold body of bag in half, allowing three horizontal rows between top edge of body and beginning of flap for attaching leather cord.

3. Join sides of body by repeating Steps 4–7 on page 48, treating doubled first and last rows as if each were now both Row 1 and Row 2.

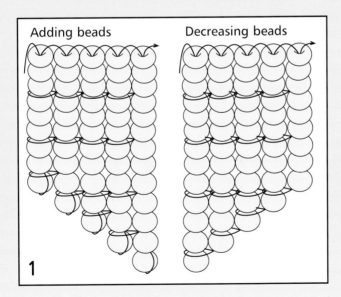

Adding beads   Decreasing beads

1

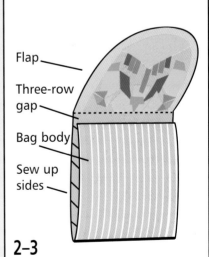

Flap

Three-row gap

Bag body

Sew up sides

2–3

Woven Bag Necklace Pattern & Key

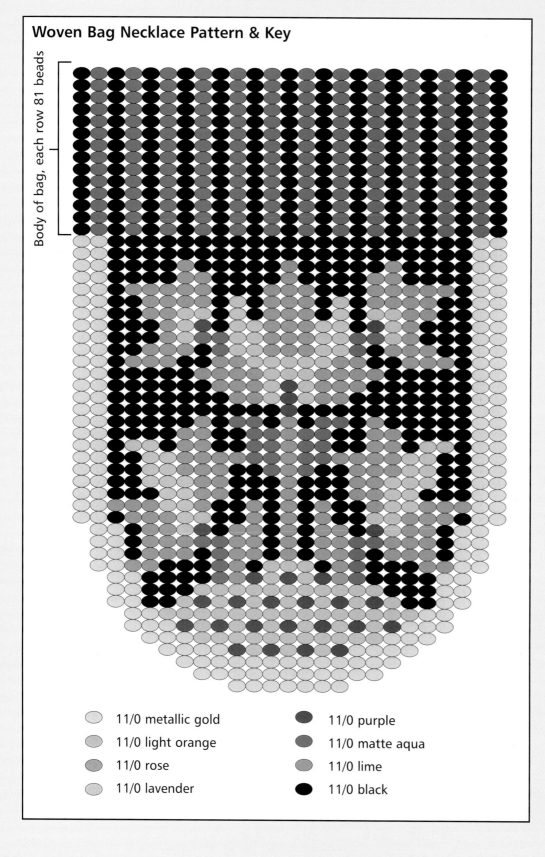

Body of bag, each row 81 beads

Key:

- ⬭ 11/0 metallic gold
- ⬭ 11/0 light orange
- ⬭ 11/0 rose
- ⬭ 11/0 lavender
- ⬤ 11/0 purple
- ⬤ 11/0 matte aqua
- ⬤ 11/0 lime
- ⬤ 11/0 black

4. Bury excess thread in weave.

5. Center leather cord on inside of bag just below flap over three horizontal rows. Whip-stitch cord onto inside of bag.

6. Refer to Steps 1–3 on page 33. Attach pressure crimps, securing firmly with glue.

7. Using needle-nosed pliers, attach rings and clasp.

Troubleshooting:
For additional threadings, refer to *Adding a New Length of Thread* on page 18.

How do I shape needle-weaving and add fringes?

This squared needle-weaving design is made up of delica beads. Because of their uniformity of shape and size, delica beads create a beautiful effect when woven. The fringes and necklace strands are made up of thoughtfully placed colors combined with ornamental 6/0 seed beads and faceted crystals.

What You Need to Get Started:

Beads:
Delica beads:
  metallic gold (462); light green (169); dark green (89); ivory (289); dark blue-lavender (1577); light blue-lavender (277); light rose (146); dark rose (80)
6 mm faceted crystals: light blue (27)
6/0 seed beads: lavender (37)

<u>Etc.:</u>
Barrel clasp: gold-finished
#9 embroidery needle
Embroidery scissors
Thread: tan

Squared Floral Necklace
Photograph on page 74.

Here's How:
1. Following Squared Floral Necklace Pattern on page 73, string beads for Row 1 from top to bottom. Skipping last bead, insert needle back through all beads. Note: The needle should emerge from the top bead of Row 1.

2. String beads for Row 2, from top to bottom. Add first fringe by continuing to string as charted from top to bottom. Skipping last bead, insert needle back through all beads on fringe. Insert needle into loop exposed at bottom of Row 1. Pull thread gently until entire second row is taut, but not tight, and beads rest against first row without puckering. Note: When forming fringes, the tension of the thread is important. Try to leave enough slack so that the fringes move freely, but not so much that there is a lot of visible thread. Part of the beauty of fringes is their motion. Lack of motion impedes the beauty of the overall design.

3. Insert needle into last three beads of Row 2, and bring thread out until it is taut, but not tight. Loop thread around Row 1 so it is nestled between corresponding beads of Row 1. Insert needle into next three beads of Row 2, bringing needle out again between subsequent beads on Row 2. Again, thread should be taut, but not tight.

4. Loop thread around Row 1 so it is nestled between corresponding beads of Row 1. Insert needle into next three beads on Row 2 and continue this looping and inserting process until thread emerges from bead 1 of Row 2.

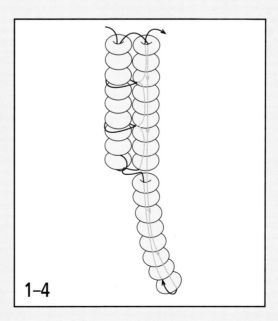

1–4

5. Repeat Steps 1–4 for all subsequent rows of pattern and fringes.

6. Cut one 24" length of thread and thread needle.

7. Attach thread at outermost top row of either side of foundation pattern by running it through several of beads in foundation until secure or by tying it onto end of thread left from weaving.

8. Slip beads on needle as indicated. Slip dark blue-lavender delica beads on needle to 8½" length. Note: There are two patterns of strands, "dots" and "Xs," which emanate from the top of rows marked on the foundation pattern.

9. Take needle through loop of one end of barrel clasp and then reinsert it into top bead of necklace strand. Run thread through all beads on strand until reaching foundation pattern.

10. Run thread through beads in foundation pattern and bring out at next marker.

11. Repeat Steps 8–10 until all strings are attached.

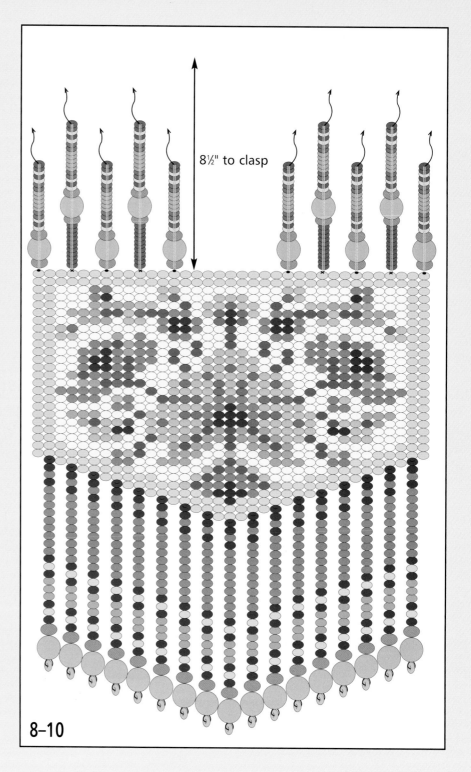

8½" to clasp

8–10

Squared Floral Necklace Pattern & Key

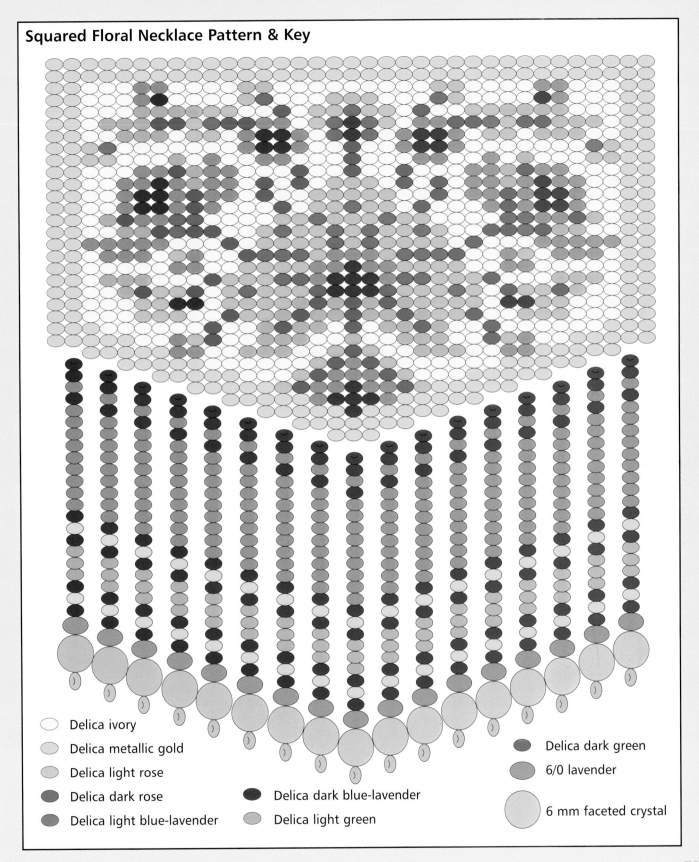

○ Delica ivory

○ Delica metallic gold

○ Delica light rose

● Delica dark rose

● Delica light blue-lavender

● Delica dark blue-lavender

● Delica light green

● Delica dark green

● 6/0 lavender

○ 6 mm faceted crystal

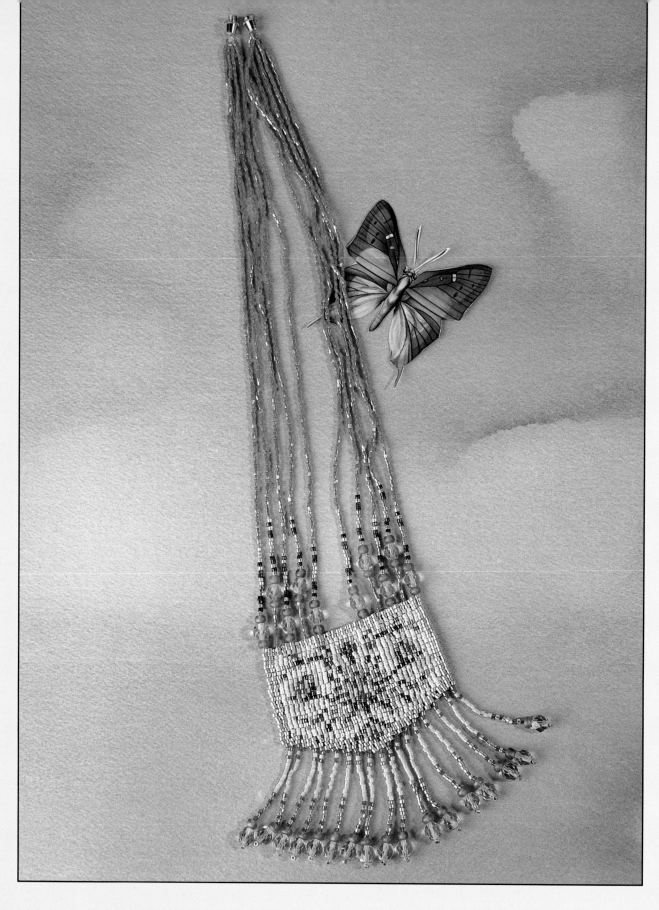

How do I create a tube with needle-weaving?

This interesting necklace uses squared needle-weaving and demonstrates how to join the weave to form a tube. It is then embellished with a turquoise drop attached to a band of bugle beads formed by double needle-weaving.

Woven Southwest Tube Necklace

Photograph on page 77.

Here's How:

Note: An arrowhead-shaped drop was used to embellish this piece, but any shaped drop will work.

1. Refer to Steps 1–14 on pages 47–49. Following Woven Southwest Tube Necklace Pattern on page 76, weave right half of piece, beginning at center row as indicated on pattern. Weave vertical rows as charted, repeating final section until length of half-strip is 8½" long.

2. Attach thread at center row (first woven row), rotate work piece 180° and repeat pattern until both ends are identical. Note: As there is no front or back to the design, rotate or flip the work piece and complete the weave in a manner that is most comfortable for you.

3. Wrap width of woven piece around clothesline, matching top and bottom beads of each vertical row.

4. Attach new thread at one end of weave. Take needle through last three beads on first row and continue through first three beads on same row. Take thread through first three beads on next row and continue through last three beads of same row. Continue weaving back and forth until entire length has been joined together.

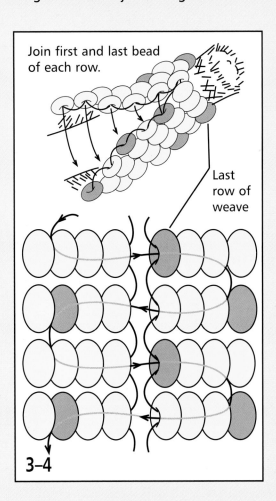

Join first and last bead of each row.

Last row of weave

3–4

What You Need to Get Started:

Beads:
#3 bugle beads: gold (18)
11/0 seed beads: dark aqua (250); light aqua (480); metallic copper (250); cream (1800); metallic gold (350)

Etc.:
Barrel clasp: gold-finished
Clothesline: ¼"-diameter, 18"-long
Craft scissors
Sewing needles (2)
Thread: tan
Turquoise carved drop

5. Trim each end of clothesline very close to end of weave.

6. Attach new thread at one end of weave. Take needle through three beads on last row of weave. Slip two cream 11/0 seed beads on needle and run needle back through first three and next three seed beads on woven row. Slip two more beads on needle and continue in this manner all around until twelve beads have been added onto weave.

7. Take needle through first two beads on row of twelve. Slip one cream 11/0 seed bead on needle and run needle back through first two and next two seed beads on row. Slip one more bead on needle and continue in this manner all around until six beads have been added on. Run thread through last six beads and pull thread taut so gap closes.

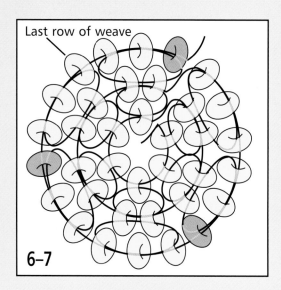

Last row of weave

6–7

8. Repeat Steps 6–7 for remaining end.

9. Sew one part of clasp onto each finished end, looping thread back through last few beads until clasp is secure. Bury thread in weave.

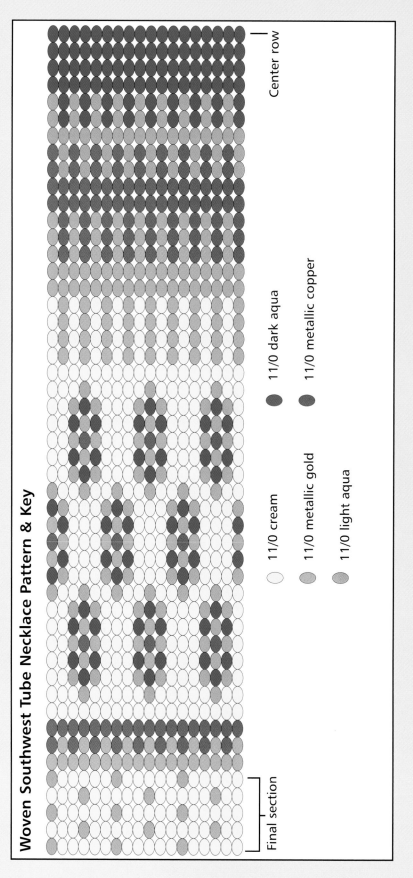

Woven Southwest Tube Necklace Pattern & Key

Center row

Final section

11/0 dark aqua

11/0 metallic copper

11/0 cream

11/0 metallic gold

11/0 light aqua

10. Cut a piece of thread 24" long and thread a needle on each end.

11. Put a bugle bead on one of the needles and pull to center of thread.

12. Slip the next bugle bead over the needle. Bring the other needle through from the opposite end of the bead and pull both needles in opposite directions, drawing the second bead in against the first.

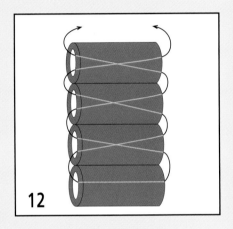

13. Repeat Step 12 until eighteen bugle beads are woven together. Join length together in a circle around center of tube necklace.

14. Sew turquoise drop onto one bugle bead in ring and bury excess thread in weave.

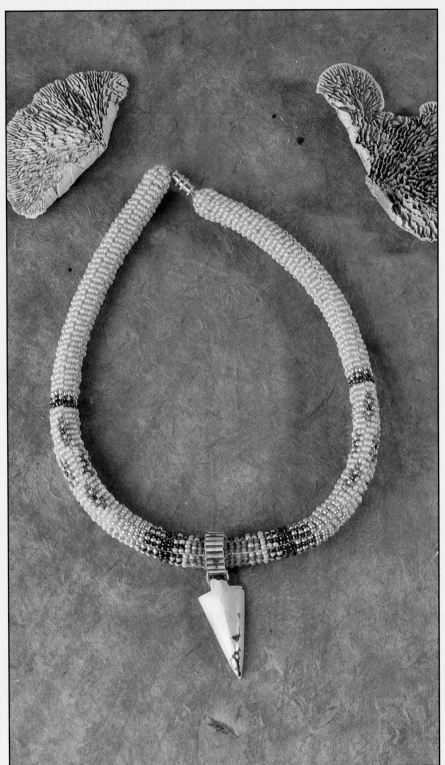

How do I embellish
brick stitch needle-weaving?

**What You
Need to
Get Started:**

Beads:
6 mm aventurine
flat beads with
hole through
length (5)
Delica beads:
cream (400);
galvanized gold
(50); galvanized
light green (80);
galvanized dark
pink (75);
galvanized light
pink (160)

Etc.:
Ear wires: gold-
finished (2)
#9 embroidery
needles (2)
Embroidery
scissors
Pin back: 1½"
Needle-nosed
pliers
4 mm rings: gold-
finished (2)
Thread: off-white

This set is worked in brick stitch, which is ideally suited to use in small jewelry items because the weave is strong and inflexible, so items hold their intended shape. This rigidity also makes it possible to attach heavier beads at the points of the design for attractive dangles.

Brick Stitch Pin & Earrings
Photograph on page 80.

Here's How:
Note: This design uses the top row of the pin as the foundation row.

1. Refer to Steps 1–6 on pages 50–51. Following Brick Stitch Pin Pattern on opposite page, form foundation (top) row. Note: The thread that would ordinarily be used to work upward will be used to sew the finished beadwork to the pin back, so do not cut it.

2. Work consecutive rows until completing row 17. Weave thread through first and second bead on row 17 and bring needle out at bottom of third bead on row to begin row 18. Continue working remaining rows until pattern is complete.

3. Using thread end at bottom of pattern, slip one galvanized dark pink delica bead, one aventurine bead, and one galvanized dark pink delica bead on needle. Run needle back through aventurine and first galvanized dark pink delica bead.

4. Take needle up through cream delica beads on right side of woven piece. Bring needle out at bottom of second to last bead on row 17.

5. Repeat Step 3 at base of row 17.

6. Take needle up through last cream delica bead on row 17. Working from right to left, weave thread in and out of each bead on row 17 until reaching second bead on row.

7. Bring needle out at bottom of bead and repeat Step 3. Bury excess thread in weave.

8. Using thread at top of pattern, whipstitch pin back onto back top edge of woven piece.

(continued on page 80)

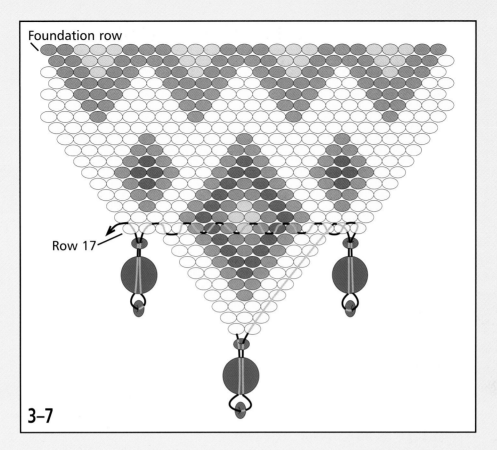

Foundation row

Row 17

3–7

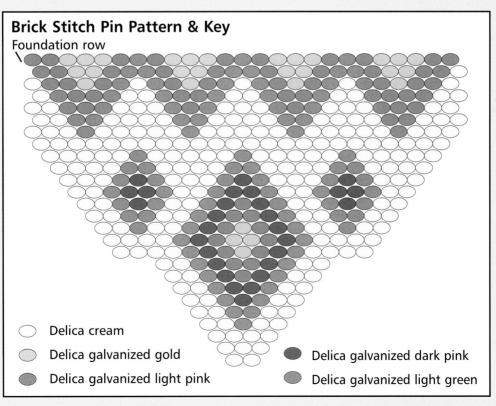

Brick Stitch Pin Pattern & Key

Foundation row

- ○ Delica cream
- ○ Delica galvanized gold
- ● Delica galvanized light pink
- ● Delica galvanized dark pink
- ● Delica galvanized light green

(continued from page 78)

9. For earrings, refer to Steps 1–7 on pages 50–51. Following Brick Stitch Earring Pattern, form foundation row. Work consecutive rows to complete one full pattern. Repeat for second full pattern.

10. Repeat Step 3 for each. Bury excess thread in weave.

11. Using thread end at top of each pattern, take needle through top two beads and sew on one 4 mm ring. Bury excess thread in weave.

12. Using needle-nosed pliers, open loop on each ear wire. Slip ring on and close loop.

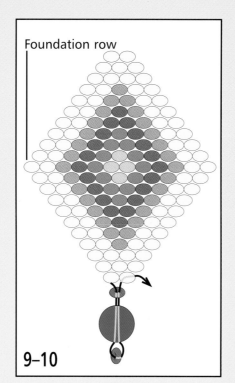

Foundation row

9–10

Brick Stitch Earring Pattern

Foundation row

CANDLEMAKING
for the first time®

Vanessa-Ann

Candlemaking for the first time

Introduction

Candles are more than just a source of light. For centuries they have been used for symbolic and religious purposes. Candles also serve as a focal point for celebrations throughout the world.

The first candles, tallow candles, were made from beef or mutton fat. These candles produced black smoke and a rancid smell. Beeswax offered a more decorative and better smelling candle. However, with the cost of beeswax being so high, only the rich or clergy could purchase these higher quality candles. Eventually, the development of paraffin and stearin increased the availability of decorative and scented candles. Through the centuries, the materials needed to create candles have advanced, while the method of creating a candle has stayed the same.

Although candles are no longer a necessity for light, their popularity is enormous. They are still used for symbolic and religious reasons. However, the use of candles in today's society has a much broader spectrum. Candles are a very versatile item. Some offer healing and relaxation through their scent. Others contain a scent that repels mosquitoes. The variety of colors and shapes in which they are available adds to their simple and timeless beauty. Candles can add a unique touch to any type of setting. Their flickering light seems to draw people together. The look of a room can be enhanced simply by the way a candle is used.

For the person who is candlemaking for the first time, here is a comprehensive guide to supplies, tools, and techniques that can be used to create fabulous decorative and functional candles.

Candlemaking can produce so many unique results. Candles such as molded, double mold, container, dipped, rolled, and gel candles can be made by almost anyone. Learn to decorate the candles you have made, using decoupaging and painting techniques. Discover contemporary ideas for decorating with candles to create a relaxed and intimate atmosphere.

Creating the finished projects shown may take some time and practice, since this is your first time candlemaking. However, once the basic techniques of candlemaking are mastered, the possibilities of creating scent, beauty, and light are endless.

This section will provide a starting point and teach basic skills. The more you practice candlemaking, the more comfortable you will feel. Allow yourself a reasonable amount of time to complete your first project—remember this is your first time. You will soon discover that the techniques are easy to master.

After you have completed the first few projects, you will be surprised by how quickly you will be able to finish the remaining projects. Take pride in the talents you are developing and the unique designs only you can create.

Getting Started

What do I need to get started?

To begin candlemaking, all you need to do is take a trip to the local craft store or candle-making supplier to find a wide array of supplies. You probably already have many of the supplies around the house.

The following list of tools and supplies is necessary for creating candles. In addition, each technique or project gives a list of other items needed for that specific project.

Candle Dye Chips—used to dye the melted wax.

Candle Molds—used to mold candles into desired shapes and sizes.

Candle Scents—used to scent the melted wax.

Candle Thermometer—used to determine the precise temperature of wax.

Containers (not shown)—used to contain soft waxes while burning.

Craft Scissors—used to trim soft candle wax and wicks.

Double Boiler—used for melting wax. Make certain water does not boil dry. *Note: There are a few different options to choose from, depending on the amount of wax being melted. A container such as a coffee can or large soup can on a small rack inside of a saucepan filled with water can be easily substituted for a double boiler.*

Hammer & Screwdriver—used to break wax into smaller pieces.

Heating Element (not shown)—used to melt wax. Use either a stove or hot plate.

Kitchen Scale—used to weigh wax.

Large Plastic Trash Bag (not shown)—used to prevent scattering chips while breaking up wax.

Liquid Measuring Cups (not shown)—used to measure liquid ingredients.

Measuring Spoons—used to measure ingredients, following manufacturer's instructions.

Metal Pouring Pot—used to contain and pour molten wax.

Metal Spoons—used to mix dyes and scents into melted wax. Use a separate spoon for each dye color.

Mold Release (not shown)—used to coat the inside of molds for easy candle removal. Vege-table oil can be easily substituted.

Mold Sealer—used to secure wick and seal wick holes in molds.

Paper Towels (not shown)—used to wipe melted wax from equipment while still warm.

Paring Knife (not shown)—used to cut soft cold wax and trim candles.

Pencils—used to hold wick in place while creating candles.

Primed Wicks—used to burn candles. These wicks have been chemically treated.

Tape Measure—used to measure candle and wick dimensions.

Double Boiler

Metal Pouring Pot

Candle Mold

Waxed Paper

Candle Thermometer

Wax

Kitchen Scale

Metal Spoon

Hammer

Candle Scent

Pencil

Candle Dye Chip

Screw Driver

Craft Scissors

Tape Measure

Mold Sealer

Primed Wick

Measuring Spoons

Waxed Paper—used to cover and protect work surface.

Waxes—used to create a candle. There are several types of wax used for candle-making: bead, beeswax, gel, blended paraffin, and paraffin.

Safety precautions

The following precautions are strongly recommended for your safety. When working with melted wax, it is a good idea to have baking soda and a fire extinguisher handy. Wax can be volatile and may ignite without warning. Please review the following items:

• Never use water to put out a wax fire. Smother the fire with baking soda.

• Use the lid to your double boiler to smother a wax fire.

• Never leave melting wax unattended. Always be aware of the wax's flash-point temperature. Keep a thermometer in the melting wax so you can be certain of the temperature.

• Never allow wax temperature to exceed 280ºF.

• Always keep children and pets away from hot wax.

• Never allow wax to drip onto heating element. It may ignite upon contact and could cause a fire.

• Never store wax anywhere near heat. Always store wax in a cool dry location.

• Avoid heating wax in a microwave. It will collect energy from the inside out and can bubble, explode, or catch fire.

• Use only fragrances and dyes designed specifically for candlemaking.

• Be aware of aluminum molds when they contain hot wax. The aluminum molds get very hot and can burn your skin.

• Always pour wax with a container that can withstand high temperatures, and that has a spout and a handle.

• If melted wax comes in contact with skin, bathe the area immediately in cold water. Peel off the wax and treat burned area as any other burn or scald.

• Do not allow water to drip into melted wax as it will burst and could burn the skin.

• Never pour melted wax down the drain.

Kinds of waxes

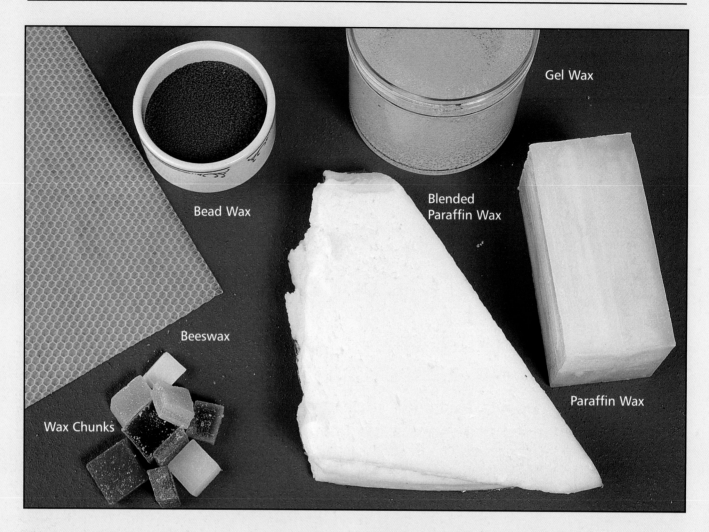

Gel Wax

Bead Wax

Blended
Paraffin Wax

Beeswax

Paraffin Wax

Wax Chunks

The most essential ingredient in a candle is wax. The type of wax used, amount of wax used, and the temperature of melted wax will effect the final look of the candle.

Waxes used to create the candles in this book include:

Bead Wax—is wax that has been granulated into small beads. It can be found in a variety of colors and scents.

Beeswax—comes in blocks or sheets. It can be natural, unbleached, or bleached white. It offers a natural honey fragrance. When added to paraffin wax, it will help to lengthen the burn time.

Blended Paraffin & Paraffin Waxes—are petroleum-based waxes. Paraffin wax can be used plain, or it can come in a variety of blends to be used in creating specific candles.

Gel Wax—is a clear gel that can be purchased at your local craft store. We have also provided the ingredients and instructions for making gel wax in the Basic Gel Candle on pages 114–115.

Wax Chunks—come in a variety of colors. They can be melted down when small portions of wax are needed. They can also be embedded into a candle for a unique look.

Working with wax

Calculate amount of wax needed (for the mold, container, or desired height of dipped candle) by filling the mold/container with water and measuring it—3 ounces of cold wax are needed for every 3½ fluid ounces of water.

Melting

Melted wax can be volatile. Prepare and use caution and safety measures when handling wax. Please refer to *Safety precautions* on page 85 before melting wax.

1. Place the block of paraffin wax into a large plastic bag, then place on a solid surface. Using hammer and screwdriver, break wax into small pieces that will fit into top of double boiler. *Note: Softer waxes can be cut with a paring knife.*

2. Make certain top section of double boiler is deep enough to accommodate length of thermometer so bulb does not touch bottom of pan. Separate top and bottom sections of double boiler. Place wax pieces into top of double boiler.

3. Fill bottom section of double boiler with water. Replace top section. Make certain water does not boil dry.

4. Set double boiler on heating element and bring water to boiling point. The wax will begin to melt, becoming a clear liquid.

5. Place thermometer in melting wax and reduce heat to medium low. If water begins to boil rapidly, reduce heat to a gentle boil to prevent water from splashing into wax container. Make certain heat is not reduced too much, as doing so will cause difficulty in keeping the temperature accurate.

6. Once wax is melted and is at the specified temperature, add stearin if necessary, dye, and scent. This may lower the temperature. Make certain wax is brought back up to temperature required.

Pouring

This book recommends that the melted wax be poured from the double boiler into a pouring pot. Using a pouring pot reduces the chance of spilling melted wax and makes filling molds or containers easier and safer. A pouring pot is not necessary when pouring large amounts of wax into another large container or when conciseness is not an issue.

Once the melted wax has reached the required temperature for candle, remove top section of double boiler from bottom section. Be aware of steam, and water dripping from bottom of top section. Carefully pour melted wax into pouring pot. Do not fill pouring pot more than 70 percent full. Replace top section.

When pouring melted wax, make certain of the following items:

• When filling a candle mold, candle container, or topping off a candle, make certain to use a pouring pot.

• Always pour melted wax carefully and slowly.

• Clean up all wax spills immediately.

• Wipe off all wax drippings on sides of double boiler or pouring pot immediately.

Additives

Sometimes when you purchase paraffin wax you will need to add hardeners or other additives to keep it from being damaged by the sun or to make it opaque. Here is a list of some additives and their purposes.

Luster Crystals—provide a brilliant sheen and opaqueness and a longer burning candle. Recommended use per two pounds of wax is one teaspoon. Luster crystals must be melted first then added to your melted wax.

Microcrystalline Wax—makes candle wax harder. Recommended use per pound of wax is two tablespoons. It must be melted first, then added to melted wax as it will not melt in the wax by itself.

Snow Wax—makes the candle wax opaque with a high luster. It also prevents hot-weather sag, increases the burning time, and improves the surface texture. Recommended use per pound of wax is one teaspoon. It is recommended that Snow wax be melted separately.

Stearin—improves the candle's burning time and gives an opaque or white appearance. Recommended use per pound of wax is two tablespoons.

Vybar—makes the candle harder and cuts down on wax shrinkage. Recommended use per pound of wax is two teaspoons. Start with one teaspoon per pound then add more if necessary It will also cause your candle to be opaque. Do not use more than the recommended amount.

Dyes

Dyes for candlemaking come in several forms: chip, flake, liquid, and powder. They all come in a broad range of colors. Colors can also be mixed and matched for endless possibilities. This book uses the dye-chip form because it is readily available and easy to use.

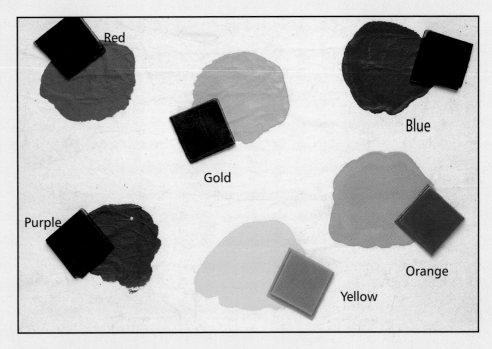

Candle Dye Tips:

• Be careful when using candle dye. Clothes and some plastic equipment can become permanently stained.

• Too much dye can affect the candle's burning qualities.

• Too much heat can cause discoloration, at time of heating or within a short time after.

• Avoid using clear wax when making a black candle. Use pieces of scrap wax, then add needed amounts of black.

Scents

Scents for candlemaking come in several forms: liquid, natural herbs, and solid-wax perfume chips. They all come in a broad range of scents. This book uses the liquid form because it is readily available and easy to use.

Candle Scent Tips:

• Add candle scent just before pouring to keep evaporation to a minimum.

• Avoid adding too much scent as this may cause mottling or pitting, making removal of candle from mold difficult.

Wicks

Wicks are what helps the candle burn. Wicks must be carefully chosen to ensure proper burning. Primed wicks are made of braided cotton and specially treated to slow the burning rate. The three basic wicks used in this book are flat-braided, square-braided, and wire-core. Pretabbed wicks are available in these basic types. The tab on a wick is used to anchor the wick to the bottom of the container.

Flat-braided Wicks—used for dipped taper candles.

Square-braided Wicks—used for square or round pillar candles.

Wire-core Wicks—used for container candles and votives. This type of wick has a metal wire center, allowing the wick to stand upright in melted wax.

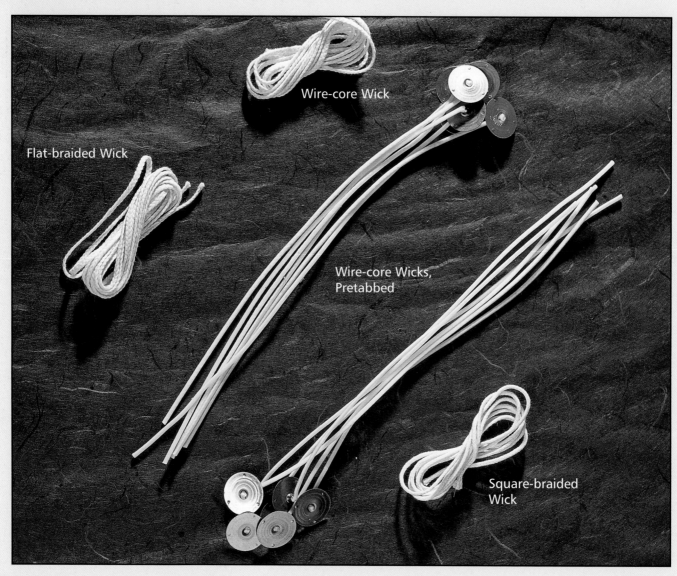

Wire-core Wick

Flat-braided Wick

Wire-core Wicks, Pretabbed

Square-braided Wick

Priming

Wicks can be purchased primed or unprimed. Prime an unprimed wick, using the following method:

1. Soak wick in melted wax for five minutes.

2. Remove saturated wick from melted wax and lay straight on waxed paper. Allow to harden.

Wick Size
The size of wick depends upon the diameter of the candle being made. Determine necessary size of wick, using the following method:

1. Using tape measure, measure diameter of mold, container, or desired thickness of dipped candle.

For candles with a burn area up to 2" in diameter, use small-sized wicks. For candles 2"–3", use medium-sized wicks. For candles 3"–4", use large-sized wicks.

Wick Length
In some cases, you may wish to leave a longer wick that can be knotted or embellished with beads and charms for a more decorative effect or for gift giving. Determine necessary length of wick, using the following method:

1. Using tape measure, measure height of mold, container, or desired height of dipped candle.

2. Add 2" to that measurement.

3. Cut length of wick to new measurement.

Molds

Candle molds can be purchased at your local craft store or from candlemaking suppliers. Molds are available in an endless variety of shapes and sizes, from simple geometrics to ornate fruits and flowers. Molds are relatively inexpensive, and their sturdiness allows for long-lasting, repeated use. They are made from acrylic, metal, plastic, or rubber.

Many household cartons and containers make excellent molds. Anything that can be peeled, pulled, or broken off from a finished candle works well. However, in this book we will be using candle molds.

Temperatures required for different types of molds

Acrylic molds	180°–210°F
Clay molds	180°–210°F
Glass molds	170°–200°F
Metal molds	180°–210°F
Plaster molds	160°–180°F
Rubber molds	160°–180°F
Tear-away molds	160°F

Cleaning candle molds

Molds should always be kept clean in order to provide the best results. Candle molds should be clean and free from old candle wax before using. Do not scrape or scratch inside of molds when cleaning them, it will mar future candles. Candle molds can be cleaned using the following three methods:

Method 1
1. Fill sink with hot water and a small amount of liquid dish soap. Allow candle molds to soak for 15 minutes.

2. Wash candle molds, being careful of any sharp edges. Dry molds thoroughly. Dry seamless candle molds upside down on a cookie sheet covered with paper towels.

Method 2
1. Place candle molds on a cookie sheet covered with paper towels in a 200°F oven for 7–8 minutes. The paper towel will absorb the melted wax.

2. Wipe off any remaining wax from candle mold immediately.

Method 3
1. Use cleaner designed for metal molds, following manufacturer's instructions.

Preparing the work space

Setting up your work space properly will make a large difference in the final results of your candles. We recommend that you work in the kitchen for ease and convenience. The following items are needed to prepare your work space: heating element, paper towels, pot holder (optional), and waxed paper.

1. Cover any surface that you will be working on with waxed paper. This will protect your work space and allow spilled wax to be reused.

2. Place additional sheets of waxed paper underneath candle molds and containers. Make certain that all items are within your reach.

3. Never allow wax to drip onto heating element. It may ignite upon contact and could cause a fire.

Cleanup

Candle cleaning kits can be purchased to aid in removing stubborn stains and wax buildup from equipment and supplies. Following are a few methods to help in cleanup after candlemaking:

• Pour excess wax into an old pan lined with waxed paper. Never pour wax down the drain. It will cool and clog the drain. Unused wax can be melted and reused.

• Place supplies such as molds and metal spoons in boiling water until wax melts. Using tongs, remove items from water. Using paper towels, wipe items clean.

• Discard old metal soup and coffee cans, and other replaceable equipment.

• Place glass items in freezer. Wax will shrink and easily pop out.

Troubleshooting

When learning a new craft, mistakes and problems will occur. However, certain problems tend to be more common among certain types of candles. Most of these problems can be corrected through practice and knowing what went wrong. Following are troubleshooting ideas in candlemaking:

Candle burning straight down the middle
• A candle made from a hard wax will burn straight down the wick, leaving the sides of the candle unmelted. The crater created will make it difficult for the flame to sustain itself. A softer wax, such as a container wax, could be used. However, using a wax with a lower melting point may create a pool of melted wax around the base of a pillar candle.

• A small, similarly scented votive or tea light could be placed in the cavity.

Candle color changes
• Wax was too hot when color was added. Avoid heating wax above 190°F that will be colored.

• Candle was exposed to direct sunlight. Many colors fade in sunlight. UV-protective additives are available.

Candle stops burning
• Additives such as color, spices, or essential oils of inferior quality can clog the wick.

Candle will not burn
• Wick was not primed. Saturate the wick with liquid wax or light it upside down to allow melted wax to prime wick.

Candle will not release from mold
• Make certain to always coat the mold with a mold release.

• A high percentage of beeswax may produce a candle that is sticky or does not shrink enough for easy release. Beeswax is less than ideal for using in molded candles.

• Place candle and mold into freezer or refrigerator for 5–10 minutes. Remove and check to see if candle releases.

• Candle may be run under hot water for release, although this may cause imperfections on the candle surface.

• Check molds for pits or dents.

Candles leaving excess wax on container walls

• Container candles burn best when they are lit for a minimum of four hours at a time. Burning a candle for short periods of time will cause unburned wax on container walls.

• Use a container wax or a wax with a lower burning point.

• Use a larger wick size.

Candle cracks

• Candle was cooled too fast.

• Candle was left in freezer too long.

Candle drips

• Wick is too small, it may not be able to absorb and burn the amount of wax melting around it.

• Wick is the wrong type for the wax blend.

• Wick is not properly centered. Check the position of the wick after candle is out and manually center it, if possible.

• Wax used was too soft and has too low of a melting point.

• Check for a draft around the flame.

Outside of candle looks old or dusty

• Polish the outside of the candle with a nylon stocking or almond oil.

• Overdip candle to renew its look.

Candle has pits and bubbles

• Wax was too cold when poured.

• Wax was poured too fast.

• Mold release was applied too heavily.

• Mold should be clean and dust-free before pouring wax.

Scent in candle is not strong enough

• Allow candle to burn one hour before judging strength of scent, because scent primarily rises from the liquid wax pool.

• Rubbing hands over the outside of a candle should activate scent in a candle that has lost fragrance on the outer surface.

Shrink wells

• This is a normal occurrence in paraffin wax blends. As wax cools, an indentation will form around the wick. Remelt remaining wax and fill to the top of indentation, making certain that wick is still centered. Try not to pour wax over the top, as this will set a line in candle. Allow wax to set. Repour wax as needed for an even candle.

• Occasionally, the shrink well comes at the bottom of the candle. You can straighten the bottom of the candle by trimming it off or melting it flat on a frying pan lined with aluminum foil.

Sides of candle cave in
• Air bubbles may be trapped inside candle. This problem can be prevented by tapping mold or perforating with a skewer around the wick to eliminate bubbles after pouring candle.

Smoking candle
• Wick is too thick.

• Wick is the wrong type for the wax blend.

• Wick is too long. Trim wick to ¼".

• Check for drafts around the flame.

Sputtering flame
• Wick is drawing from an air or oil pocket that has formed in the candle. This problem can be prevented by tapping mold or perforating with a skewer around the wick to eliminate bubbles after pouring candle.

• Pouring from a wet container may allow water to drop inside wax and form a water pocket.

Unintentional mottling or snowflake pattern
• Wax was too cold when poured.

• Candle was cooled too slowly.

• Too much stearin was added.

Weak flame or drowning wick
• Wick is too small.

• Wick is too loose in the candle.

• Melting point of the wax is too high for the size of wick used.

Care of finished candles

• Keep lighted candles out of reach from children and pets.

• Never leave candles unattended.

• Store candles in a cool, dry, dark place. Make certain they are placed flat in a drawer or box to prevent warping.

• Clean dusty or dirty tapers or pillars by wiping them with a nylon stocking. If candles seem a bit dry, wipe them with a small amount of vegetable oil.

• Avoid exposing candle to direct sunlight or artificial light for an extended period of time.

• Refrigerate or freeze candles before using them to make them burn slowly and evenly.

• Carve away enough wax with a sharp paring knife to expose the fresh wick if a wick becomes too short to light. Shave ¼" of the wax from the top of the candle so the wick will be exposed to the air. Gently shape and smooth the cut edges of the candle with the heat of another flame.

• Extinguish candles that are smoking or have burned down to within 2" of the holder.

• Fit candles snugly into holders. Candles that are too lose or too tight may tip over.

• Extinguish candles with a candle snuffer or by blowing gently.

How do I make a candle using a candle mold?

Candles can be molded into a variety of shapes and sizes. Today's molds are made from a variety of different materials, each type offering certain advantages and disadvantages. This basic molded candle was created with a pillar mold for a simple yet elegant look.

Basic Molded Candle

Here's How:
1. Prepare work space. Refer to *Preparing the work space* on page 93.

2. Melt wax in double boiler until it reaches 194º–198ºF. Refer to *Melting* on page 87. Proceed with Steps 3–4 while wax is melting.

3. Cut appropriate sized wick to length. Refer to *Wick Size* and *Wick Length* on page 91.

4. Prepare mold, using the following technique:

a. Lightly coat inside of mold with mold release.

b. Thread wick through hole in bottom of mold.

c. Cover hole and secure end of wick on outside of mold with mold sealer to prevent any leaking that may occur when the wax is poured.

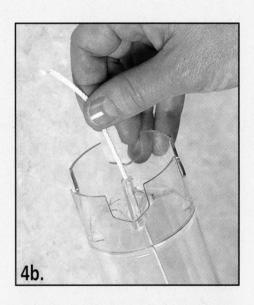

4b.

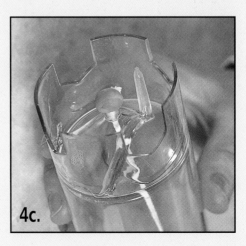

4c.

d. Tie opposite end of wick around a pencil. Place pencil on top rim of mold. Make certain that wick is centered and taut. If wick is not taut, tighten wick around pencil.

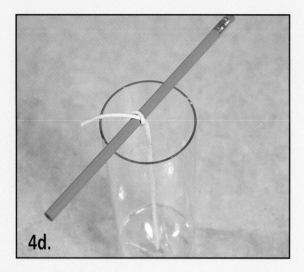

4d.

5. Using pouring pot, pour melted wax into the mold until mold is 90 percent full. Refer to *Pouring* on page 88. Allow wax to set. Make cer-tain to set aside a small amount of that particular wax in empty soup can to top off the candle.

5

6. As wax cools, an indentation will form around the wick. Top off candle, using the following technique:

a. Remelt remaining wax and fill to the top of indentation, making certain that wick is still centered. Try not to pour wax over the top, as this will set a line in candle. Allow wax to set.

6a.

b. Repour wax as needed for an even candle. Allow wax to set.

7. Remove candle from mold, using the following technique:

a. Remove pencil. Remove mold sealer. Tip mold upside down. Candle should slide out on its own. If it does not work, place mold with candle in freezer for 5–10 minutes. Remove from freezer. Tip mold upside down. Candle should slide out on its own.

8. Trim wick at top of candle to ¼". Trim wick at bottom of candle flush with base.

How do I make a candle a different color using dye?

What You Need to Get Started:

Candle dye chip: med. blue
Candle thermometer
Craft scissors
Double boiler
Empty soup can
Metal pouring pot
Metal spoon
Mold: pillar
Mold release
Mold sealer
Pencil
Pillar-blend paraffin wax (1 lb)
Primed wick: square-braided

Wax can be dyed in a wide spectrum of colors from intense jewel tones to light cream satin. If colored candles are left in direct sunlight, they will begin to fade. This summer blue candle was made by using a medium blue dye chip.

Basic Dyed Candle

Here's How:

1. Prepare work space. Refer to *Preparing the work space* on page 93.

2. Melt wax in double boiler until it reaches 190°F. Refer to *Melting* on page 87. Proceed with Steps 3–4 while wax is melting.

3. Cut appropriate sized wick to length. Refer to *Wick Size* and *Wick Length* on page 91.

4. Prepare mold. Refer to Step 4 on pages 97–98.

5. Dye wax, using the following technique:

a. Add one dye chip to melted wax. Mix well.

5a.

6. Using pouring pot, pour melted wax into the mold until mold is 90 percent full. Refer to *Pouring* on page 88. Allow wax to set. Make certain to set aside a small amount of that particular wax in empty soup can to top off the candle.

7. Top off candle. Refer to Step 6 on page 98.

8. Remove candle from mold and trim wick. Refer to Steps 7–8 on page 98.

How do I make a candle fragrant using a scent?

What You Need to Get Started:

Candle dye chip: ivory
Candle scent: vanilla
Candle thermometer
Craft scissors
Double boiler
Empty soup can
Metal pouring pot
Metal spoon
Mold: round pillar, 1½" x 9½"
Mold release
Mold sealer
Pencil
Pillar-blend paraffin wax (1 lb)
Primed wick: square-braided

Candles offer more than just light. A scented candle has the ability to set the mood, create an atmosphere, and evoke memories. With just one whiff of this vanilla candle, we can be transported to our childhood and a favorite famous French vanilla dessert.

Basic Scented Candle

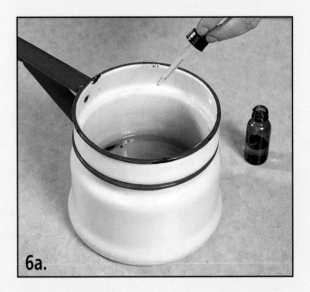

6a.

Here's How:

1. Prepare work space. Refer to *Preparing the work space* on page 93.

2. Melt wax in double boiler until it reaches 194°–198°F. Refer to *Melting* on page 87. Proceed with Steps 3–4 while wax is melting.

3. Cut appropriate sized wick to length. Refer to *Wick Size* and *Wick Length* on page 91.

4. Prepare mold. Refer to Step 4 on pages 97–98.

5. Dye wax. Refer to Step 5 on page 99.

6. Scent wax, using the following technique:

a. Add 1–3 drops of candle scent to melted wax. Mix well. *Note: Fragrance is added last to keep evaporation to a minimum.*

7. Using pouring pot, pour melted wax into the mold until mold is 90 percent full. Refer to *Pouring* on page 88. Allow wax to set. Make certain to set aside a small amount of that particular wax in empty soup can to top off the candle.

8. Top off candle. Refer to Step 6 on page 98.

9. Remove candle from mold and trim wick. Refer to Steps 7–8 on page 98.

How do I make a candle using a container?

What You Need to Get Started:

Candle dye chip: purple
Candle scent: lilac
Candle thermometer
Container: glass
Container-blend paraffin wax (1 lb)
Craft scissors
Double boiler
Empty soup can
Metal pouring pot
Metal spoon
Primed wick: pre-tabbed, wire core
Wick sticker

An alternative to making a candle in a mold is making one in a decorative container that will house the candle. Container candles are attractive, functional, and versatile. The glass containers on the facing page have found a new life as candle containers. Make certain that the container can withstand the pouring temperature of the melted wax.

Basic Container Candle

Here's How:

1. Prepare work space. Refer to *Preparing the work space* on page 93.

2. Melt wax in double boiler until it reaches 160º–165ºF. Refer to *Melting* on page 87. Proceed with Steps 3–4 while wax is melting.

3. Cut appropriate sized wick to length. Refer to *Wick Size* and *Wick Length* on page 91.

4. Dye wax. Refer to Step 5 on page 100.

5. Scent wax. Refer to Step 6 on page 102.

6. Apply wick sticker to bottom of wick tab, then to inside bottom center of clean container.

7. Tie opposite end of wick around a pencil. Place pencil on top rim of mold. Make certain that wick is centered and taut. If wick is not taut, tighten wick around pencil.

8. Using pouring pot, pour melted wax into the container until container is 90 percent full. Refer to *Pouring* on page 88. Allow wax to set. Make certain to set aside a small amount of that particular wax in empty soup can to top off the candle.

9. Top off candle. Refer to Step 6 on page 98.

10. Trim wick at top of candle to ¼".

How do I make a candle using the dipped method?

What You Need to Get Started:

Candle dye chip: blue
Candle scent: blueberry
Candle thermometer
Craft scissors
Dipping vat: 5" x 12"
Double boiler
Metal spoon
Pencil
Taper-blend paraffin wax (4 lb)
Wick: flat-braided

A dipped taper candle is made by repeatedly dipping a wick into melted wax. The longer the taper is, the more time it will need to cool in the dipping process. The dipped tapers featured opposite were dipped more than 30 times.

Basic Dipped Taper Candles

Here's How:

1. Prepare work space. Refer to *Preparing the work space* on page 93.

2. Melt wax in double boiler until it reaches 158°F. Refer to *Melting* on page 87.

3. Dye wax. Refer to Step 5 on page 100.

4. Scent wax. Refer to Step 6 on page 102.

5. Pour wax into dipping vat.

6. Make dipped candle, using the following technique:

a. Cut wick to desired height of candle times two plus 2". Center and drape wick over pencil. Hold wick in center. Dip two ends into melted wax, up to 1" from pencil. Wait for sixty seconds. Remove wick from wax, making certain that the two ends do not touch.

6a.

b. Hold candles over dipping vat and allow candles to harden. This takes only a few minutes. Repeat dipping. After 3–4 dippings, use fingers to straighten wicks and candles as necessary.

c. Continue, dipping a little shorter than previous dipping.

d. Trim drips from bottom of candle several times during dipping process.

e. Repeat dipping, hardening, and trimming until candles have reached desired thickness. *Note: To give candles a glossy top coat, increase heat to 180°F and dip one last time.* Hang candles and allow to set.

7. Trim wick in center to separate candles or leave candles connected for storing or displaying.

Dipped Taper Candle Tip:
For ease in the dipping process as candles become thicker, you may need to remove the pencil and continue dipping by hand. Make certain that fingertips do not touch the melted wax.

How do I make a candle using beeswax?

Rolled beeswax candles are easy to make. Simply roll a beeswax sheet around a wick. The beeswax sheets are imprinted with honeycomb design and offer a delicious, yet natural scent. These candles were made from colored beeswax sheets.

What You Need to Get Started:

Beeswax sheet:
  8¼" x 16¾"
Blow dryer
Craft knife
Craft scissors
Primed wick:
  square-
  braided
Ruler

Basic Rolled Beeswax Candle
Photograph on page 111.

Here's How:
Note: Beeswax candles tend to develop a powdery residue. Remove residue by blowing the candle with a blow dryer.

1. Prepare work space. Refer to *Preparing the work space* on page 93.

2. Place beeswax sheet on work surface. Using craft knife and ruler, cut beeswax sheet lengthwise into three equal sections approximately 2¾" wide.

3. Using craft scissors, cut wick ¾" longer than one short edge of sheet.

4. Using blow dryer, warm beeswax until it becomes soft and pliable.
Continued on page 110.

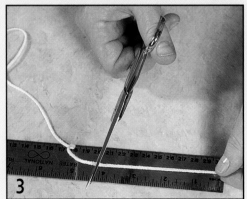

Continued from page 43.

5. Press wick into short edge, leaving ¾" length at one edge of beeswax. Begin rolling, making certain wick is firmly in place after the first roll.

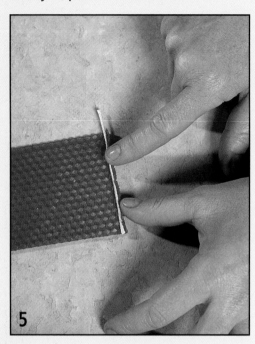

6. Continue rolling candle. *Note: The tighter the candle is rolled, the longer it will burn.*

7. When first section is completely rolled, place it on second section, with seams together, and continue rolling.

8. Repeat for remaining section.

9. When rolling is complete, press free edge into side of candle, smoothing in place with fingers.

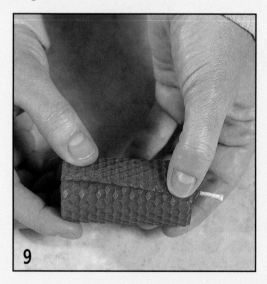

10. Trim wick at top of candle to ¼".

Bead Wax Candle Tip: As candle burns, a solid pool of wax will form around wick. More beads can be added at future lightings.

112

How do I make a candle using bead wax?

Bead wax is a fun and easy wax to create a candle. There is no melting of wax or thermometers to watch. Bead wax can be mixed or layered for a colorful candle. This elegant candle was created by spooning copper bead wax into a glass container.

What You Need to Get Started:

Bead wax:
  copper
Container: glass
Craft scissors
Metal spoon
Primed wick:
  pretabbed,
  wire core
Wick sticker

Basic Bead Wax Candle

Here's How:

1. Prepare work space. Refer to *Preparing the work space* on page 93.

2. Cut appropriate sized wick to length. Refer to *Wick Size* and *Wick Length* on page 91.

3. Apply wick sticker to bottom of wick tab, then to inside bottom center of clean container.

4. Spoon bead wax into container until full. Make certain to keep wick centered.

5. Trim wick at top of candle to ¼".

How do I make a candle using gel wax?

What You Need to Get Started:

Blow dryer
    (optional)
Candle scent:
    apple
Candle
    thermometer
Container: glass
Double boiler
Measuring cup
Measuring spoon
Metal pouring
    pot
Metal spoon
Mineral oil (16 oz)
Pencil
Primed wick:
    wire-core
Resin: CP9000
    (25 grams)

Gel wax can be made from scratch in your kitchen or it can be purchased. Whichever one you decide upon, the result will be the center of conversation, because of its transparency. Gel wax can be cubed, shredded, rolled, bubbly, or smooth. These candles appear as if the wick were floating in their contem-porary containers.

Basic Gel Candle

Here's How:

1. Prepare work space. Refer to *Preparing the work space* on page 93.

2. Using metal spoon, mix mineral oil and resin in double boiler. Allow to set at room temperature for one hour, stirring occasionally.

3. Melt resin mixture slowly, until it reaches 200°–210°F. Hold at this temperature for one hour or until gel is completely smooth like consistency of corn syrup. *Note: Never let the temperature of mixture exceed 230°F as the gel may scorch.*

4. Cut appropriate sized wick to length. Refer to *Wick Size* and *Wick Length* on page 91.

5. Scent wax. Refer to Step 6 on page 102.

6. Dip one end of wick into gel wax. Place wax-covered end in container and hold to bottom center, allowing wick to adhere to container.

7. Tie opposite end of wick around pencil. Place pencil on top rim of container. Make certain that wick is centered and taut. If wick is not taut, tighten wick around pencil.

8. Using pouring pot, pour melted gel wax into the mold until mold is 90 percent full. Refer to *Pouring* on page 88. Allow wax to set. *Note: If candle should shift or appears bumpy on top, use blow dryer to heat trouble area until flat.*

9. Remove pencil and trim wick at top of candle to ½".

6

Gel Wax Candle Tips:
Achieve a variety of effects using the following temperatures for gel wax:
180°–190°F lots of bubbles
190°–200°F fair amount bubbles
200°–210°F few to no bubbles

To ensure the gel wax is bubble free, heat container in a preheated oven at 150°F for 10 minutes before using.

How do I use a two-piece candle mold?

What You Need to Get Started:

Candle dye chip: pale green
Candle scent: apple
Candle thermometer
Craft scissors
Double boiler
Empty soup can
Metal pouring pot
Metal spoon
Mold: two-piece, apple
Mold release
Mold sealer
Mold-blend paraffin wax (1 lb)
Primed wick: square-braided

Two-piece molds offer a whole new variety of candles that can be created. They are easy to use. A ball mold can be used to create a billiard ball, a baseball or an orange. Just remember to secure the mold pieces tightly together.

Country Apple Candle

Here's How:

1. Prepare work space. Refer to *Preparing the work space* on page 93.

2. Melt wax in double boiler until it reaches 180°F. Refer to *Melting* on page 87. Proceed with Steps 3–4 while wax is melting.

3. Cut appropriate sized wick to length. Refer to *Wick Size* and *Wick Length* on page 91.

4. Separate mold pieces. Prepare wo-sided mold, using the following technique:

a. Lightly coat inside of mold with mold release.

b. Thread wick up through hole in bottom piece of mold.

c. Thread wick up through hole in top piece of mold. Attach mold pieces tightly together.

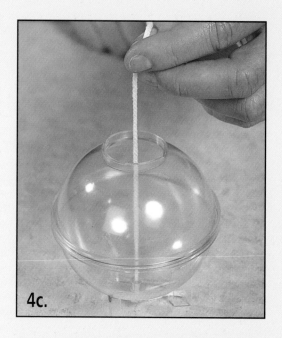

4c.

d. Cover hole and secure end of wick on outside of mold with mold sealer to prevent any leaking that may occur when the wax is poured.

e. Tie opposite end of wick around the rod that is included with two-piece mold. Place rod in grooves at top of mold. Make certain that wick is centered and taut. If wick is not taut, tighten wick around rod.

5. Dye wax. Refer to Step 5 on page 100.

6. Scent wax. Refer to Step 6 on page 102.

7. Using pouring pot, pour melted wax into the mold until mold is full. Refer to *Pouring* on page 88. Allow wax to set. Make certain to set aside a small amount of that particular wax in empty soup can to top off the candle.

8. Top off candle. Refer to Step 6 on page 98.

9. Remove candle from mold by separating mold pieces. Remove candle.

10. Trim wick. Refer to Step 8 on page 98.

Two-piece Candle Tip:
Two-piece candle molds can oftentimes leave seam lines on the candle. These lines can be easily removed. Holding a paring knife at a right angle on candle seam, turn candle until the entire seam is removed. Buff with a nylon stocking.

How do I create a candle with multiple wicks?

What You Need to Get Started:

Candle dye chip: white
Candle scent: rose
Candle thermometer
Craft scissors
Double boiler
Empty soup can
Metal pouring pot
Metal spoon
Mold: large round
Mold release
Mold sealer
Pencils (3)
Pillar-blend paraffin wax (2 lb)
Primed wicks: pretabbed, square-braided (5)
Wick sticker

A multiwick candle is created by spacing several wicks equal distances apart. This multiwick candle contains five wicks. Think of the magic a candle flame provides to a room, then multiply this effect times five.

Multiple-wick Candle

Here's How:

1. Prepare work space. Refer to *Preparing the work space* on page 93.

2. Melt wax in double boiler until it reaches 194°–198°F. Refer to *Melting* on page 87. Proceed with Steps 3–6 while wax is melting.

3. Cut appropriate sized wicks to length. Refer to *Wick Size* and *Wick Length* on page 91.

4. Lightly coat inside of mold with mold release. Cover hole on outside of mold with mold sealer to prevent any leaking that may occur when the wax is poured.

5. Apply wick sticker to bottom of wick tabs. Apply first wick in center of mold. Apply remaining wicks evenly spaced between center wick and around outside edge of mold.

6. Tie opposite ends of wicks around pencils. Place pencils on top rim of mold. Make certain that wicks are

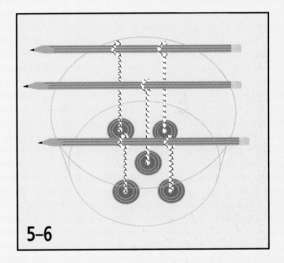

5–6

straight and taut. If wicks are not taut, tighten wicks around pencils.

7. Dye wax. Refer to Step 5 on page 100.

8. Scent wax. Refer to Step 6 on page 102.

9. Make a multiple-wick candle. Refer to Steps 5–7 on page 98.

10. Trim wicks at top of candle to ¼".

How do I create a candle with snowflake effect?

What You Need to Get Started:

Candle dye chip:
  red
Candle scent:
  pomegranate
Candle
  thermometer
Craft scissors
Double boiler
Empty soup can
Measuring spoons
Metal pouring pot
Metal spoon
Mold: large heart
Mold release
Mold seal
Mold-blend
  paraffin
  wax (1 lb)
Pencil
Primed wick:
  square-braided
Snowflake oil
  (2½ tb)

Simply add snowflake oil to your melted wax to achieve a snowflake effect. The candle featured on the facing page with its snowflake blotches and spots of white would have been considered a mistake 20 years ago. It would have been remelted for another attempt. However, this type of candle is now considered chic.

Snowflake Candle

Here's How:

1. Prepare work space. Refer to *Preparing the work space* on page 93.

2. Melt wax in double boiler until it reaches 194°–198°F. Refer to *Melting* on page 87. Proceed with Steps 3–4 while wax is melting.

3. Cut appropriate sized wick to length. Refer to *Wick Size* and *Wick Length* on page 91.

4. Prepare mold. Refer to Step 4 on pages 97–98.

5. Add snowflake oil to wax. Mix well.

6. Dye wax. Refer to Step 5 on page 100.

7. Scent wax. Refer to Step 6 on page 102.

8. Make a heart-shaped candle. Refer to Steps 5–8 on page 98.

Snowflake Candle Tips:
The lesson to be learned from the origination of the snowflake design is that mistakes made during the candlemaking process can oftentimes become a new technique.

It should also make you more willing to try something a little different than what the instructions state. After you have worked with the candlemaking process and are comfortable with the techniques, try changing the dyes, the amounts, or the sequence. The result may be that you create a new technique or design.

How do I make a multicolored layered candle?

What You Need to Get Started:

Candle dye chips: green, ivory
Candle scent: apple
Candle thermometer
Craft scissors
Double boiler
Empty soup can
Metal cans (2)
Metal pouring pot
Metal spoon
Mold: 1" votive
Mold release
Mold sealer
Mold-blend paraffin wax (1 lb)
Pencil
Primed wick: square-braided

A multicolored layered candle is made by pouring different colored waxes into the mold/container in layers. The number of colored layers depends on your own personal taste. Create a candle with several thin colored layers or a couple of thick layers as shown on the facing page.

Layered Candle

Here's How:

1. Prepare work space. Refer to *Preparing the work space* on page 93.

2. Melt wax in double boiler until it reaches 194°–198°F. Refer to *Melting* on page 87. Proceed with Steps 3–4 while wax is melting.

3. Cut appropriate sized wick to length. Refer to *Wick Size* and *Wick Length* on page 91.

4. Prepare mold. Refer to Step 4 on pages 97–98.

5. Divide and pour melted wax into two metal cans.

6. Dye wax a different color in each can. Refer to Step 5 on page 100.

7. Scent wax. Refer to Step 6 on page 102.

8. Using pouring pot, pour melted wax into the mold until mold is 50 percent full. Refer to *Pouring* on page 88. Allow wax to set.

9. Pour remaining color of melted wax into mold until 90 percent full. Allow wax to set. Make certain to set aside a small amount of that particular wax in empty soup can to top off the candle.

10. Top off candle. Refer to Step 6 on page 98.

11. Remove candle from mold and trim wick. Refer to Steps 7–8 on page 98.

123

How do I make an embossed candle?

What You Need to Get Started:

Candle dye: white
Candle scent:
   vanilla
Candle
   thermometer
Corrugated or
   ridged
   cardboard
Craft scissors
Double boiler
Duct tape
Empty soup can
Metal pouring pot
Metal spoon
Mold: square
   metal
Mold sealer
Mold-blend paraf-
   fin wax (1 lb)
Pencil
Primed wick:
   square-braided
Tape measure

A simple way to emboss a candle is to use corrugated cardboard. Corrugated cardboard comes in different-sized ridges and textures to fit your personal taste. The embossed candle on the facing page has a sleek contemporary look.

Corrugated Candle

Here's How:

1. Prepare work space. Refer to *Preparing the work space* on page 93.

2. Melt wax in double boiler until it reaches 180°–199°F. Refer to *Melting* on page 87. Proceed with Steps 3–6 while wax is melting.

3. Cut appropriate sized wick to length. Refer to *Wick Size* and *Wick Length* on page 91.

4. Lightly coat inside bottom of mold with mold release.

5. Using tape measure, measure height and circumference of mold. Using craft scissors, cut cardboard to these dimensions, making certain corrugated ridges are vertical. Trim edges where necessary to fit cardboard tightly inside mold. Tape long edges together on noncor-rugated side, with corrugated side facing inward. Place cardboard into mold.

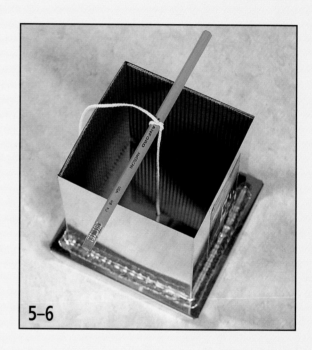

5–6

6. Prepare wick in mold. Refer to Step 4b–d on pages 97–98.

7. Dye wax. Refer to Step 5 on page 100.

8. Scent wax. Refer to Step 6 on page 102.

9. Using pouring pot, pour melted wax into the mold until mold is 90 percent full. Refer to *Pouring* on page 88. Allow wax to set. Make certain to set aside a small amount of that particular wax in empty soup can to top off the candle.

10. Top off candle. Refer to Step 6 on page 98.

11. Remove pencil. Remove mold sealer. Using fingers, tap sides of mold. Pull cardboard from sides and remove from mold. If it does not work, place mold with candle in freezer for 5–10 minutes. Remove from freezer. Tip mold upside down. Candle should slide out on its own.

12. Using craft scissors, cut and peel cardboard from candle. *Note: The cardboard may leave* *layers of paper on the candle, giving the candle a textured look.*

13. Trim wick at top of candle to ¼". Trim wick at bottom of candle flush with base.

Corrugated Candle Tip:
If you do not want the textured look that the corrugated cardboard leaves on the candle, a rubber mold can be purchased that will give the embossed look without the paper.

What kind of items can I embed in gel wax?

Any item that can withstand hot temperatures without melting can be placed in a gel wax candle. The possible trinkets and various containers that can be used to create a gel wax candle are endless. At a glance, the glass container opposite looks like it is simply holding a collection of seashells. But look again . . . it is a candle.

What You Need to Get Started:

Blow dryer (optional)
Candle scent: lavender
Candle thermometer
Container: glass 10"
Double boiler
Measuring cup
Measuring spoon
Metal pouring pot
Metal spoon
Mineral oil (16 oz)
Pencil
Primed wick: flat braided
Resin: CP9000 (25 grams)
Seashells: large bag

Seashell Gel Candle

Here's How:

1. Make gel wax. Refer to Steps 1–3 on page 115.

2. Cut appropriate sized wick to length. Refer to *Wick Size* and *Wick Length* on page 91.

3. Scent wax. Refer to Step 6 on page 102.

4. Prepare wick. Refer to Steps 6–7 on page 115.

5. Arrange seashells as desired in container. Make certain that wick is centered and taut. If wick is not taut, tighten wick around pencil.

6. Using pouring pot, pour melted gel wax into the container until container is 90 percent full. Refer to *Pouring* on page 88. Allow wax to set. *Note: If candle should shift or appears bumpy on top, use blow dryer to heat trouble area until flat.*

7. Remove pencil and trim wick at top of candle to ¼".

Embedded Gel Candle Tips:
Try embedding costume jewelry, dried botanicals, pennies, rocks, or marbles into a gel wax candle.

Several items along the same theme can be embedded into a gel candle.

How do I embed purchased wax shapes into a candle?

What You Need to Get Started:

Candle thermometer
Craft scissors
Double boiler
Metal pouring pot
Metal spoon
Mold: tapered cup
Mold release
Mold seal
Mold-blend paraffin wax (1 lb)
Pencil
Primed wick: square-braided
Wax stars: clear (lg. bag)

Wax shapes can be embedded in a candle by simply filling the mold with them and adding melted wax. This Star-filled Candle was created using clear wax stars and clear melted wax for a natural luminous effect.

Star-filled Candle

Here's How:
1. Prepare work space. Refer to *Preparing the work space* on page 93.

2. Melt wax in double boiler until it reaches 194°–198°F. Refer to *Melting* on page 87. Proceed with Steps 3–5 while wax is melting.

3. Cut appropriate sized wick 4" longer than height of mold. Refer to *Wick Size* and *Wick Length* on page 91.

4. Prepare mold. Refer to Step 4 on pages 97–98.

5. Place wax stars as desired into mold from bottom to top, making certain wick remains centered. Make certain that many of the stars touch the side of the mold and extend above the mold.

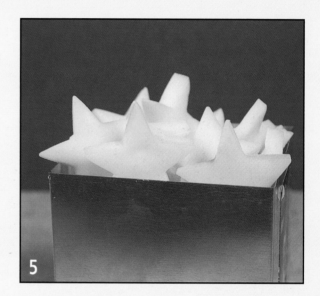

6. Using pouring pot, pour melted wax into the mold until mold is 90 percent full. Refer to *Pouring* on page 88. Allow wax to set.

7. Remove candle from mold. Refer to Step 7 on page 98.

8. Trim wick at top of candle to 3". Trim wick at bottom of candle flush with base. *Note: Remember to trim wick to ¼" before burning.*

Wick Tip: Small ornaments or trinkets can be tied onto the end of wicks for a personal touch when giving your handmade candles away. Tell recipient to trim wick to ¼" before burning.

How do I embed just one or two wax shapes into a candle?

What You Need to Get Started:

Candle dye: olive green
Candle scent: eucalyptus
Candle thermometer
Container: shallow plastic 8" x 8"
Cookie cutters: round; star
Craft scissors
Double boiler
Empty soup can
Freezer
Metal can
Metal pouring pot
Metal spoon
Mold: square pillar
Mold release
Mold seal
Paper towels
Pencil
Pillar-blend par-affin wax (1 lb)
Primed wick: square-braided
Spatula

Embedding wax shapes in a candle takes a little more time and patience than a basic molded candle. However, the final result is worth it. These unique candles were created using the same technique, yet each has a look all its own.

Rustic Embedded Candle

Here's How:

1. Prepare work space. Refer to *Preparing the work space* on page 93.

2. Melt wax in double boiler until it reaches 194º–198ºF. Refer to *Melting* on page 87. Proceed with Steps 3–5 while wax is melting.

3. Cut appropriate sized wick. Refer to *Wick Size* and *Wick Length* on page 91.

4. Prepare mold. Refer to Step 4a–c on page 97. Allow remain-ing portion of wick to hang over side of mold.

5. Place mold in freezer for 30 min-utes. *Note: The reaction between the cool mold and the melted wax will cause a white film on the finished candle, creating a rustic look.*

6. Using pouring pot, pour wax to a depth of ½" into plastic container. Refer to How do I pour melted wax? on page 17. Allow wax to cool, but not set.

7. Using cookie cutters, cut entirely through layer of wax for one shape each. Do not remove.

8. Dye remaining wax in double boiler. Refer to Step 5 on page 100.

9. Scent wax. Refer to Step 6 on page 102.

10. Using spatula, remove shapes from container. Set aside.

11. Remove mold from freezer. Using paper towels, make certain to remove any traces of water in mold. *Note: If water drips into melted wax, it will pop and could burn the skin.*

12. Using pouring pot, pour melted wax into the mold until mold is 90 percent full. Wait 3–5 minutes until a thin film appears on surface.

13. Using paring knife, cut ½" in from edges around top of mold. Remove film from center and place film back in double boiler. Immediately pour remaining wax in the mold back into double boiler and remove from heat. *Note: This will leave a thin layer of wax on sides of mold.*

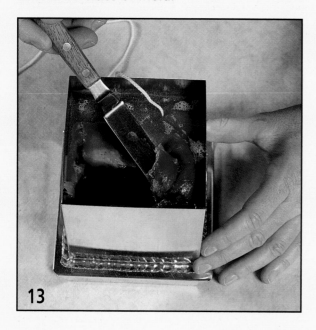

14. Using paper towels, clean off rim of mold.

15. Gently, press wax shapes into thin layer of wax around sides of mold as desired. Make certain to embed shapes into wax but do not break through thin wax layer.

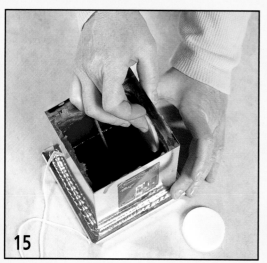

16. Tie remaining portion of wick around a pencil. Place pencil on top rim of mold. Make certain that wick is centered and taut. If wick is not taut, tighten wick around pencil.

17. Check temperature of melted wax in double boiler. Make certain it is 130°–140°F. Adjust as necessary.

18. Using pouring pot, pour melted wax into the mold until mold is 90 percent full. Make certain to set aside a small amount of that particular wax in empty soup can to top off the candle. Allow wax to set.

19. Top off candle. Refer to Step 6 on page 98. Repour wax as needed for an even candle. Allow wax to set.

20. Remove candle from mold and trim wick. Refer to Steps 7–8 on page 98.

How do I make a double-molded candle?

A double-molded candle is a shell of wax that holds a candle. As the candle burns down, the flame will light up the shell. Here, the golden glow of apples brings back memories of fall and hot apple cider.

What You Need to Get Started:

Candle dye chip: gold
Candle scent: apple cinnamon
Candle thermometer
Craft knife
Double boiler
Dowel
Dried botanicals: cinnamon sticks; dried apples; dried berries; dried leaves
Empty soup can
Metal pouring pot
Metal spoon
Mold: large, rigid, round
Mold release
Mold seal
Mold-blend paraffin wax
Paper towels
Pillar candle: gold to fit inside of mold with 1" all around

Double-molded Candle

Here's How:

1. Prepare work space. Refer to *Preparing the work space* on page 93.

2. Melt wax in double boiler until it reaches 165º–185ºF. Refer to *Melting* on page 87. Proceed with Step 3 while wax is melting.

3. Lightly coat inside of mold with mold release. Cover hole on outside of mold with mold sealer to prevent any leaking that may occur when the wax is poured.

4. Dye wax. Refer to Step 5 on page 100.

5. Scent wax. Refer to Step 6 on page 102.

6. Create candle mold. Refer to Steps 12–14 on pages 131–132.

7. Gently, press some dried botanicals into thin layer of wax as desired. Make certain to embed into wax but do not break through thin wax layer.

8. Place pillar candle in center of mold.

9. Place remaining botanicals in mold.

10. Check temperature of melted wax in double boiler. Make certain it is 165º–185ºF. Adjust as necessary.

Continued from page 133.

11. Using pouring pot, pour melted wax into the mold until mold is 90 percent full. Allow wax to cool, but not set. Make certain to set aside a small amount of that particular wax in empty soup can to top off the candle.

12. Using dowel, press down any items that may float to the top or out of place. Allow wax to set.

13. As wax cools, a cavity will develop around the top edge. Refer to Step 6 on page 98. Repour wax as needed for an even candle. Allow wax to set.

14. Remove candle from mold. Refer to Step 7 on page 98.

How do I make a candle tart?

Candle tarts are a wickless type of candle that are melted in a special container. They can be made in various shallow molds, muffin tins, and tart pans—hence the name "candle tart." The candle tarts featured on page 136 were made in tea-light candle molds and offer a lovely lavender scent.

What You Need to Get Started:

Candle dye chip: white
Candle scent: lavender
Candle thermometer
Container-blend paraffin wax (1 lb)
Craft scissors
Double boiler
Dried lavender
Metal pouring pot
Metal spoon
Mold: tea-light
Mold release

Candle Tart

Here's How:
Note: Candle tarts can be made in various molds such as a metal petit four tin. Any type of tin can be used as long as it has a smooth surface with openings that are wider than the bases. This allows for easy melting.

1. Prepare work space. Refer to *Preparing the work space* on page 93.

2. Melt wax in double boiler until it reaches 180ºF. Refer to *Melting* on page 87. Proceed with Step 3 while wax is melting.

3. Lightly coat inside of mold with mold release.

4. Dye wax. Refer to Step 5 on page 100.

5. Scent wax. Refer to Step 6 on page 102.

6. Sprinkle and stir dried lavender into melted wax.

7. Using pouring pot, pour melted wax into the mold until full to create candle tart. Refer to *Pouring* on page 88. Allow wax to set.

8. Remove candle tart from mold. Refer to Step 7 on page 98.

Candle Tart Tip:
Dye and scent candle tarts to match the occasion or upcoming season.

How do I make a floating candle?

Floating candles are small candles with tops that are wider than their base—like a bowl. Floating candles, glittering in a container of water, are extremely attractive. However, they are even more stunning when incorporated into a theme as featured on facing page.

What You Need to Get Started:

Candle dye chip: brown
Candle paint: gold metallic
Candle scent: pine
Candle thermometer
Craft scissors
Double boiler
Hot water
Metal pouring pot
Metal spoon
Mold: floating, pinecone
Mold release
Mold sealer
Mold-blend paraffin wax (1 lb)
Paintbrush: small
Primed wick: wire core
Stearin (1 tb)
Wicking needle

Floating Candles

Here's How:

1. Prepare work space. Refer to *Preparing the work space* on page 93.

2. Melt wax in double boiler until it reaches 180°–194°F. Refer to *Melting* on page 87. Proceed with Steps 3–4 while wax is melting.

3. Cut wick 1" higher than mold. Refer to *Wick Size* and *Wick Length* on page 91.

4. Lightly coat inside of mold with mold release.

5. Add stearin to melted wax. Mix well.

6. Dye wax. Refer to Step 5 on page 100.

7. Scent wax. Refer to Step 6 on page 102.

8. Using pouring pot, pour melted wax into the mold until full. Refer to *Pouring* on page 88. Allow wax to set.

9. Remove candle from mold. Refer to Step 7 on page 98.

Floating Candle Tip:

Make certain that molds for floating candles are containers with openings wider than the bases. They can come individually or in sets of four or six.

10. Dip wicking needle into hot water long enough to warm needle. Using wicking needle, pierce a hole through center of each candle. *Note: The hole should be a clean one, small enough to insert wick, but not large enough that wick slides out.* Immediately place wick through hole. The melted wax around the hole will seal the wick in place.

11. Using paintbrush, daub paint onto tips of pinecone candle.

12. Trim wick at top of candle to ¼".

How do I make a stacked candle?

**What You
Need to
Get Started:**

Baking sheets (2)
Candle dye chips:
  magenta; pink
Candle scent:
  cinnamon
Candle
  thermometer
Cookie cutter:
  heart
Craft scissors
Double boiler
Metal cans (2)
Metal pouring pot
Metal spoons (2)
Mold-blend
  paraffin wax
  (1 lb)
Pastry brush
Primed wick:
  square-braided
Spatula
Vegetable oil
Wick tab
Wicking needle

A stacked candle can be created in any desired shape. This stacked candle was created using a heart-shaped cookie cutter and a thin layer of wax. The thickness of the shapes depends on the depth of wax placed into the baking sheet. With all the possible shapes and colors, the fun will never end.

Stacked Heart Candle

Here's How:

1. Prepare work space. Refer to *Preparing the work space* on page 93.

2. Melt wax in double boiler until it reaches 180°F. Refer to *Melting* on page 87. Proceed with Step 3 while wax is melting.

3. Using pastry brush, brush baking sheets with vegetable oil.

4. Using pouring pot, divide and pour wax into two cans. Refer to *Pouring* on page 88.

5. Dye wax pink in one can and magenta in remaining can. Refer to Step 5 on page 100.

6. Scent wax in each container. Refer to Step 6 on page 102.

7. Pour one can of melted wax onto baking sheet to ¼" depth. Pour remaining can of melted wax onto remaining baking sheet.

8. Allow wax to cool, but not set. Using cookie cutter, cut entirely through layers of wax. Do not remove.

9. Using wicking needle, pierce a hole through center of each heart. Allow wax to set.

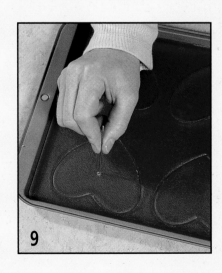

139

10. Using spatula, remove hearts from baking sheets.

11. Thread 12" length of wick onto wicking needle. Apply wick tab to one end of wick.

12. Using wicking needle, thread wick through heart holes. Stack hearts in color groups of three hearts, on top of each other.

Stacked Heart Candle Tip:
Stacked hearts are individually movable after assembly. Be careful when moving stacked hearts; because of their thinness, they are easily broken and/or chipped.

How do I use whipped wax?

What You Need to Get Started:

Candle dye chip:
   yellow
Candle
   thermometer
Double boiler
Measuring spoons
Metal can
Metal fork
Metal spoon
Paraffin wax (1 lb)
Pillar candle:
   round, yellow
Spatula
Stearin (1 tb)

Whipped wax can be used to create various decorative candles such as a snowball candle or an ice cream sundae candle. The candle featured on the facing page was covered with whipped wax to resemble a frosted cake.

Whipped Candle

Here's How:

1. Prepare work space. Refer to *Preparing the work space* on page 93.

2. Melt wax in double boiler until it reaches 140°F. Refer to *Melting* on page 87.

3. Add stearin to melted wax. Mix well.

4. Dye wax. Refer to Step 5 on page 100.

5. Pour melted wax into metal can. Allow wax to cool until a thin film appears on surface. *Note: The wax will first set on the top and around the sides and bottom of can.*

6. Using fork, whip wax until thick and foamy. *Note: This may take 5–10 minutes.*

7. Using spatula and working one area at a time, apply generous amount of whipped wax to candle. Continue until candle is covered. *Note: Whipped wax must be applied when warm. If wax cools too much, melt it down and begin again.*

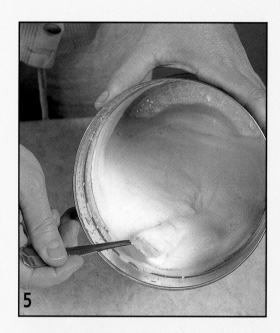

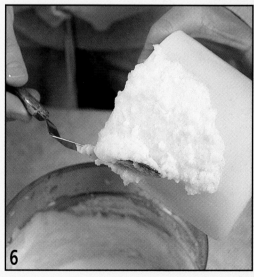

Whipped Candle Tip:
Candles also can be dipped into the whipped wax, using the following method:
Holding onto wick of candle, dip into whipped wax in one smooth motion.

142

How do I use melted wax to decoupage a candle?

There are many ways to enhance the surface of a candle to create a more interesting appearance. The candle featured on the facing page has been decoupaged using melted wax and decorative paper, then gold leafing has been added for an extra touch of class.

What You Need to Get Started:

Candle thermometer
Cloth: soft
Craft scissors
Dipping vat: deep enough to accommodate enough wax to submerge candle
Double boiler
Gold leafing
Motifs: paper
Nylon stocking: soft
Paintbrush: soft
Paper towels
Paraffin wax (½ lb)
Permanent marker
Pillar candle: square, white
Water
Waxed paper

Decoupaged Candle

Here's How:
Note: This method of decoupage should only be used with 3"-diameter candles or larger. Trim away sides as candle burns down.

1. Prepare work space. Refer to *Preparing the work space* on page 93.

2. Trim motifs to fit candle.

3. Melt wax in double boiler until it reaches 194ºF. Refer to *Melting* on page 87. Proceed with Step 4 while wax is melting.

4. Prepare dipping vat using the following technique:

a. Place candle in dipping vat and fill dipping vat with water until it covers the candle. Hold candle down, as it will float to the top. Remove candle.

b. Using permanent marker, mark water level on outside of dipping vat. Pour water out. Using paper towels, dry candle and dipping vat thoroughly.

5. Pour melted wax into dipping vat to 1" depth over mark on vat.

6. Holding onto wick of candle, dip entire candle into melted wax in one smooth motion. Remove and place candle on waxed paper.

7. Quickly adhere motifs onto candle. Smooth as needed. Holding onto wick, dip entire candle into melted wax in one smooth motion. Remove and place candle on waxed paper.

8. Allow wax to set. *Note: The candle will look cloudy when it comes out but will dry clear.*

9. Using paintbrush and a tapping motion, adhere gold leafing to remaining sides of candle. Adhere leafing around top edges of candle.

10. Using cloth, buff and distress leafing as desired.

11. Using nylon stocking, buff candle for a smooth, shiny finish.

How do I add pressed flowers to a candle?

What You Need to Get Started:

Candle
  thermometer
Dipping vat: deep
  enough to
  accommodate
  enough wax
  to submerge
  candle
Double boiler
Glue pen with
  sponge
  applicator
Multiple-wick
  candle: cream
Paraffin wax
  (½ lb)
Pressed flowers

Pressed flowers can turn a plain candle into an eyecatching decoration. This multiple-wick candle was decorated by gluing pressed flowers onto the candle, then dipping it into melted wax to seal. This method can be applied to any smooth-surfaced candle.

Pressed-flower Candle

Here's How:

1. Prepare work space. Refer to *Preparing the work space* on page 93.

2. Melt wax in double boiler until it reaches 180°F. Refer to *Melting* on page 87. Proceed with Steps 3–5 while wax is melting.

3. Prepare dipping vat. Refer to Step 4 on page 143.

4. Arrange pressed flowers on candle as desired.

5. Using glue pen, apply glue to back of pressed flowers. Adhere pressed flowers to candle. *Note: Pressed flowers can be carefully repositioned if glue is still wet.*

6. Pour melted wax into dipping vat 1" depth over mark on vat.

7. Holding onto wicks of candle, dip entire candle into melted wax in one smooth motion. Remove and place candle on waxed paper.

8. Press down any flowers or leaves that protrude through the wax.

9. Allow wax to set.

Pressed-flower Candle Tip:
Pressed-flower candles can be made even more attractive by scenting the wax to complement the flowers used.

How do I decorate a candle with paint?

What You Need to Get Started:

Candle paints:
   burgundy;
   cream; lt. green;
   med. green;
   silver; lt. yellow
Foam plate
Paintbrushes: #4
   flat; #1 liner
Tapered candle:
   lavender

Painting is an excellent way to decorate your candle because of the smooth canvas provided. This lavender candle was painted with simple yet beautiful flowers. Follow the painting diagrams provided or create your own meadow of flowers.

Painted Candle

Here's How:

1. Pour a quarter-sized amount of silver paint on foam plate.

2. Dip finger in paint and rub randomly over candle.

3. Repeat Steps 1–2 using burgundy paint and overlapping part of silver paint.

4. Load flat paintbrush with cream paint. Paint flower petals on candle as desired.

5

6. Load flat paintbrush with burgundy paint. Shade behind flower center.

4

6

5. Load liner with lt. yellow paint. Paint oval in center of petals for flower center.

147

7. Load half of flat paintbrush edge with lt. green paint. Load other half with med. green paint. Stroke brush on plate to soften colors. Paint leaves on candle.

8. Load liner with med. green paint. Paint a vein in each leaf. Allow to dry.

How do I give my candle a cracked appearance?

A candle can be given a cracked appearance by a method called overdipping. Cracking of the top layer is done by placing the overdipped candle in the freezer. When an overdipped candle is cracked, it reveals the candle's true color underneath. The candle featured on the facing page shows light-colored cracks against the dark-colored candle for a dramatic look.

What You Need to Get Started:

Candle dye chip: dk. brown
Candle paint: dk. brown
Candle thermometer
Dipping vat: deep enough to accommodate enough wax to submerge candle
Double boiler
Foam plate
Freezer
Metal spoon
Nylon stocking: soft
Paper towels
Permanent marker
Pillar candle: square, tan
Sponge brush
Taper-blend paraffin wax (1 lb)
Water

Cracked-finished Candle

Here's How:

1. Place candle in freezer for two hours.

2. Prepare work space. Refer to *Preparing the work space* on page 93.

3. Melt wax in double boiler until it reaches 180°F. Refer to *Melting* on page 87. Proceed with Steps 4–5 while wax is melting.

4. Pour two quarter-sized amounts of dk. brown paint on foam plate.

5. Dip sponge in paint. Sponge on candle. Repeat until candle is covered. Allow candle to dry for a few minutes and, while paint is still tacky, place in freezer on waxed paper for 20 minutes.

6. Dye wax. Refer to Step 5 on page 100.

7. Prepare dipping vat. Refer to Step 4 on page 143.

8. Holding onto wick of candle, dip entire candle into melted wax in one smooth motion. Repeat dipping two additional times. Remove and place candle on waxed paper.

9. Place candle in freezer for two hours. *Note: The longer the candle is left in freezer, the more cracks will appear.*

10. Allow candle to come to room temperature. Using fingers, carefully press the outside of the candle to smooth out any air bubbles.

11. Using nylon stocking, buff candle for a smooth, shiny finish.

How do I embellish wicks?

Embellish a wick by simply attaching a treasure or trinket onto the end. Embellished wicks add a special touch to the unique candles that you have created. Embellish a candle wick with something that makes a statement about yourself or the candle that you have created, making something common-place look extraordinary.

Embellished Wicks

Here's How:
1. Embellish wicks as desired.

2. Make certain to remove embellishments and trim wick to ¼" before burning.

Embellished Wicks Tips:
The purpose for making a fancy wick is to add a little something special when the candle you are making is to be a gift. Design the wick to complement the candle—if there are seashells in the wax, you can drill tiny holes in miniature shells and string them from the wick's end. Try using an assortment of beads, buttons, or pieces of vintage broken jewelry. Embellish the wick by braiding it with embroidery floss, speciality yarns or threads, or thin ribbon.

You never know when a new idea for wick decorating will appear, so make the wicks longer than necessary—they can always be trimmed if you choose to keep the candle rather than giving it as a gift.

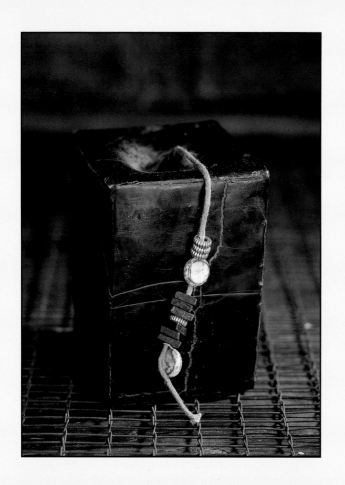

POLYMER CLAY
for the first time®

Syndee Holt

Polymer Clay for the first time

Introduction

Polymer clay is more than just a space-age modeling material—it is a worldwide community of people dedicated to art, science, chemistry, and each other. It's one of the few art mediums where information is shared freely, via the Internet, videos, books, magazines, and guilds. They are artists, doctors, authors, teachers, and scientists—all drawn together by this medium as friends and clay mentors. My friends will be dropping in from time to time to add to your journey.

Polymer clay is a plastic material first designed over thirty years ago for doll-making and molding. We've now expanded the techniques to include everything from cane-making (creating patterns in the clay), stamping, textures, faux stone, faux metals, transfers, and multimedia collage, to name a few. Artists are even turning the material on the lathe and throwing it on the potter's wheel. Because the baking temperature is so low, you can cover almost any other material with polymer clay to create new lamps, boxes, vases, frames, etc. It is waterproof, fade-proof, and durable.

I do need to warn you, though. Working with polymer clay is addictive. You'll live, breathe, and think clay 24 hours a day. You'll begin to see colors, textures, and ideas everywhere. And you'll wake up at 2 a.m. with the idea to put them all together with your precious clay. AND once you do, you will be rushing to your computer, phone, or guild to share "the newest idea" with your other clay buddies. Personally, I couldn't ask for a better way to live!

Naturally, this means other things in life, like jobs, housework, cooking, children, family, and friends have to fight for our attention. But, don't overlook them—they are wonderful sources of ideas, support, and most important—tools!

First, we will go over some of the basic information for polymer clay. Next, I will show you some of the basics of doing "canework," or patterned clay. Then we will try using some molds and textural techniques.

Please feel free to vary the colors suggested for projects and even the projects themselves. It is important to us in polymer clay that we teach technique not design. In this way, we can cause the greatest amount of growth in our medium. When I teach a polymer clay basics class, there is a small surprised reaction from the students about this freedom but it has its rewards. There is a time when I just sit quietly and watch. My students are empowered with the techniques I've taught them, and they are so busy adapting these techniques to their needs and tastes that they don't notice that I've ceased teaching and started learning from them!

Getting Started

First, get over the idea that this is difficult. There are three things I can count on to happen in each beginning class I teach. First, everyone will be very impressed with my beads until they cut open their first canes and find themselves saying, "That's it? That's all there is to it?" Then, about midway through, they will start looking at my once impressive pile of beads and say, "Oh, okay, I see it now." And then, finally, someone will suddenly look up and announce, "That's it. I'm calling in sick to work tomorrow." Guaranteed.

Tools

Gathering tools for working with polymer clay is quite a lot of fun and fairly inexpensive. There are some basic tools that you will use for each clay project. There are also a wide variety of additional tools available that can help you create some incredible textures and effects.

Basic Clay Tools: There are not a lot of materials needed to create with polymer clay—a few blocks of clay, something to make the clay flat, a sharp blade, a work surface, and an oven for baking. Note: Any tool or surface used for clay should not be used for food.

Tools to Flatten Clay—
    Acrylic rod
    Brayer
    Pasta machine, clay-dedicated
       (recommended)
    Rolling pin
    Wallpaper blades
    Water glass

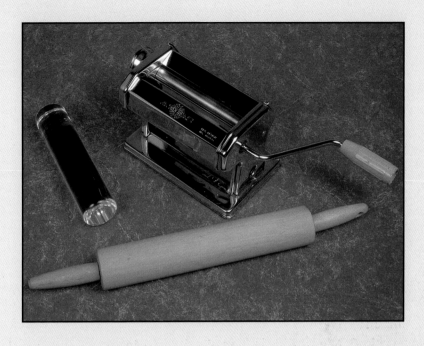

Tools to Cut Clay—
    Craft knife
    Unimpeded edge blades for caning:
        Clay blades
        Ripple-cut blades
        Tissue blades
        Wallpaper blades

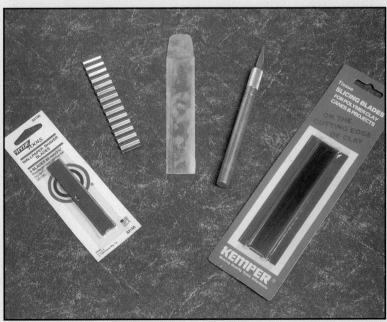

Working Surfaces—
   Acrylic sheets
   Baking parchment
   Ceramic tiles
   Drafting vellum
   File folders
   Index cards
   Poster board
   Smooth, nonporous, nonfood surfaces

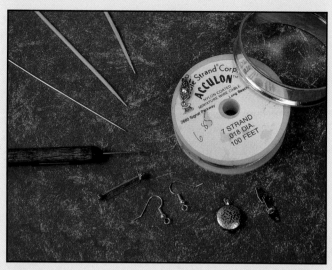

Sandpaper—wet sanding to prevent dust is strongly recommended. The really high-grade sandpapers can be found at automotive stores.

Garage Tools—nails and screws for textures; pliers for assemblage; flood lights for 2 a.m. work; and burnt out light bulbs for vessel shapes.

Ovens—
   Convection oven
   Home oven (for occasional baking)
   Toaster oven
   NO microwave

Additional Tools: You won't find an enormous amount of items marketed specifically for clay—we borrow from all media—from painters and sculptors, to metal workers and wood workers, to our children's toy boxes and our tool boxes. Once you begin to recognize potential clay tools, the garage will never look the same to you.

Piercing Tools—large needles, small knitting needles, piercing tools, and bamboo skewers.

Jewelry Findings—Stringing materials for beadwork; regular store-bought findings for assemblage; or make your own.

Kitchen Tools—empty jars for making covered vessels; old forks make great texture tools; and old spoons work well for braying down transfers.

Toy-box Tools—plastic dinosaurs for fossils, action figures and small dolls for hand and face molds; old crayons to chop up and mix in the clay—Lindley Hunani showed us that trick; soft-lead colored pencils to color transfers and baked clay.

Backyard Tools—rocks, sticks, and bark for textures; sand and dirt to mix into clay; leaves for textures and molds; and dried flowers for mixing into translucent clay.

Choosing Clay

There are several brands of clay available. I will tell you from my experience with these brands of clay what I think of them.

FIMO: This is a stiff, stiff, stiff clay. Get the food processor ready for this clay. The colors are okay but reds and blues darken when baking. The tensile strength is moderate to good.

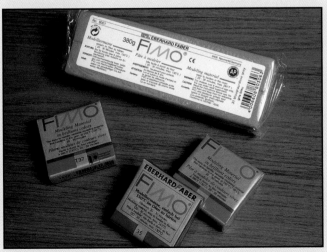

Sculpey: This is a basic modeling clay. It is chalky and very soft in its raw state. It only comes in white. Its tensile strength is not great. However, this is a good clay to paint on. It bakes very hard.

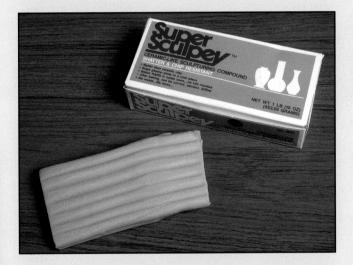

Super Sculpey: This is the darling of sculptors and doll-makers. Its tensile strength is moderate. The texture of this clay is smoother and its color is translucent beige.

Sculpey III: This is the top children's modeling clay. It is available in great colors, very easy to work with, and its tensile strength is moderate. It is soft enough for children to use quite easily. Sculpey III bakes to a very hard surface. It is the preferred clay of my children. The Sculpey Clay

Kits for children are wonderful—the instructions include nonverbal pictures and there is plenty of clay included. If I don't give these for birthday gifts, I can expect a disappointed look from the birthday child.

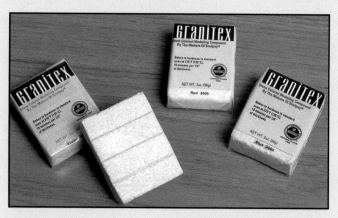

Sculpey Super Flex: We're talking pure un-adulterated fun here. This clay is flexible after it bakes. There are 50 tub toys in my bathtub that are a testament to this. It is currently available in eight colors and in kit form.

Sculpey Premo: This clay is my favorite. American polymer artists, led by my friend Marie Segal of the Clay Factory, in conjunction with the Polyform team, designed this clay. It is pasta-machine-ready and also has excellent tensile strength. It is available in wonderful colors with intense color saturation. NOW, you know why it's my favorite!

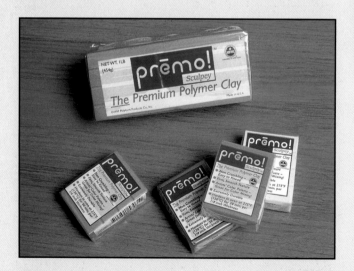

Liquid Sculpey: Oh boy, this is truly amazing stuff. It's not available on the general market—see the list of websites in the back. "LS," as it is referred to on the internet is available in opaque white and transparent. You can pour it, paint it, or drizzle it.

Sculpey Granitex: This is a material that was designed to imitate stone. It has moderate tensile strength and mixes well with Sculpey Premo. The nylon fibers in this clay preclude caning with it.

Cernit: This is another doll-maker's clay. It is a moderately stiff clay and most colors are translucent. It doesn't cane well unless mixed with other clays. Cernit and Sculpey III mixed 1:1 makes a great caning clay.

All these clays can be intermixed together. Just remember that if you do mix them for a cane, you need to keep the consistency of the clays the same throughout the cane.

Safely Using Polymer Clay

Even though the clays are AP certified non-toxic, we follow basic safety procedures for petroleum-based products:

• Any tool or surface you use for clay should not be used for food.

• Anything created or covered with clay should not be used for food or food handling.

• Wash hands after handling the clay and before eating to remove the plasticizer.

• Bake outside when possible. Ventilate interior rooms when baking inside.

• NEVER exceed recommended baking temperatures.

• Check the oven for stray clay pieces after removing baking trays.

• Be aware of repetitive-motion injuries. If you are experiencing hand or arm discomfort, PUT THE CLAY AWAY for awhile. This is particularly important when working with stiffer clays.

• Some artists wear latex gloves when handling the clay. I use them only to prevent fingerprints.

• Some of the clay pigments will come off on hands, so use lighter colors first.

• Cover, wrap, or bag the clay to keep pets and pet hair out of the clay.

Conditioning the Clay

All techniques and projects in this book call for clay that has already been conditioned and is ready to work with. All polymer clays on the market contain polymer fibers. These little fibers just love to connect with each other, providing durability and the magic of the clay. When you purchase the clay, these fibers are all jumbled up like uncombed hair. We want the fibers all smoothed out and going the same way when we use them, so we do what is called "conditioning" before we use any polymer clay. Well conditioned clay will not have rough edges when rolled through a pasta machine and will stretch slightly before breaking when you pull on it. Soft clay is the result of conditioning—all clays need this process.

Conditioning the clay by hand: Cut the clay block in half, then cut each half into three pieces. Begin rolling one of these pieces into a ball, roll into a snake, fold it in half to form a ball, and repeat until the clay feels flexible and it stretches.

Conditioning the clay using a clay-dedicated pasta machine: Cut slices off the block of clay. Roll a slice through the pasta machine. Fold the clay in half and roll it through again, folded side first to force the air out. As each piece becomes workable, add another piece off the block.

Conditioning the clay using a clay-dedicated food processor: Fortunately the newer clays have allowed us to do without this method. But if you have some particularly stiff clay, chop it up and put it into a clay-dedicated food processor or chopper and whirl away. You may even add a few drops of mineral oil, baby oil, or diluent to help soften the clay. Clay conditioned in a food processor looks like cottage cheese. When conditioned this way and pressed into small balls, turquoise clay resembles stone nuggets.

Conditioned clay will maintain its flexibility for several hours and will remain more flexible than unconditioned clay for several days.

Rolling Sheets of Clay

This should be titled "I'm going to tell you everything it took me months to figure out about a pasta machine."

Rolling the clay out by hand: Always work on a nonporous surface so you can peel the clay up. Baking parchment, drafting vellum, index cards, and file folders all work well.

Begin by rolling the clay in all four directions with a flattening tool. I have used acrylic rods, water glasses, and books. Experiment until you find what works best in each situation.

If you are going to create a very thin sheet of clay, "sandwich" the clay between drafting vellum or baking parchment.

Note: Go slowly! The clay will stick to work and tool surfaces if you try to press down too much.

Rolling the clay using a pasta machine: Remember that if you use the machine for clay, it is dedicated to this medium. Do not make pasta with it after using it for clay.

Use a manual pasta machine. A motor can be attached to it later if you wish.

We like to use a pasta machine imported from Italy. It has seven to nine thickness settings on it. The settings are adjustable with the dial on the side.

We typically refer to the settings as they are numbered, #1 being the thickest and #7 the thinnest.

Start with a #1 setting and then move to the smaller settings. This will keep the clay in a workable squared size and shape.

Make certain to roll the clay through the pasta machine folded side first to force out air.

Note: I do not clean the pasta machine. I just run scrap clay through it before rolling a critical color, such as white. All the other little bits of color just mix in.

For the Sake of Reference
I thought it might be convenient to show you exactly the width of the sheets I will be talking about in these projects. For the sake of expediency, I usually refer to the sheets by the number on the pasta machine that makes that particular width.

#1 or ⅛"

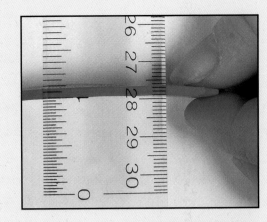

#2 or ³⁄₃₂"

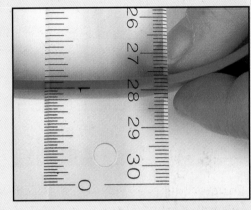

#3 or ¹⁄₁₆"

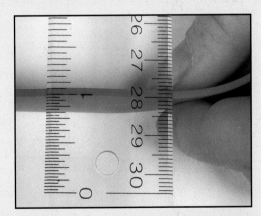

#4 or ³⁄₆₄"

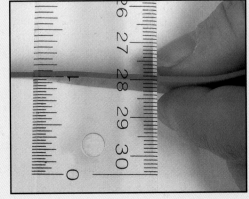

161

#5 or ¹⁄₃₂"

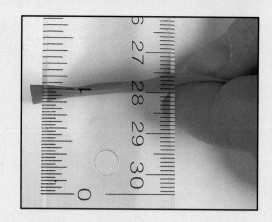

I tend to use numbers #1, #3, and #5 the most. If you are using a pasta machine, you may want to compare the sheets your machine makes to mine as they can differ from one machine to another by as much as one sheet thickness.

> PLEASE NOTE THAT ALL PROJECTS ARE USING CONDITIONED CLAY AND A PASTA MACHINE.

Troubleshooting with Clay

Here are some helpful hints just in case you should run into any problems when working with polymer clay.

Clay is too hard: A plasticizer or diluent can be added to soften the clay. Chop up the clay and add just a few drops of mineral oil, baby oil, or diluent to the clay. Allow the clay to sit for one hour before mixing.

Clay is too soft: Soft clay can be "leached" to remove some of the excess plasticizer. Place sheets of clay between layers of absorbent paper like blank newsprint or simply leave the package open for a couple of days.

Clay just keeps crumbling: Remember that both heat and ultraviolet rays will affect the clay. Do not leave the clay in the car all day, on top of the oven, or in front of a window. Also, buy only from a reputable source that has handled and stored the clay correctly. I once walked into a bead store, which had its clay selection displayed in the front window. I never went back.

Clay turns dark in the oven: Check the baking temperature and do a test piece again. You may be scorching the clay.

Need green clay but don't have any: Do you have blue and yellow clays? Do not be afraid to mix your own colors. Buy a color-mixing chart or take a color theory class if you just cannot figure out that ecru is three parts white and one part raw sienna.

Baking the Clay

The clay must be properly baked to complete the polymerization process. There are lots of opinions on just how to achieve this. I use the technique that my friend and mentor, Marie Segal, has devised. She was instrumental in the formulation of the Sculpey Premo clay and she is a wealth of information about polymer clay.

1. Check the baking temperature of your oven with a thermometer. Does it bake hotter or cooler than indicated temperature? Adjust the suggested starting temperature accordingly.

2. Place a sheet of conditioned clay, rolled on #1, on a piece of baking parchment, an index card, or a file folder.

3. Place the clay and the paper on a clay-dedicated cookie sheet and place them in a cold oven.

4. Turn the oven to 200° for 10 minutes. This allows the entire piece to heat to an even temperature before polymerization of the surfaces.

5. After 10 minutes, turn the oven up to 275°, adjusted according to your oven thermometer, for 15 more minutes.

6. Turn the oven off and allow the piece to cool in the oven.

7. When the piece is cool, the polymerization process will be complete. You should be able to bend the piece and flex it a reasonable amount without cracking or breaking it.

Note: The baking times will vary according to the thickness of the piece. Thicker pieces will require more baking time. Check your oven frequently.

Baking Tips

Always bake the clay in a well-ventilated room. There should be a mild plastic odor when it bakes. If it starts to become bitter smelling, it is probably scorching or burning.

If you are baking large areas of white clay, tent them with foil—just like you would tent a turkey—to keep the white areas from scorching.

Items can be rebaked. In fact, many of the more complex techniques require several bakings.

Whenever possible, allow the pieces to cool in the oven. This is especially important with pieces that have a lot of bulk to them. Cracks can appear in the outside layers of clay if large items are not cooled slowly. If small cracks occur, put them back into a warm oven. The cracks often close on their own.

If you are baking in your home oven and you are concerned about the fumes there is a simple method of containment:

1. Purchase two foil roasting pans (the same size).

2. Line one roasting pan with some file folders or index cards and place the pieces inside.

3. Place the remaining roasting pan upside down on top of the first pan. Clip them closed with sturdy clothespins or gator clips.

4. Bake.

5. When the pans have cooled enough to touch, take them outside and remove the clips. The clay will be baked and the fumes will not be inside your house.

Making Basic Canes

Polymer canework has its roots in millifiore glass beadwork. Essentially, you are creating a one-dimensional picture or pattern in three dimensions. When you make the cane smaller (we call this "reducing the cane"), those polymer fibers will slip on themselves and retain the pattern. Once the pattern is created and reduced to the dimension you want it to be, you can slice the cane like slicing cookie dough and use the pieces for beads or for decorating other items. The pattern is created on the INSIDE and you do not see it until you cut the cane open.

There are five basic patterns to canework. Clockwise from left, they are the bull's eye, the Skinner blend, the banner, the pinroll, and the checkerboard.

Reducing & Reshaping a Cane

Good technique for cane reduction forces all the layers of clay to move at once and reduces distortion and waste. There are as many techniques for cane reduction as there are canes. Marie Segal showed me the following method.

To reduce a round cane:

1. Pick the cane up in the middle with your left hand. Place it in the area between your right thumb and forefinger and wrap your remaining fingers around the bottom half of the cane.

2. Now squeeze. Move your hands up the cane and squeeze again.

3. When you get to the top, turn the cane over. Starting at the middle, begin squeezing. Repeat in this manner to end of the cane. Note: I know it looks a mess now, but remember the magic is inside.

4. Roll the cane on the work surface to smooth it out and reduce it a little more to the largest diameter desired.

To reshape and reduce a square cane:
1. Convert a round cane to a square by pressing on all four sides of the round cane to create a square shape.

2. Using the lengths of your thumbs and fore-fingers, squeeze in the middle and squeeze out to each end. Note: Square canes are easier to cut without distortion than round canes.

3. Use an acrylic rod or brayer to even the sides and sharpen the edges.

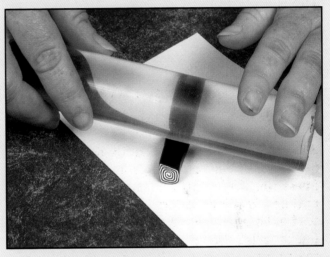

To reshape and reduce a triangular cane:
1. Convert a round cane to a triangular cane, beginning with the round cane slightly larger than you want the finished cane.

2. Set the cane on the table and pinch up one side of the cane.

3. Roll the cane over, and pinch up the other two sides.

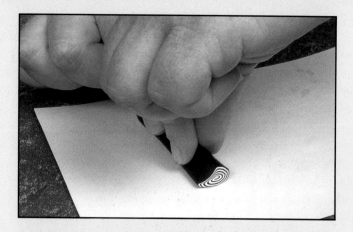

4. Smooth out the edges of the triangle by sliding your fingers down the cane from the middle to the edges. This will also help reduce the cane.

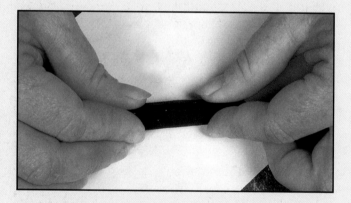

To reshape and reduce an oval cane:
1. Reduce the round cane to the size desired for the oval cane.

2. Using an acrylic rod or brayer, lightly roll down the top of the cane to flatten it into an oval.

166

Allowing the Clay to Rest

As mentioned previously, the softness of the clay is enhanced as a result of the conditioning process. Climate, temperature, and the warmth of your hands are also factors. Once you build a cane, it is recommended to allow the cane to "rest" for 15–30 minutes unless specified otherwise. This time allows the fibers to re-create their contacts and the fillers and binders to solidify once again. Resting also allows for cleaner cuts and less distortion in the pattern of the cane.

Using Molds

If canework causes you to see images in a different way, wait until you play with molds. Ready-made molds are available for purchase in crafts stores. However, we can also make our own original molds at home. We make molds of almost everything. Note: When making molds it is important to remember artist ethics and honor any applicable copyrights.

Simple Molds: Use scrap clay as the mold material. The mold masters, Judi Maddigan and Maureen Carlson, suggest forming the clay into a soft point and placing the point of clay into the deepest part of the mold. Note: Both Judi and Maureen have excellent websites listed as links of the San Diego Guild website.

Premo Sculpey clay seems to have a "memory" for detail. Use a mold of unbaked Premo for the impression if you are in a hurry or do not want a permanent mold. Katherine Dewey showed me this little trick one year in Dallas.

Mold Release: A mold release is used to protect the original item being molded. The mold release is also used to help keep the clay being molded from sticking to the mold. Use baby powder, water, or a petroleum-based vinyl protectant as common mold releases. Apply the release agent to either the mold or the surface of the clay to be molded.

Using Rubber Stamps with Polymer Clay

Rubber stamps work very well with this medium. Look for well-defined images on the stamps to create fairly deep impressions.

Use a mold release to protect the stamps and aid in achieving a clean impression.

Heat-set inks work superbly with the clay. If you have not used these inks before, they are inks that do not "set" until heat is applied. Thus, you can cure the clay and set the ink in one baking.

The inks can be embossed into the surface or stamped onto the smooth surface of the clay. Heat-set ink and stamps were used to make the fabulous pin below.

Using Translucent Heat-embossing Powders with Polymer Clay

Remember that a little of these powders goes a long way. You can use your fingers to apply these powders directly to the raw clay.

A small paintbrush can be used to create a soft layer of the powders, but the paintbrush does not control the powder very well, so be very careful.

My favorite tool for applying the powder is a small rubber sculpting chisel. This little tool allows you to "paint" the surface of the clay and create a straight line of powder.

This translucent heat-embossing powder can be applied to the raw surface of the clay before baking. It also can be mixed into the clays for a very subtle metallic effect.

This powder also can be mixed into a surface sealant, resulting in a lovely glistening effect that is perfect for leaves and fairies.

Sanding Polymer Clay

Always use wet sandpaper and sand under water as much as possible. My expert, Jami Miller, says to soak the sandpaper for at least an hour before use.

The most common grits are the very high-end grits—300, 400, and higher. You can use a few of the lower grits if you need to take a lot off the surface right away. The very high-end grits are available at auto parts stores for car painting.

Begin with the lowest grit and sand in all four directions for at least one to two minutes. Continue this process with each higher grit. The finer grit you use, the better the finish will be.

Polymer clay can be polished on a polishing wheel after sanding. Use only a muslin wheel and no polishing paste.

This beautiful necklace was made by Dottie McMillan and was sanded and polished after baking. The jade was created of mostly translucent clay with a little green, burnt ochre, and purple.

Finishing Polymer Clay

Sealants for Polymer Clay: There are sealants, called glazes, available for finishing or sealing the clay.

I prefer to use a water-based varathane in the clear satin finish. It has no smell and it is nearly invisible on the surface of the clay. Take care not to apply too much in one coat as it can cause a milky effect.

Some floor waxes are polymer-based products that can be rubbed or brushed onto the surface. You can also dip the whole piece like these large molded beads I made.

Antiquing Polymer Clay: There are many ways to "antique" the surface of the clay. We have used brown acrylic paint in several projects.

Marie Segal made this lovely pendant by painting the entire surface with heat-set ink, curing it, and then sanding off the surface, producing a neat inlay of pigment without any residual pigment on the upper layers.

How do I make a pinroll cane?

The pinroll is perfect for covering a small candleholder. Give new life to an older candleholder or embellish a new plain glass candleholder. They make excellent gifts.

Small Candleholder

Here's How:

1. Roll a #1 sheet from ½ package of the white clay.

2. Cut the biggest rectangle possible from this sheet of clay.

3. Repeat Step 1 with ½ package of the black clay.

4. Place the white rectangle on the black and trim the edges to match.

5. Place the sandwiched rectangle of clay with the black side down. This will make the outside layer of the pinroll black.

6. Trim the two short ends of the rectangle to 45˚, so that the white layer is slightly shorter than the black.

7. Pinch up one of the short ends and slowly roll the rectangle up. Push the ends back into the cane as they spread out.

8. Gently roll the cane on the work surface to seal the outside.

7

12

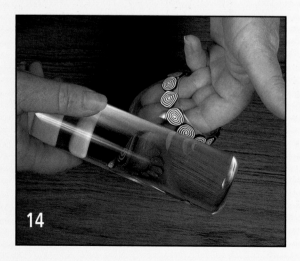

14

9. Refer to *Reducing & Reshaping a Cane* on page 164. Reduce the cane to the first desired size. Allow the cane to rest for 10–15 minutes.

10. Cut the cane for the first time right in the middle, as this should produce the least distorted image.

11. Cut thin slices from the cane.

12. Gently press the slices evenly into place around the upper edge of the candleholder.

13. Repeat Steps 11–12 for the bottom edge of the candleholder.

14. Using a water glass or acrylic rod, press and smooth the slices into place.

15. Refer to *Baking the Clay* on page 162. Bake the covered candleholder. Allow to cool. Note: The clay will adhere to the glass without adhesives. However, if you decide you don't like the configuration or just wish to change it after baking, just peel the clay off.

How do I resize and reshape a pinroll cane?

**What You
Need to
Get Started:**

Basic clay tools
Nail clippers
Needle tool:
  long, thin
Premade pinroll
  cane
Round-nosed
  pliers
Sculpey Premo
  clay in 2 oz.
  package: black
  or contrasting
  color (small
  amount)
T-pin and French
  loop wire for
  earring
  assembly

Remember, once you create a cane, you can resize and reshape all of it or portions of it for different uses. I have the habit of saving portions of cane for later use. Earrings make quick and easy small projects to start your new jewelry collection. You can make them as simple or elaborate as you wish.

Pinroll Earrings

Here's How:
1. Refer to *Reducing & Reshaping a Cane* on page 164. Reduce ¼ of the cane to ¼" diameter.

2. Cut two ¼"-thick slices from the cane.

3. Reshape the rest of the cane to form a triangle.

4. Cut two ¼"-thick slices from the triangular cane.

5. Using the needle tool, pierce each bead by twisting it halfway through the bead. Complete the pierce from the other side of the bead.

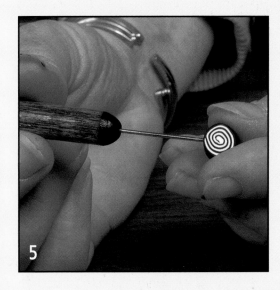

6. For coordinating beads, form some small balls and some flattened balls from the contrasting color of clay and pierce them.

7. Refer to *Baking the Clay* on page 162. Bake the beads. Allow to cool.

8. Place the beads on the T-pin as desired.

9. Using the pliers, trim the T-pin to ¼" longer than the stack of beads.

10. Grip the top of the T-pin. Roll the pliers to form a circle.

11. Thread the French loop wire on and close the loop.

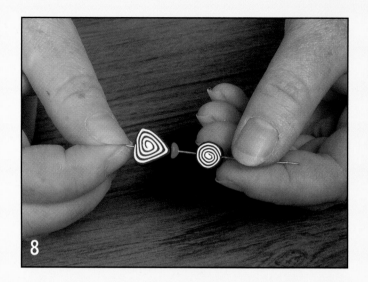

How do I recombine the pinroll cane?

What You Need to Get Started:

Basic clay tools
Napkin rings:
    ceramic, metal,
    or wood
Sculpey Premo clay
    in 2 oz.
    packages:
    ultramarine blue
    (1); turquoise (1)

This project is an excellent demonstration of the combination and recombination of basic patterns to create a lovely new life for an old set of napkin rings.

Napkin Rings

Here's How:

1. Refer to Steps 1–8 on page 169. Make a pinroll cane from ultramarine blue and turquoise clays.

2. Refer to *Reducing & Reshaping a Cane* on page 164. Reduce the pinroll cane to ½" diameter. Allow the cane to rest 20–30 minutes.

3. Cut the cane into four equal pieces.

4. Stack the four cane pieces together to make a square.

5. Roll a small long snake from the turquoise clay. Cut the snake into five equal pieces. Place one piece in the intersection of the four canes.

6. Place remaining snake pieces in the outside intersections of the canes. This creates a Spanish tile effect. Gently press the pieces together.

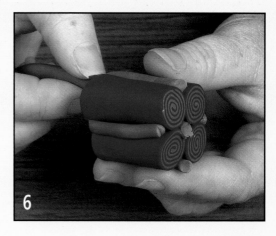

7. Reduce for a square cane. We now have an intricate design from our simple pinrolls.

8. Cut thin slices from the cane.

9. Press the slices onto the outside of the napkin rings.

10. Using an acrylic rod, smooth the cane slices in place, taking care not to smear the designs.

11. Refer to *Baking the Clay* on page 162. Bake the napkin rings. Allow to cool.

7

How do I turn the pinroll cane inside out?

What You Need to Get Started:

Basic clay tools
Necklace clasp
Needle tool:
 long, thin
Round-nosed
 pliers
Sculpey Premo
 clay in 2 oz.
 packages:
 black (1);
 ecru (1);
 gold (1)
Stringing
 material
T-pin and French
 loop wire for
 earring
 assembly

Two of my favorite people showed me two of my favorite techniques. Marie Segal showed me the Inside-out cane technique and Mike Buessler showed me how to create the Mobius bead. Both techniques work with almost any cane pattern, but I prefer them with this particular pattern.

Mobius Bead

Here's How:

1. Refer to Steps 1–8 on page 169. Make two pinroll canes from black and ecru clays.

2. Refer to *Reducing & Reshaping a Cane* on page 164. Reduce the pinroll canes to ½" diameter. Allow the canes to rest 20–30 minutes.

3. Cut one cane right in the middle. Cut one piece of the cane in half lengthwise.

4. Cut these two halves lengthwise again, creating quarters of the original cane.

5. Reassemble these pieces inside out.

6. Roll a snake from the gold clay. Place the snake in the center of the four cane pieces to fill the area. Gently press the pieces together.

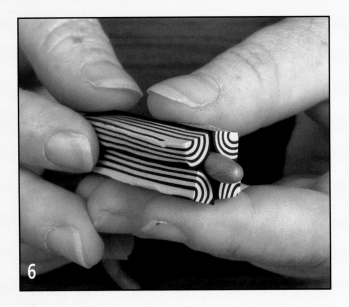

7. Roll a #5 sheet from the remaining black clay.

8. Place the cane pieces on the black sheet of clay. Trim the sheet of clay behind one long edge of the cane. Trim up the two sides of the sheet, using the ends of the cane as a guide.

9. Roll the cane pieces up in the black clay until the edges touch. Roll it back slightly and look at the surface of the black clay. There will be a dent where the leading edge of the black clay touched itself. Trim the black clay at the dent. Lightly roll the cane on the work surface to seal the wrap.

10. Reduce for a ¾"-square cane.

11. Cut several thin (less than ⅛") slices from the cane. Set aside some slices for filler beads.

12. Make Mobius beads by holding two opposite corners of one slice with your right thumb and forefinger. The slice should look diamond shaped between your two fingers.

13. Reach from behind the slice and touch the two opposite corners with your left thumb and forefinger.

14. Gently pull your two hands apart while folding the opposite corners toward each other. You have now created a wonderful three-dimensional shape that looks like an animal print. Allow the beads to rest for a few minutes.

15. Repeat Steps 12–14 for number of Mobius beads desired.

16. Make round filler beads of consistent size, by rolling a snake first and cutting it into equal sized pieces. Roll each piece into a ball.

17. Cut several slices from the remaining pinroll cane for filler beads.

18. Using the needle tool, pierce each filler bead and each Mobius bead by twisting it halfway through the bead. Complete the pierce from the other side of the bead, resealing the points of the Mobius beads as they are pierced.

19. Refer to *Baking the Clay* on page 162. Bake the beads. Allow to cool.

20. Refer to Steps 8–11 on page 171. Place beads as desired for earrings.

21. Place the beads onto stringing material to length desired.

22. Attach necklace clasp to ends of stringing material to create a necklace.

Design Tips:

The Mobius beads work best with a fresh cane that is still well-conditioned. If the points come apart, apply a dot of super strength craft adhesive to seal them.

A pinroll does not have to be just two colors—try three colors rolled together.

Try making the layers rolled together different thicknesses.

Pinrolls recombined together do not have to be from the same cane. Use complementary or contrasting colored canes together.

Use a very thin layer of a lighter color or white to separate two dark colors.

Try mixing embossing powder into the clays before making the pinrolls. The embossing powders will "bloom" when they are baked. They will show more when baked, so remember, a little goes a long way. Mix lighter colored powders into darker clays and darker colored powders into lighter clays. My favorite Mobius bead is made up of dark blue clay with white embossing powder pinrolled with white clay that is mixed with dark blue embossing powder.

Inside-out canes do not have to be from the same cane. Mix and match was never so fun.

How do I make a bull's eye cane?

What You Need to Get Started:

Acrylic frame: clear, small
Basic clay tools
Index cards (2)
Sculpey Premo clay in 2 oz. packages: black (2); fuchsia (1); green (1); orange (1)

Bull's eye canes are the most creative of the basic canes. They can be simple or elaborate, bold or subtly colored. The frame project described here has become one of my favorite creations. I now have little bull's eye frames all over the house and I'm considering making a bull's eye "frame" for my computer monitor

Clay Frame

Here's How:

1. Roll a little less than half of the fuchsia clay into a ball. Elongate the ball into a 1½"- to 2"-long cylinder.

2. Roll a #1 sheet from half of the black clay. Roll a #5 sheet from this sheet of clay.

3. Refer to Steps 8–9 on page 175. Wrap the fuchsia cylinder with the sheet of black clay. Note: The resulting cane is called a bull's eye.

5. Roll another #5 sheet from the black clay. Wrap it around the bull's eye cane.

6. Roll a #3 sheet from the orange clay. Wrap it around the bull's eye cane.

7. Finally, roll another #5 sheet from the black clay. Wrap it around the bull's eye cane. Roll the cane on the work surface to seal the wraps.

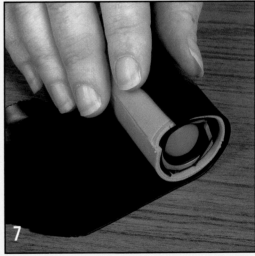

4. Roll a #3 sheet from the green clay. Wrap it around the bull's eye cane.

8. Refer to *Reducing & Reshaping a Cane* on page 164. Reduce the bull's eye cane to ¾" diameter.

9. Cut the cane right in the middle and reduce one piece to ½" diameter. Allow the cane to rest for at least 30 minutes.

10. Roll a #3 sheet from the remaining black clay. Place the acrylic frame, face down, on the sheet of clay.

11. Cut the clay slightly larger than the frame to allow for minimal shrinkage.

12. Cut one index card to form a template the size of the photo area of the frame. Center this on the black clay and cut around the edge of the index card. This will form the clay frame background of the project. Keep the clay frame on the index card.

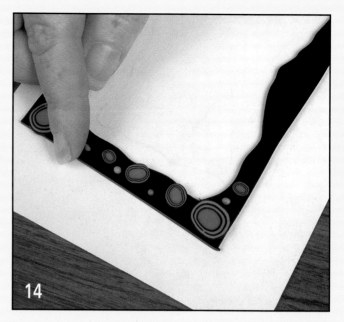

16. Glue the clay frame onto the acrylic frame.

13. Cut thin slices from the cane and place them randomly on the clay frame.

14. Embellish the clay frame further with little dots of fuchsia, green, and orange clays.

15. Refer to *Baking the Clay* on page 162. Place the decorated clay frame on the second index card and bake, taking care to keep the frame flat. Allow to cool. Note: The acrylic frame does not go in the oven.

How do I add a banner to the bull's eye cane?

What You Need to Get Started:

Basic clay tools
Needle tool: large
Phillips screw-
   driver: small
Premade bull's
   eye cane: 2"
   long, ¾"
   diameter
Sculpey Premo
   clay in 2 oz.
   packages:
   colors used for
   the bull's eye (⅓
   package each);
   black, ecru, or
   white (⅓
   package)

The banner technique is a quick, easy way to achieve a striping effect. I like to use it for making buttons. Made from Sculpey Premo polymer clay, they are very sturdy and can withstand many cycles through the washer and dryer. Years ago, I made buttons for a denim shirt. The denim is now faded, but the buttons are still pristine.

Bull's Eye Buttons

Here's How:

1. Roll clay colors, including those used in the bull's eye cane, into balls.

2. Flatten the clay balls into little "pillow" shapes. Note: The pillows do not need to be the same thickness, but roughly the same shape and size.

3. Stack the pillows on top of each other, alternating the contrasting light and black color, if desired.

4. Slightly press the stack together and cut in half.

5. Restack the two halves on top of each other. Set the stack on the work surface and press it out to the same size you began with. This will have the effect of compressing the layers together.

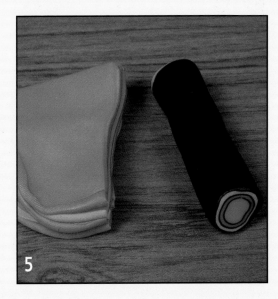

6. Cut the stack in half and repeat Step 5.

7. Cut the stack in half again. Observe that the layers are now fine stripes of color. Note: The intricacy of the striping is controlled by the number of times Steps 4–5 are repeated.

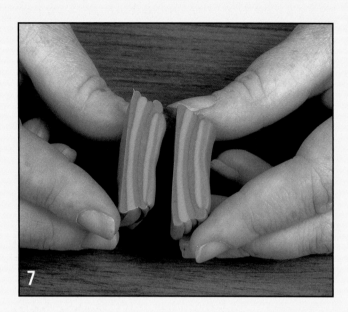

8. Compare the stack to the bull's eye cane. Select the side of the stack that most closely matches the length of the cane. Cut ⅛"-thick slices of the stack.

9. Place these slices around the outside edge of the cane, alternating the striping and allowing the slices to touch but not overlap. Trim the last slice lengthwise to fit, if necessary.

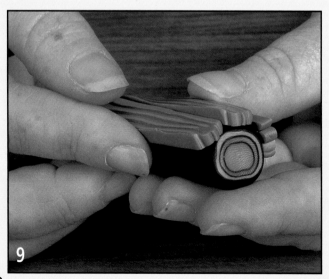

10. Gently roll the cane on the work surface to seal. Slightly reduce the cane.

11. Cut the cane right in the middle. At this point, add a thin wrap of color to the outside if desired. Allow the cane to rest 15–20 minutes.

12. Cut ³⁄₁₆"- to ¼"-thick slices from the cane to make buttons. If desired, round the edges of the buttons with your finger.

13. Using the large needle tool or a phillips screwdriver, create the thread holes. Angle the holes toward the outside to help strengthen the thread and button.

14. Refer to *Baking the Clay* on page 162. Bake the buttons. Allow to cool.

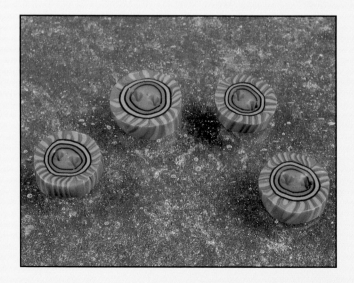

How do I use the banner cane?

What You Need to Get Started:

Basic clay tools
Leftover banner cane
Necklace clasp
Needle tool: long
Sculpey Premo clay: colors of the banner cane (scraps)
Stringing material

The uneven striping effect created by the banner technique perfectly yields itself to wonderful twisted beads. These beads are great made into a piece of jewelry, when alternated with coordinating pinroll beads. made into a piece of jewelry,

Twisted Beads

Here's How:

1. Cut a ¼"-thick slice from the leftover banner cane.

2. Evenly twist the slice.

3. Cut the twist into desired lengths.

4. Roll small balls from the solid colors of clay. Press them onto the ends of the twists, making end caps and completing the beads.

5. Using the needle tool, pierce each bead by twisting it halfway through the bead. Complete the pierce from the other side of the bead.

6. Refer to Baking the Clay on page 19. Bake the beads. Allow to cool.

7. Refer to Steps 21–22 on page 175. Place the beads onto stringing material to length desired and attach necklace clasp to create a necklace.

How do I make a checkerboard cane?

There are many ways of making a checkerboard cane, but this method creates the cleanest pattern. The technique for covering pens can be used with any cane or combination of canes.

Checkerboard-covered Pen

Here's How:

1. Roll a #1 sheet from black and white clays.

2. Cut a 1¼" square from the black sheet of clay.

3. Place the black square on the white sheet and trim to match.

4. Repeat Steps 2–3, alternating between the black and white clays until you have six layers or a square block of alternating layers of color. Note: The top and bottom layers must be different colors.

5. Gently press the stack together. Do not use too much pressure as this could disturb the precision of the layers.

6. Turn the stack on its side so the layers are now vertical.

7. Carefully cut ⅛"-thick slices from the stacked clay. Note: I sometimes cool my stack in the refrigerator before beginning this step.

8. Flip every other slice and restack, taking care to line up the top and bottom of the cane. The colored squares should alternate into a checkerboard.

9. Refer to *Reducing & Reshaping a Cane* on page 164. Reduce for a square cane to ½" diameter.

10. Using a pair of pliers, remove the ink cartridge from the pen.

11. Cut thin slices from the checkerboard cane.

12. Press the slices around the barrel of the pen, avoiding overlapping the slices, but trimming them to fit. The thinness of the slices will determine the finished diameter of the pen.

13. Slowly roll the covered pen barrel on the work surface to seal the canes together.

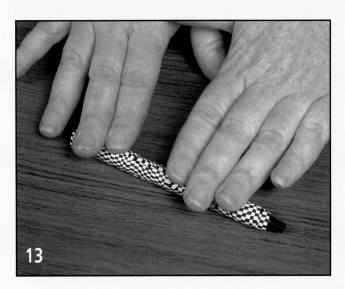

14. Trim the bottom edge of the clay to the end cap of the pen.

15. Pull the top edges together and pinch to cover the top of the pen.

16. Refer to *Baking the Clay* on page 162. Bake the covered pen for 20 minutes. Allow to cool.

17. Replace the ink cartridge after the pen has cooled.

Troubleshooting:
   This type pen can withstand the heat of the oven quite well, while the styrene, or clear plastic pens cannot. If you have a pen you would like to cover, remove the ink from it and put it in the oven at 275° for a few minutes to determine if it will be applicable.

How do I make a blended cane using the Skinner method?

What You Need to Get Started:

Basic clay tools
Brass light switch cover
Needle tool: large
Sculpey Premo clay in 2 oz. packages: cobalt blue (1); fluorescent green (1); white (3)

Judith Skinner knew there had to be a simple mathematical formula for gradating colors. Here is the technique she devised. I congratulate her for radically reforming the caning process, and I never do this technique without thanking Judith, whether I'm talking to a roomful of people or my cats in the garage.

Color-blended Light Switch Cover

Here's How:
1. Roll a #1 sheet from the blue and white clays.

2. Cut a triangle from the blue sheet of clay.

3. Cut a matching triangle from the white sheet of clay.

4. Place the two triangles together to form a rectangle. Press the edges together to help hold the two pieces of clay together.

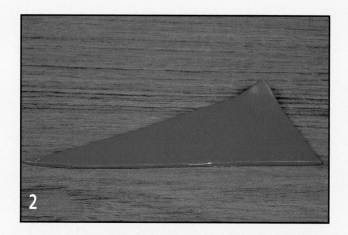

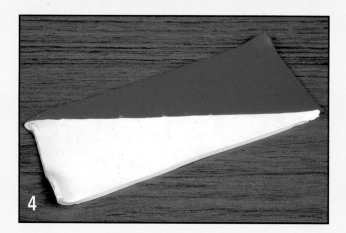

5. Fold the clays lengthwise and roll a #1 sheet. Keep folding and rolling, the SAME way. It takes several passes through the machine to get a nice blend. Note: At first it appears that you have just created a mess, but do not give up. You determine when the blend is sufficient.

6. Turn the blended sheet 90° and roll a #5 sheet.

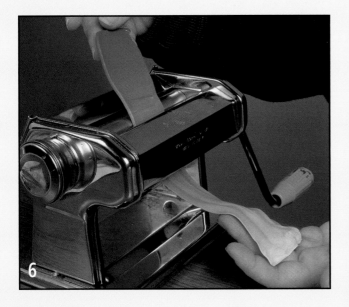

7. Refer to Steps 7–8 on page 169. Roll the blend into a pinroll. If a lighter color is desired on the inside of the roll, begin rolling there.

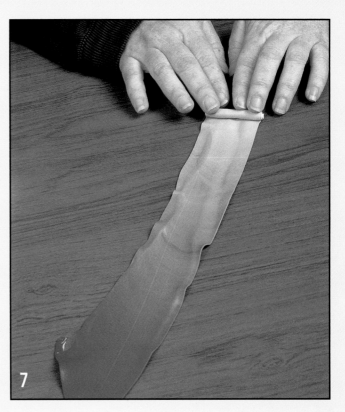

8. Roll a #5 sheet from the outside color. Wrap the sheet around the cane to maximize the effect of the blend.

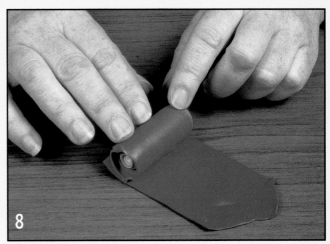

187

9. Repeat Steps 1–8 for the green and white clays.

"Thank you, Judith."

10. Refer to *Reducing & Reshaping a Cane* on page 164. Reduce the canes to ½". Cut the canes right in the middle and reduce one piece of each cane to a smaller size.

11. Roll a #1 sheet from remaining white clay. Roll a #3 sheet from this sheet of clay.

12. Place the brass light switch cover as a template face down on the clay. Trim the hole for the switch. Trim the clay around the brass light switch cover, leaving ¼" selvage.

13. Fold the selvages over the light switch cover and trim off excess clay.

14. Turn the cover so it is right side up. Using the needle tool, place the screw holes. Make an offset for the screw head to fit.

15. Cut thin slices from the canes. Press the slices onto the white clay. Note: From a distance, the effect will look like bubbles. This effect is great for the bathroom or spa switch.

16. Refer to *Baking the Clay* on page 162. Bake the light switch cover. Allow to cool.

17. Pop the clay off the brass cover. Note: Sculpey Premo is strong enough to endure without breakage—even in the boys' room.

Troubleshooting:

If the clay forms a bubble between the brass cover and the clay, eliminate it by putting the brass cover with the baked clay back into the oven and warming it. Remove the assembly while it is still warm and place it face down on a flat, heat-proof surface with a large heavy book on it until it cools.

Design Tips:

Double-up the triangles of color to get more gradated clay for larger canes.

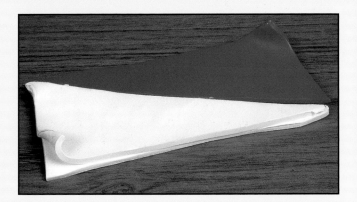

Use more than two colored triangles to create wonderful multicolored, air-brushed effects. Make the triangles in the shape below to use more than two colors. Marie Segal excels at this, creating spectacular effects in minutes.

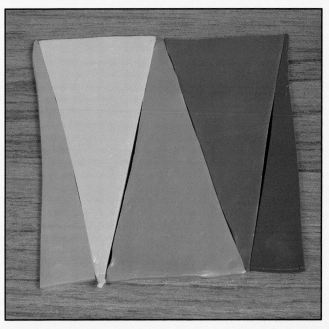

Try various color combinations, using the Skinner technique.

How do I make
3-D chain-linked canes?

**What You
Need to
Get Started:**

Basic clay tools
Basic jewelry
 findings
Necklace clasp
Needle tool: long,
 thin
Sculpey Premo
 clay in 2 oz.
 packages:
 pearl blue (2);
 ecru (2);
 pearl green (2)
Stringing material

Several years ago, I took a class with Pier Volkos where she showed us her lantern bead technique. I have always loved the dimensionality of that technique, so I played with it and came up with a linked effect that is spectacular in blended colors.

3-D Chain-linked Necklace

Here's How:
1. Refer to Steps 1–8 on page 169. Make a pinroll cane from ¾ package each of blue and ecru clays. Refer to *Reducing & Reshaping a Cane* on page 164. Reduce the cane to ½" diameter.

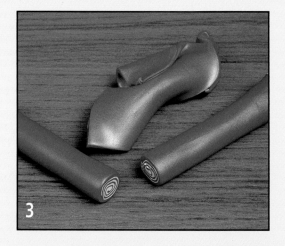

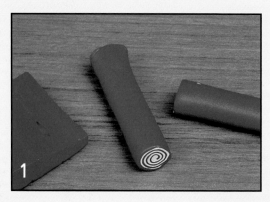

2. Make a pinroll cane from ¾ package each of green and ecru clays. Reduce the cane to ½" diameter.

3. Refer to Steps 1–6 on page 186. Blend a little ecru clay into the blue clay. Make a pinroll cane from this blend and ecru clay. Allow all canes to rest 30 minutes.

4. Cut two ³⁄₁₆"-thick slices from the blue cane. Place these two slices right next to each other so that they touch.

5. Cut a ³⁄₁₆"-thick slice from the green cane. Cut this slice in half and place the two pieces so that each half bridges the two blue slices from center to center, creating a linked bead.

6. Repeat Steps 1–5 with the other colors to create a couple of beads from each.

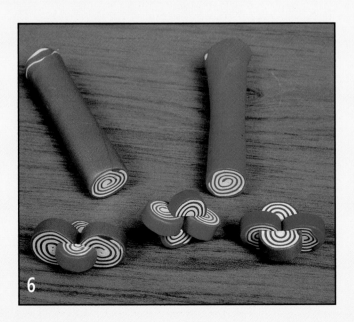

7. Using the needle tool, pierce each bead by twisting it, halfway through the length of the bead. Complete the pierce from the other side of the bead.

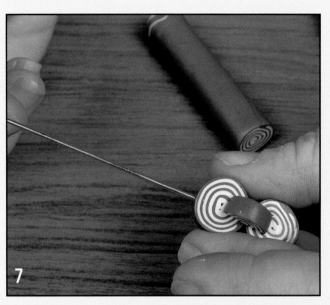

8. To make a couple of single lantern beads (Pier Volkos style), cut two slices in half and attach the four halves to a cylinder of color.

9. Using the needle tool, pierce each bead by twisting it, halfway through the central cylinder of the bead. Complete the pierce from the other side of the bead.

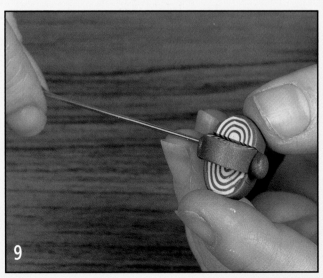

10. Cut slices from the remaining pinroll canes for additional beads. Reduce some of these canes to create smaller beads for placement at the top of the necklace.

11. Refer to Baking the Clay on page 19. Bake the beads. Allow to cool.

12. Refer to Steps 21–22 on page 175. Place the beads onto stringing material to length desired and attach necklace clasp to create a necklace.

Design Tips:

The same type bead can be made with blended canes, unblended canes and checkerboard cane, and whatever combinations you can think of.

The links hold up quite well if the canes are fresh when you put them together and then allow them to sit overnight before baking. I imagine this allows the separate pieces of polymer to bond together better. I have had to repair a only few of my linked beads with super strength craft adhesive.

192

How do I make a heart-shaped cane?

What You Need to Get Started:

Basic clay tools
Needle tool: long, thin
Premade pinroll canes
Sculpey Premo clay in 2 oz. package: coordinating color (1)
T-pin and French loop wire for earring assembly

I used a heart-shaped cane one year for Valentines Day. I didn't know at the time that hearts are supposedly one of the most difficult shapes to cane! Sometimes ignorance is bliss.

Heart Earrings

Here's How to Make a Pinroll Heart:
1. Refer to *Reducing & Reshaping a Cane* on page 164. Reduce the pinroll cane to ½" diameter.

2. Cut two 1"–3" long pieces from cane, depending on the amount of cane available and how many hearts you wish to produce.

3. Place the two pieces of cane side-by-side and lightly press them together.

4. Pull the bottoms of the two canes together in a point with your fingers. You will need to work your fingers down the cane to do this. After the point is achieved, slide your fingers down the cane to smooth out the pointed shape.

5. If the top of the heart got too pressed together, set the back of the blade in the middle of the canes and lean it out to each side to re-accent the two parts of the heart. Allow the cane to rest.

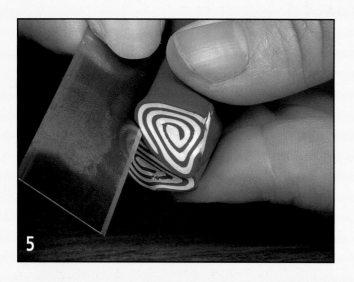

6. Cut thin slices from the cane.

7. Make small beads by rolling a snake from coordinating colored clay first and cutting it into equal-sized pieces. Roll each piece into a bead.

8. Using the needle tool, pierce each bead by twisting it halfway through the bead. Complete the pierce from the other side of the bead, resealing the points as they are pierced.

9. Refer to Steps 7–11 on page 171. Place beads on earring findings.

How do I make a simple flower cane?

What You Need to Get Started:

Basic clay tools
Drawer pulls:
  round, ceramic
  or wooden
Sculpey Premo
  clay in 2 oz.
  packages:
  cobalt blue (2);
  green (1);
  orange (1);
  cad yellow (2)

This pattern is perfect for drawer pulls or buttons. Kids love this pattern. One of those days when I have nothing but time, I would like to try making it from Sculpey III Glow-In-the-Dark colors with a black background.

Flower Drawer Pulls

Here's How:

1. Refer to Steps 1–3 on page 179. Roll a cylinder from ½ package of yellow clay. Roll a #1 sheet from green clay. Wrap the sheet of green clay around the cylinder to make a bull's eye cane.

2. Refer to *Reducing & Reshaping a Cane* on page 164. Reduce the cane.

3. Cut the cane into five equal pieces. Assemble the pieces.

4. Repeat Steps 2–3.

5. Reduce this cane to ½" diameter and set aside. Note: You have now made a lace cane.

6. Refer to Steps 1–7 on page 186. Make a blended cane from ¾ package each of orange and yellow clays to create a blend from orange and yellow. Begin rolling at the yellow end of the sheet.

7. Wrap this cane with a #5 sheet made from the remaining orange clay.

6–7

Note: Note: We are assembling the cane vertically now, instead of horizontally.

10

8. Reduce this cane to ¼" diameter.

9. Cut the cane into five equal pieces. Stand these five pieces up so that they touch each other, creating the "petals."

11. Roll a snake from ½ package of blue clay. Reshape the snake to form a triangle. Cut the triangle into five equal pieces.

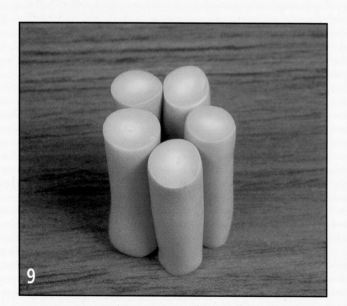

9

11

10. Determine the center of the five petals and adjust the lace cane to fit into this space. Place the lace cane into the center of the petals.

12. Place a triangle of blue between each petal. Note: The triangle should be wider at the base of the triangle and about as deep as the space of the petal.

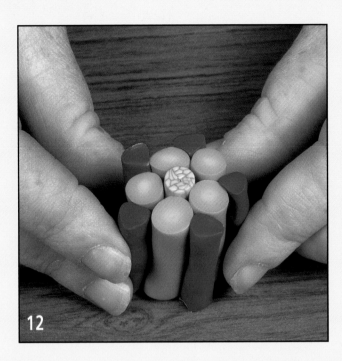

13. Wrap a #1 sheet of blue clay around the outside of this clay assemblage.

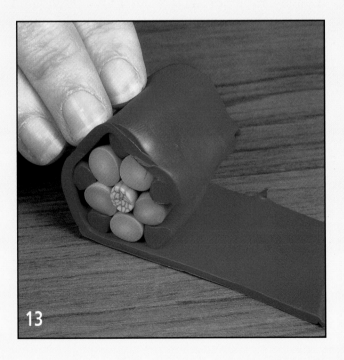

14. Reduce the cane down to 1" diameter. Note: The diameter of the cane depends on the size and condition of the drawer pull.

15. Cover the entire drawer pull with a #1 sheet of blue clay.

16. Cut a ⅛"-thick slice from the cane. Center the cane slice on the top of the covered drawer pull.

17. Gently roll the drawer pull in your hands, blending the cane slice into the covered drawer pull.

18. Refer to *Baking the Clay* on page 162. Bake the covered drawer pulls. Allow to cool.

How do I make a millefiori bead?

Millefiori is the famous Italian technique for lampworked glass beads. The glass artist touches a rod of glass containing a flower pattern to a molten bead, leaving a small part of the rod attached to the new bead. This is where the canework concept comes from.

What You Need to Get Started:

Backpack clip kit with header pin
Basic clay tools
Premade flower cane
Round-nosed pliers
Sculpey Premo clay in 2 oz. package: color of the cane or a complementary color

Millefiori Backpack Clip

Here's How:

1. Refer to *Reducing & Reshaping a Cane* on page 164. Reduce the premade cane to ¼" diameter.

2. Roll a 1"-diameter ball from selected color of clay.

3. Cut thin slices from the flower cane.

4. Place the slices in a random fashion, completely covering the ball.

5. Cup your hands and slowly roll the cane-covered ball, blending the cane slices into the original ball. Frequently reverse the direction of the roll.

6. Using the needle tool, pierce the ball by twisting it halfway through. Complete the pierce from the other side of the ball.

7. Refer to *Baking the Clay* on page 162. Bake the ball. Allow to cool.

8. Place the ball on the header pin.

9. Using the pliers, trim the pin to ¼" longer than ball.

10. Grip the top of the pin. Roll the pliers to form a circle.

11. Thread the backpack clip on and close the loop.

198

How do I make a star cane?

What You Need to Get Started:

Basic clay tools
Pin back: 1"
Sculpey Premo clay in 2 oz. packages: cobalt blue (2); ultramarine blue (1); cad yellow (2); zinc yellow (1)

You can never have too much star cane. Star shapes are prevalent throughout the history of art, and are popular today in all sorts of media.

Moon & Stars Lapel Pin

Here's How to Make a Basic Star:

1. Refer to Steps 1–3 on page 181. Roll a cylinder from one package of cad yellow clay. Roll a #1 sheet from zinc yellow clay. Wrap the sheet of zinc yellow clay around the cylinder to make a bull's eye cane.

2. Refer to *Reducing & Reshaping a Cane* on page 164. Reshape the bull's eye cane to form a triangle.

3. Reduce the triangle cane so each side is ¼" wide.

4. Cut the triangle cane into five equal pieces.

5. Stand the pieces on end in a circle so that the bottom two points touch and the other point is facing out.

7. Determine the center of the five triangles and adjust the cylinder to fit into this space. Place the cylinder into the center of the triangles. Set this formation aside.

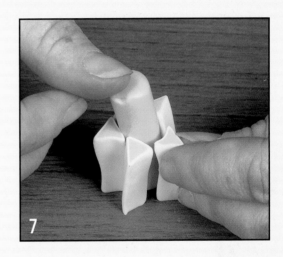

8. Roll a 1"-diameter ball from blue clay. Flatten the clay ball to a cylinder.

9. Reshape the cylinder to form a triangle.

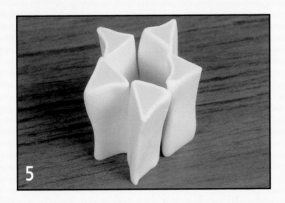

6. Roll a cylinder from cad yellow clay.

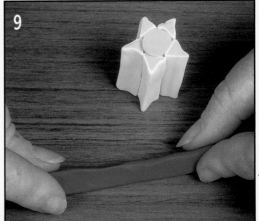

10. Reduce the triangle cane so each side is ¼" wide.

11. Cut the triangle into 10 equal pieces and fit two pieces between each arm of the star.

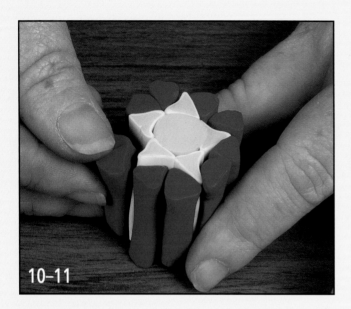

12. Roll a #1 sheet from blue clay. Wrap the sheet of blue clay around the assemblage to "pad" the pointed arms.

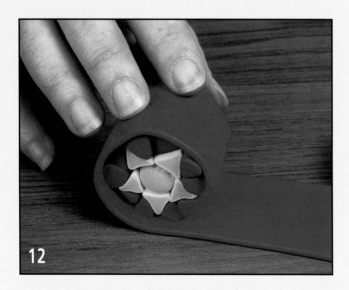

13. Reduce the entire cane to ⅜" diameter.

14. Cut the cane right in the middle. Set aside.

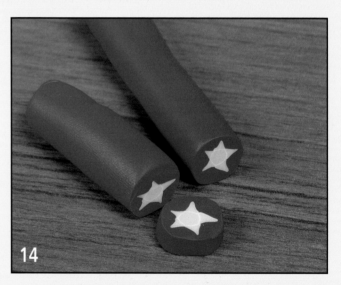

15. Roll a #1 sheet from ¼ package of cad yellow clay.

16. Place a 2"-diameter round form on the sheet. Cut the clay around the form.

17. Reposition the form on the clay so that a crescent shape is formed. Cut it out. Note: The sharper the edge of the form, the easier it is to trace around it.

18. Cut ⅛"-thick slices from the star cane. Apply the slices on top of and leading away from the crescent. Note: Back the projecting pieces with a #4 sheet of blue clay attached to the crescent to support the design if it gets really freeform away from the crescent.

19. Refer to *Baking the Clay* on page 162. Bake the assemblage. Allow to cool.

20. Place the pin back onto the back of the crescent. Attach the pin back by placing a small piece of clay over the flat part of the pin back, creating a "bandage." Rebake the clay. Allow to cool.

Design Tip:
    No one says the star has to be a solid color. Try making it with blended canes, patterned canes or leftover canes in the center portion.

How do I make a face cane?

I found some face drawings in my five-year-old son's backpack and they were exactly what I was looking for—bold, simple, funky, and easy. You can make the faces different colors and vary their expressions and hair, or combine them with little polymer shirts, or see where your imagination takes you.

Funny Faces Barrette

Here's How to Make the Ecru Boy:
1. Roll a small snake from black clay.

2. Roll two sheets from white clay. One at a time, wrap the sheets around the black snake.

3. Roll a #4 sheet from black clay. Wrap the sheet around the black and white clay combination.

4. Refer to *Reducing & Reshaping a Cane* on page 164. Reduce the cane to ¼" diameter or slightly smaller.

5. Cut two 2"-long pieces from the cane for the eyes.

6. Roll a #1 and a #3 sheet from ecru clay. Wrap the #1 and then the #3 sheet of ecru clay around each piece of eye cane.

7. Stand the two canes up. Cut a slice off part of the #3 sheet at the seam. Note: This cut is what keeps the eyes round when reducing the cane.

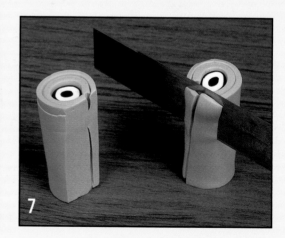

202

8. Roll a cylinder from ecru clay. Reshape the cylinder to form a triangle. Cut two pieces from the triangle and place these pieces between the eye canes at the top and bottom. Notice that the shape is a rectangle again.

9. Roll a ⅜"-diameter cylinder from ecru clay.

10. Trim this cylinder to the length of the eye cane and cut it in half lengthwise.

11. Roll a #5 sheet from black clay. Wrap the sheet around one of the ecru halves, taking care not to cover the flat portion and creating a mouth piece.

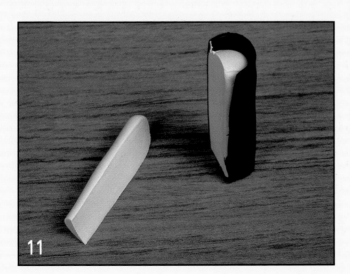

12. Attach the mouth by centering it under the eyes and slightly pressing the assemblage together.

13. Place two triangles of ecru on either side of the mouth to bring the assemblage back to a round shape. Note: Always try to bring the assemblages back to the shape into which you plan to reduce the cane.

14. Roll a #1 sheet from ecru clay. Wrap the sheet around the bottom half of the assemblage from cheek to cheek.

15. Roll a #5 sheet from black clay. Roll a #4 sheet from ecru clay. Create the crewcuts by stacking the sheets. Cut the stacked layers to different heights and assemble them together on the top of the head. Note: Make certain to vary the height of the layers for tousled hair.

16. Roll a #5 sheet from black clay. Wrap the black sheet from one side of the hairline, under the face, to the other.

17. Reduce the cane to diameter desired. Cut slices as desired.

Here's How to Make the Purple Girl:

Note: The little purple girl has Skinner blended cheeks added to her assemblage. She is decked in curls on top.

1. Refer to Steps 1–12 for *Here's How to Make the Ecru Boy* on page 202. Assemble the face cane substituting violet clay for ecru clay.

2. Refer to Steps 1–7 on page 186. Make a blended cane from fuchsia clay and white clay proportionate to the size of the face cane.

3. Roll a small cylinder from the violet clay. Reshape the cylinder to form a triangle. Tuck the triangle into the area formed by the mouth and the eyes.

4. Set the blended canes into the assemblage for cheeks. Complete the shape with a couple more small triangles of violet clay.

5. Refer to page 169. Make a pinroll cane from violet clay rolled with black clay for the hair.

6. Refer to *Reducing & Reshaping a Cane* on page 164. Reduce the pinroll cane and cut it into several pieces.

7. Add the pieces of the pinroll cane to the top of the face for curly hair.

8. Roll a #1 and a #5 sheet from black clay. Wrap the #1 sheet over the hair. Wrap the #5 sheet from one side of the hairline, under the face, to the other.

9. Reduce the cane to diameter desired. Cut slices as desired.

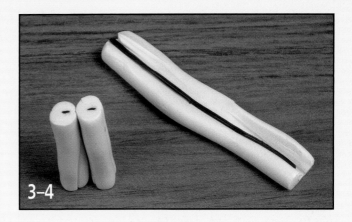

Here's How to Make the Boy with Tongue:
1. Mix yellow and white clays 3:1. Roll a ½"-diameter cylinder from this mix for the eye cane.

2. Cut the cylinder in half lengthwise.

3. Roll a #5 sheet from black clay. Cut and insert a small strip from the sheet between the two halves of the cylinder and center it within the cylinder.

4. Gently press the cylinder back together and roll it on the work surface to the size desired to begin construction.

5. Refer to Steps 7–8 for *Here's How to Make the Ecru Boy* on page 202. Begin assembling the face, substituting yellow clay mix for ecru clay.

6. Roll a cylinder of red clay the same size as one of the eyes.

7. Trim the cylinder to the same height as the face assemblage.

8. Make a cut lengthwise down the center of the cylinder. This cut should be just one third of the way through.

9. Insert the straight edge of a #5 sheet of black clay into this cut and trim it flush with the cylinder.

10. Gently press the cylinder back together and roll it on the work surface, without reducing it.

11. Stand the cylinder up. Cut a slice off part of the cylinder to give it a flattened edge. The black insert should be roughly centered in the flat edge now.

12. Wrap the bottom rounded portion of the cylinder with a #5 sheet of black clay.

13. Roll a #3 sheet from black clay. Cut and place a portion of the sheet to cover and extend beyond the flattened edge of the cylinder.

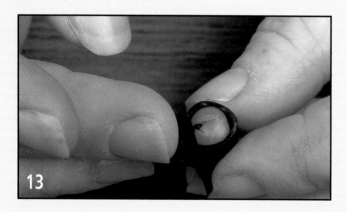

14. Roll a #3 or #4 sheet from yellow clay mix. Wrap the sheet around the tongue to even out the black, "padding" the tongue and supporting that upper lip of black clay .

15. Refer to Steps 13–17 for *Here's How to Make the Ecru Boy* on page 202, substituting the yellow clay mix for ecru clay. Add the tongue assemblage to the face assemblage and complete the face cane.

Here's How to Make the Orange Boy:
1. Mix orange and white clays 3:1.

2. Refer to Steps 1–17 for *Here's How to Make the Ecru Boy* on page 202. Assemble the face cane substituting orange clay mix for ecru clay.

Here's How to Make the Barrett:
1. Roll two #1 sheets from the black clay. Stack the sheets for the base. Trim as desired.

2. Cut slices from the face canes and arrange them on the base. Decorate the exposed base with small dots of colored clay.

3. Refer to *Baking the Clay* on page 162. Bake the clay right on the surface of the barrette. Allow to cool.

4. Pop the clay off the barrette. Using craft adhesive, adhere it back onto the barrette for more durability.

How do I use clay molds?

Baby powder
Basic clay tools
Brass light switch
  cover
Clay mold: leaf
Granitex clay:
  black (1); blue
  (2); green (1)
Needle tool: large

Clay molds produce a variety of fast and easy clay shapes that can be used as individual pieces of art or to embellish a larger project. This decorative light switch cover and the leaves that are on it are made from a premade stone-effect clay called Granitex. The light switch cover appears to have been sculpted from colored granite.

Leaf Light Switch Cover

Here's How:
1. Roll a #3 sheet from the blue clay and place it on the work surface.

2. Place the brass light switch cover as a template face down on the clay. Trim the hole for the switch. Trim the clay around the brass light switch cover, leaving ¼" selvage.

3. Fold the selvages over the light switch cover and trim off excess clay.

4. Turn the cover so it is right side up. Using the needle tool, place the screw holes. Make an offset for the screw head to fit.

5. Roll the green clay into a slightly pointed ball. Dust the clay ball or the mold with baby powder. Press the clay

ball into the leaf mold. Slice across the surface of the mold to remove the excess clay.

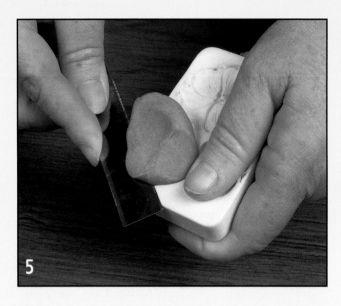

6. Remove clay from the mold by lightly pressing the excess clay onto the back of the clay still in the mold. The clay in the mold should stick to the excess enough to lift it out of the mold.

7. Place the leaves onto the blue clay and press to make surface contact.

8. Refer to *Baking the Clay* on page 162. Bake the light switch cover. Allow to cool.

9. Pop the clay off the brass cover.

Design Tip:
For autumn leaves, try blending small amounts of gold, orange, and red clays into the green Granitex.

How do I use household objects to make a reverse impression?

What You Need to Get Started:

Acrylic paint: brown
Baby powder
Basic clay tools
Brass light switch cover
Brush: small
Cotton cloth
Needle tool: large
Plastic dinosaurs or plastic ferns: small
Rock for texturing
Sculpey Premo clay in 2 oz. packages: ecru (2)

Don't overlook household objects—such as those found in your children's toy boxes—as resources for wonderful textures and molds. I once had a student bring an antique Chinese chop, or signature stamp, to class. The image was of a carp fish. We made a reverse mold of the image and created some wonderful pieces with it.

Fossils Light Switch Cover

Here's How:

1. Roll a #3 sheet from the ecru clay and place it on the work surface.

2. Place the brass light switch cover as a template face down on the sheet. Trim the hole for the switch. Trim the clay around the brass light switch cover, leaving ¼" selvage.

3. Fold the selvages over the light switch cover and trim off excess clay.

4. Turn the cover so it is right side up. Using the needle tool, place the screw holes. Make an offset for the screw head to fit.

5. Using the rock, texture the entire surface of the clay. If desired, add a small amount of organic material such as dirt to the surface of the clay as you texture. Note: My round rock is perfect for this procedure. Since it is sandstone, it actually embeds sand into the clay as I use it.

5a

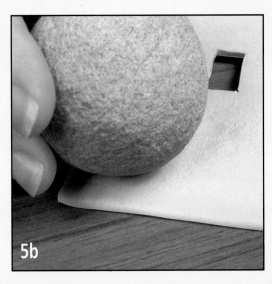

5b

6. Dust the dinosaurs or ferns with baby powder and press them into the surface of the clay. Roll them slightly to get a full impression.

7. Refer to *Baking the Clay* on page 162. Bake the light switch cover. Allow to cool.

8. Pop the clay off the brass cover.

9. Mix the paint with a little water and wash the surface of the baked clay, allowing the paint to pool in the depressions.

10. Using the cotton cloth, lightly wipe the surface.

11. Repeat Steps 9–10 until you are pleased with the effect.

Troubleshooting:

Watch out for small text written on the dinosaurs. It won't show up until they are baked and antiqued. I don't think you would really find "Made in China" in any prehistoric wall art.

Design Tips:

Experiment with this technique by making or covering pendants, pens, magnets, etc.

Look for molding possibilities in unexpected places. Once, I went looking in the bathtub. Low and behold, there was a perfect little plastic fish. I did some modification on it and made a mold. The result was pretty satisfying.

How do I make a mold?

I live at the beach and finding interesting shells to use for molds is a part-time summer job for my boys. Don't overlook barnacles and interesting rocks, either.

What You Need to Get Started:

Acrylic paint: brown
Baby powder
Basic clay tools
Box, round: cardboard, metal, or wooden
Brush
Cotton cloth
Craft adhesive: all purpose
Sculpey III or Super Sculpey: scraps
Sculpey Premo clay in 2 oz. packages: ecru (3)
Shells: several different shapes and sizes

Seashell Box

Here's How:

1. If using a wooden or cardboard box, prepare the surface by painting a layer of all purpose craft adhesive on it and allowing it to dry. This will help the clay to adhere to the nonporous surface.

2. Prepare the molds by making a flattened ball of the Sculpey III or Super Sculpey scrap clay that is about ¼" larger all around than the shell.

3. Dust the outside of the shell with baby powder and press it evenly into the clay.

4. Remove the shell by lifting up on both ends of the shell at once and pulling straight up.

5. Refer to *Baking the Clay* on page 162. Bake the mold. Allow to cool.

6. Roll a #3 sheet from ecru clay and place it on the work surface. Place the top of the box lid face down on the sheet of clay. Trim around the lid, leaving enough clay to cover the sides of the lid.

7. Fold the clay down around the sides of the lid and trim. You may have to overlap the clay, like wrapping a package. Press these overlaps and trim off the excess.

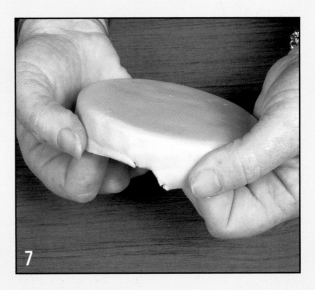

8. Roll another #3 sheet from ecru clay and cover the sides of the box, leaving the upper edge free of clay so the lid still fits on the box.

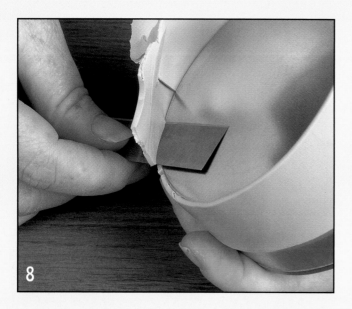

9. Roll a #4 sheet from ecru clay. Place the box on this sheet. Trim around the box to cover the bottom of the box. Smooth the edges of the bottom into the side edges of clay.

10. Using the rock, texture the clay surfaces, except the bottom. Make a couple of uneven

areas for a more natural feel. Add some "organic materials" to the surface if desired. Note: Remember that my "magic" sandstone rock leaves particles of dirt and sand behind.

11. Roll a slightly pointed ball from ecru clay and dust the surface of the point with baby powder. Press the point into the shell mold and trim off the excess clay.

12. Use the excess clay to "lift" the clay from the mold.

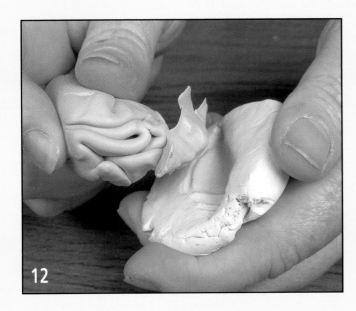

13. Place the clay shells on the surface of the clay-covered lid as desired. Press shells into place when satisfied with the design.

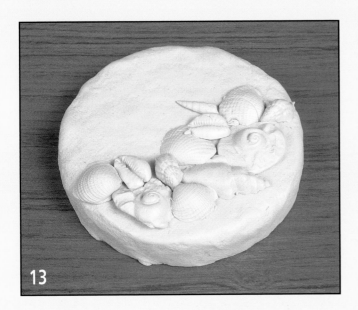

14. Using another smaller piece of rock, blend and feather the edges of the shells into the surface clay so they appear to be formed out of the rock surface.

15. Refer to *Baking the Clay* on page 162. Bake the box. Allow to cool.

16. Mix the paint with a little water and wash the surface of the box, allowing the paint to pool in the depressions.

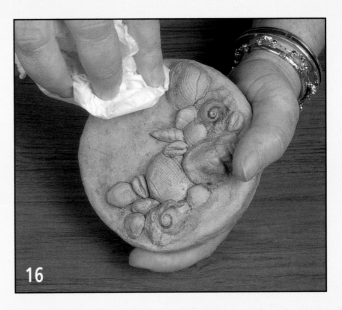

17. Lightly wipe the surface with the cotton cloth.

18. Repeat Steps 16–17 until you are pleased with the effect.

Design Tips:
Use Sculpey III or Super Sculpey for these shell molds as these clays give a rougher texture to the surface of the shells, similar to unpolished shells.

Several small shells can be molded on one larger piece of scrap clay. It is easier to find the mold among your supplies if you do this.

Cut the excess clay from the molded clay after removing it from the mold. This gives a more random edge to the mold.

I have made everything with these shells—light switch covers, necklaces, picture frames, and my favorite napkin rings.

The paint tends to grab the surface more if the clay is warm. So for a heavy coat of antiquing, try treating the clay before it is completely cooled.

How do I use colored pencils with clay?

What You Need to Get Started:

Basic clay tools
Colored pencils: soft lead
Composition metal leaf: color desired (small amount)
Cotton cloth
Round or square form
Rub-on gilt: gold
Sandpaper: fine grit
Sculpey Premo clay in 2 oz. package: pearl (1)
Varathane and brush

Colored pencils are not just for paper. They work very well with the clay medium, too. With pencils, you can quickly decorate the surface of the clay. Pearl colored clay shows through the pencil and causes the pencil to appear pearlized.

Rainbow Coasters

Here's How:
1. Roll a #1 sheet from the pearl clay large enough to accommodate the round or square form.

2. Place the form on the sheet. Cut the clay around the form. Repeat for a set.

3. Sprinkle small pieces of the composition metal leaf on the surface of the clay. Rub the metal leaf into place with your finger, blending the colors across the clay.

4. Refer to *Baking the Clay* on page 162. Bake the coasters. Allow to cool.

5. Using colored pencils, color the surface in any pattern desired. Color in both directions, right over the surface of the leaf, to ensure even color.

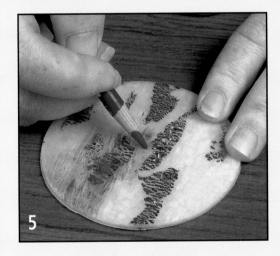

6. Using a cotton cloth, blend the colors slightly. If needed, reapply the pencil and blend again.

7. Using the fine-grit sandpaper, sand the edges of the coasters.

8. Apply rub-on gilt on the edges of the coasters.

9. Seal the surface and edges with varathane.

Design Tips:

Blend pencil colors into each other in different patterns. Try stripes, following the order of the colors in a rainbow or spots of colors over the entire coaster.

Color only a portion of the coaster, contrasting the clay and metal leaf.

How do I use rubber stamps with clay?

What You Need to Get Started:

Basic clay tools
Bracelet blank
Rubber stamps: small
Sculpey Premo clay in 2 oz. package: black (1)
Surface sealant
Texturing tools
Translucent heat-embossing powders: antique bronze; super copper; brilliant gold

Rubber stamps brushed with a translucent, heat-embossing powder yield incredible textures on clay. With the use of texturing tools and coordinating powders, black clay takes on the appearance of antiqued bronze. Your friends will have to look closely to see that you are not wearing a piece of ancient art.

Stamped Bracelets

Here's How:

1. Roll a #4 sheet from black clay and place it on the work surface.

2. Lightly press the bracelet blank onto the clay to get an impression of the bracelet edges.

3. Trim the clay around the impression. Press the clay into place onto the bracelet blank.

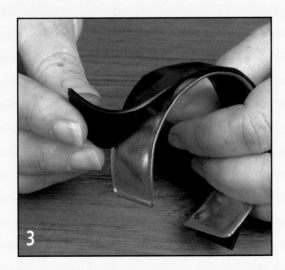

4. Using the texturing tools, randomly texture the surface of the clay, leaving some blank areas as desired.

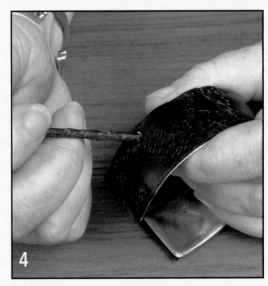

5. Lightly rub gold translucent heat-embossing powder over the stamp. Randomly press the stamp into the textured surface of the clay.

6. Randomly layer the remaining translucent heat-embossing powders with your fingers, over-lapping the colors to create depth.

7. Refer to *Baking the Clay* on page 112. Bake the bracelet. Allow to cool.

8. Pop the clay off the bracelet blank. Glue it onto the surface of the blank, so the bracelet can flex for fit.

9. Using the surface sealant, seal the clay.

Design Tips:

Apply as much or as little color as desired. Vary the color of the powder and vary the image.

Use this combination of techniques to create anything from bracelets, to boxes, to light switch covers.

How do I make clay look metallic?

What You Need to Get Started:

Acrylic paint: black
Basic clay tools
Brush: small
Pen: round barrel, any color
Pin back
Rubber sculpting chisel: small
Sculpey Premo clay in 2 oz. packages: gold (small amount); silver (1)
Surface sealant
Translucent heat-embossing powders: antique bronze; super copper; brilliant gold

One of my favorite variations of this technique is silver-work. I've used this combination for bracelets, boxes, pins, and even a Christmas ornament.

Metallic Brooch

Here's How:
1. Roll a #1 sheet from the silver clay and place it on the work surface.

2. Cut the clay to create a geometric shape. Note: This is an excellent use for kitchen sets of cutters.

3. Using the back of the blade, draw several lines on the clay to create random geometric areas.

4. Remove the ink cartridge from the pen cylinder. Using the different parts of the pen, create designs within the geometric areas without having adjoining areas with the same pattern.

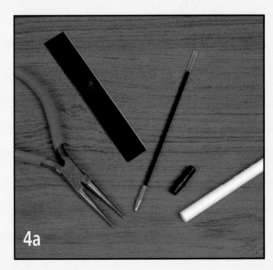

Using the point of the ink cartridge, make the small holes. Using the opposite end of the ink cartridge, form the smaller circles. Using the empty pen cylinder, form the larger circle.

5. Once you have the textures in place, determine which areas will be which color, without having adjoining areas of the same color. Using the chisel, apply the translucent heat-embossing powders in nice even strokes. Watch the tip of the chisel to make certain you do not pick up too much powder at once. Leave some areas without powder, so that the silver shows also.

6. Refer to Step 20 on page 201. Apply the pin back with a bandage of clay to the back of the brooch.

7. Refer to *Baking the Clay* on page 162. Bake the brooch. Allow to cool.

8. Mix the paint with a little water and wash the surface of the clay, allowing the paint to pool in the depressions.

9. Lightly wipe the surface with the cotton cloth.

10. Repeat Steps 7–8 until you are pleased with the effect. Allow to dry.

11. Seal the clay with a sealant of your choice.

Design Tip:
Back the textured piece with a larger piece of textured clay. Use contrasting shapes and colors.

How do I use scrap clay?

What You Need to Get Started:

Basic clay tools
Cookie cutter:
  heart
Craft adhesive:
  super strength
Drafting vellum
  or baking
  parchment
Pin back
Premade canes:
  end pieces in
  any color and
  any pattern,
  reduced to no
  larger than 1/2",
  in a variety of
  diameters
Rubber sculpting
  chisel: small
Sculpey Premo
  clay: scraps
Translucent
  heat-embossing
  powder: gold

Nothing need go to waste with this medium. Here are a few ways to use both scrap clay and leftover end pieces of cane.

Pretty Patchwork Pins

Here's How:
1. Roll a #3 sheet about 3" x 4" from scrap clay.

2. Cut very thin slices from the canes. Place the slices on the clay sheet, completely covering the surface and leaving as little space as possible between the cane slices.

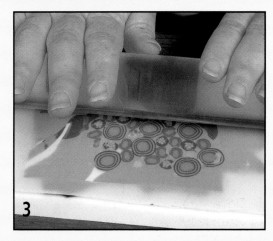

4. Carefully lift the parchment or vellum to see if there are any obvious seams still showing.

3. Place the parchment or vellum over the piece. Rub gently to blend the edges of the canes together.

5. Repeat Steps 3–4 as needed.

6. Using the cookie cutter, cut a heart from this patterned clay.

7. Using the rubber sculpting chisel, apply a little powder all along the edge of the heart if you wish to disguise the scrap clay below the canes.

8. Refer to *Baking the Clay* on page 162. Bake the clay heart. Allow to cool.

9. Using super strength craft adhesive, adhere the pin back onto the back of the heart.

Design Tips:

Refer to Step 20 on page 201. Finish this pin more professionally by applying a bandage of clay to the pin back.

The finished product can be any shape you desire.

Use the same method to make an egg-shaped Easter pin, such as the one shown below, or let your imagination be your inspiration!

How do I make a Natasha bead?

**What You
Need to
Get Started:**

Needle tool: long
Premade canes:
    end pieces
Sculpey Premo
    clay: assorted
    scraps

This is one of the most documented and versatile techniques for using scrap clay. It is named after the woman who first described it on the world wide web. The other name for this technique is the Mirror Bead.

Natasha Bead

Here's How:

1. Roll snakes from each piece of scrap clay. Bundle the snakes and canes together.

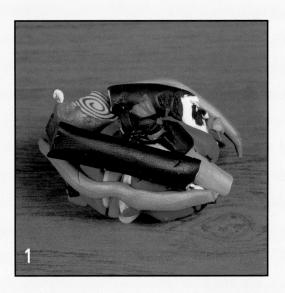

2. Twist these bundles together tightly. The tighter you twist the finer the detail.

3. Using your fingers and an acrylic rod, form the twist into a rectangle. Cut the rectangle into smaller segments if desired.

4. Cut the rectangle in half lengthwise. Cut each of these two pieces in half lengthwise again. You now have four pieces from the original rectangle.

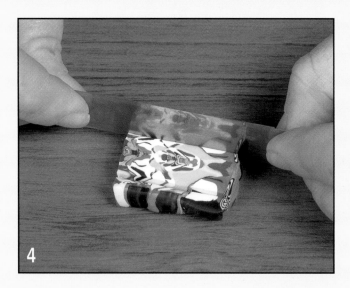

5. Rearrange the four pieces, turning them around to turn the piece inside out. Each side should be a different mirror image.

6. Using your hands and the acrylic rod, smooth the seams.

7. Trim the two ends. Top the ends with flattened balls of clay or pinch the edges together.

8. Using the needle tool, pierce each bead by twisting it halfway through the bead. Complete the pierce from the other side of the bead.

9. Refer to *Baking the Clay* on page 162. Bake the beads. Allow to cool.

Design Tips:

   Try using Skinner blends in this process as they are spectacular.

   Use a ripple blade to cut the four pieces and yield an entirely different effect.

RUBBER STAMPING
for the first time®

Carol Scheffler

Rubber stamping for the first time

Introduction

Welcome to the world of rubber stamping! I am delighted to introduce you to what I promise will become a fulfilling and exciting hobby. You will be making cards, gifts, decorative items for your home, and a host of other projects that will look terrific and give you a great sense of accomplishment. And the best part is, you can start right now!

When I look back over my own early ex-periences with this craft, I realize that the initial attraction for me was that I could create beautiful projects without having to draw. Someone else has done the drawing for you. You have the fun of taking their image and making it come to life through the magic of rubber stamping.

You will be amazed by the variety of images available. There are thousands of rubber stamps to suit every imaginable style. Everything from adorable to elegant, primitive to victorian, ab-stract to realistic—the choices are endless. As you become comfortable with the craft and gain confidence as a stamper, your own style will develop naturally, but I recommend that you continue to experiment with all different sorts of images and stamping techniques. Stretching yourself in your craft keeps it interesting and gives you a chance to discover new sides of your creative self.

An undeniable appeal of this craft is the fact that you can complete a great looking project in minutes. You don't need to survive a three month course or struggle through labor in-tensive projects, only to be disappointed with the results. My guess is that by tonight you will have created a project that you will be proud of.

Stamped artwork comes together quickly. Many of the projects in this book can be made in

10 minutes or less. Even most of the advanced projects will take you less than an hour. If you are like me, craft projects are accomplish-ed in stolen moments, between paying bills and driving carpool. A fast project is a real plus!

With all the crafting I do, rubber stamping is the craft I always return to. In trying to figure out why, I come up with one overriding reason. Versatility. Rubber stamping can be used on practically every project I want to tackle— making a memory book, crafting a new lamp shade for the bedroom, designing a sweatshirt for one of my daughters, or creating a special birthday card for a friend. With rubber stamps, I can achieve so many different looks, all with professional polish.

But be forewarned—rubber stamping is addictive. You will start to play with your stamps and lose track of time and the next thing you know, it is 2:00 a.m. But the creative satisfaction and the chance to forget about "real life" and become totally engrossed in a project is worth a little sleep deprivation!

Getting Started

Basic Materials

For the most basic rubber stamp project, you will need just a few tools.

1. Brush art markers in a variety of colors, dye-based ink pads in rainbow and/or solid colors, paper, and rubber stamps (acrylic mounted, foam mounted, or wood mounted).

To create more sophisticated projects, you will also need the following tools.

2. A craft knife, a cutting mat, decorative-edged scissors, and a ruler.

3. A bone folder, card stock in a variety of colors, paper in a variety of patterns, and paper adhesive (double-sided tape, dry bond, or paper glue).

4. Dual-tipped brush art markers in a variety of colors, colored pencils, and a black permanent ink pad (not shown).

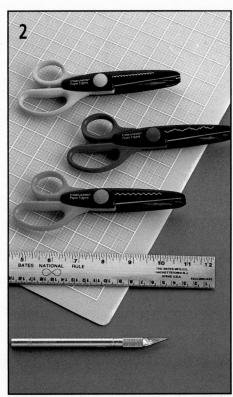

Materials to Create Special Effects

To accomplish the following special effects, you should also purchase the following materials.

1. *To heat-emboss*—pigment ink pads (rainbow and/or solids), a heat gun, and embossing powder (clear, metallic, colored, or specialty).

2. *To layer paper*—a paper cutter (with or without a variety of cutting blades), decorative-edged scissors, hole and shape punches, and textured and handmade papers.

3. *To give a soft-colored effect*—a sponge, watercolor pencils, chalks, and a watercolor paint set.

4. *To embellish your artwork*—brass charms, raffia, buttons or whatever in-spires you!

5. *To add sparkle*—ultrafine glitter, double-sided tape, a glue marker or pen (not a glue stick), sparkle glue in a squeeze bottle, and glittery adhesive-backed paper (not shown).

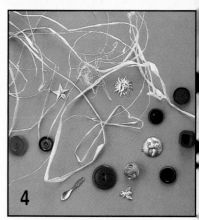

6. *To create interesting backgrounds*—a rubber brayer, a sponge brayer (not shown), wedge-shaped makeup sponges, round utility sponges (not shown), patterned papers (not shown), metallic markers, a white correction pen . . . experiment with other tools that you find!

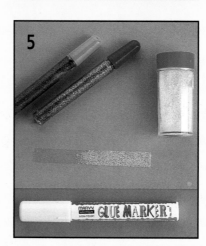

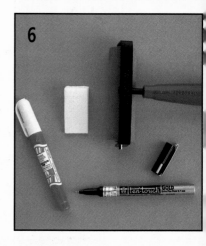

7. *To create dimension*—adhesive foam tape or dots, corrugated cardboard, a paper crimper, and dimensional paints.

8. *To stamp on fabric*—fabric paint (not shown), bold-faced fabric stamps (not shown), sponge brushes, cotton swabs, fabric ink pads, fabric markers, and your fabric item.

One of the wonderful things about rubber stamping is that getting started does not require a large investment of money. Average-sized, wood-mounted stamps cost between $4.00–$8.00. Foam-mounted sets of five to eight stamps cost about $10.00. Dye-based ink pads cost about $4.50. A prepackaged set of 10 cards and envelopes costs about $5.00. A package of 12 brush art markers costs about $18.00.

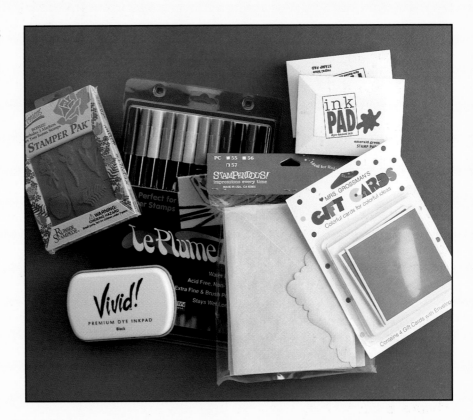

Setting up a work space

Always stamp on a stack of scrap paper or newsprint. The soft padding of the paper helps you achieve a better impression when you print the image. The paper will protect the work surface from possible ink smears and is also a good place to try out a stamp to help you decide whether to incorporate it into your work.

Have a damp paper towel sitting on a plastic plate nearby to wipe off the excess ink on the stamp once you have finished using it. You may also want to have handy a dry paper towel or cloth towel to dry off the stamp once you have cleaned it.

If you are using markers, store them standing with the tips down in a mug or similar container so that they don't roll away from you. Gather the stamps you have chosen and the paper and . . . begin!

Cleaning your stamps

Most ink will clean off stamps easily with a damp paper towel. Pigment ink may need a little scrubbing with an old toothbrush to come completely clean. Stubborn ink can be treated with a small amount of window cleaner diluted in water. Avoid submerging the stamp in water or else the glue holding everything together will start to dissolve. Permanent inks must be cleaned off with a solvent cleaner made for this purpose.

Storing Materials

All ink pads and markers are best stored upside down. This keeps the ink on the top of the pad or marker tip where you need it. Papers should be stored flat and in a place where they will be kept clean. Keep all stamping materials out of direct sunlight and away from dust.

Stamps should be clean and dry when you put them away. They should be stored flat, rubber die side down.

Different parts of a stamp

All stamps consist of a piece of rubber into which an image has been impressed (known as a die), a piece of foam cushion, and a mount. The mount is the handle, so to speak, with a picture of the image (the index) glued or printed on top of it. Mounts can be made of wood, foam, or acrylic block.

1. *Wood-mounted stamps*—These stamps are a bit more expensive, but many stamping artists like the sturdy feel of the wood.

2. *Foam-mounted stamps*—These stamps are much less expensive, but stamp very nicely.

3. *Acrylic-mounted stamps*—These are transparent, allowing the stamping artist to see exactly where the image is being printed. There are not many stamps available with acrylic block mounts and they can be as expensive as wood-mounted stamps.

Some stamps are also mounted onto a wheel (not shown), allowing for a continuous printing of an image as you roll it along.

Basic kinds of stamps

There are basically three kinds of stamps: bold-faced, highly detailed, and outline. Each one has its own look and requires a different approach to inking. While there are no hard and fast rules, I have provided some guidelines as to which inking techniques will consistently produce the best results. However, I encourage you to experiment on your own and develop a sense of what appeals to you.

1. *Bold-faced stamps*—A bold-faced stamp has a wide expanse of raised rubber. Detail is usually minimal. These stamps can be inked with a single color, but they look wonderful when colored with a few different brush art markers, or inked with a rainbow pad. Try inking a bold-faced stamp with a pigment pad or pigment ink markers. Then print and heat-emboss the image—the bold image looks very dramatic when it is raised and shiny.

2. *Highly detailed stamps*—These stamps have a great amount of detail in the rubber die. Images may have a lot of stippling or fine lines incorporated into them to provide realistic detail. Printing a highly detailed image is best achieved by using a dark-colored ink. Heat-embossing these printed images works best if you use a very fine embossing powder called a "detail embossing powder."

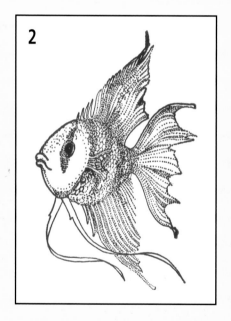

3. *Outline stamps*—Outline stamps, also known as cartoon stamps, are simple outlines of images without much detail. They work well when the outline is printed and then the interior is colored in with markers, pencils, or paints. Outline stamps work well when the printed image is heat-embossed.

Choosing the right paper

There is a seemingly infinite variety of paper available to the stamp artist and choosing the right paper can seem tricky. Each paper has its own qualities which make it more or less appropriate for a certain project.

If you want your artwork to last for generations, make certain your paper is acid free, archival, or pH neutral. Papers made without these specifications can yellow, become brittle, and fade over time. Archival quality papers and card stocks are readily available in craft and rubber stamp stores.

Here is a guide to help you in your paper selection:

1. *Card stock paper*—This is the paper you will select most often. It is a smooth, heavy-weight paper that comes in a wide variety of colors and patterns and is also available in matte (not shiny) and glossy finishes. Glossy-finish card stock is exciting for stamping artists to use because it makes colors look vibrant. It can be a little slippery to stamp on and may take a little getting used to.

Stamping with pigment inks on glossy card stock requires heat-embossing to permanently set the ink. If pigment ink is not heat-embossed on glossy card stock, it will not dry and, consequently, will smear.

Card stock takes ink beautifully and has a substantial feel to it, giving your work a professional look. Usually it is sold in 8½" x 11" sheets. You should purchase a variety of colors for constructing your own cards and for use in paper layering.

You will also find prepackaged folded cards with envelopes in craft and rubber stamp stores. They are a great choice for the beginner because they come in a variety of sizes and colors and are ready to use.

2. *Text-weight paper*—This is a lightweight paper that is most similar in weight to computer paper. It is available in a wide variety of colors and patterns. You can adhere it to the top of card stock as an embellishment or use it to make your own stationery.

3. *Cover-weight paper*—This is slightly heavier and thicker than text-weight paper and is a great choice for stationery.

4. *Fancy paper*—Marbleized papers; corrugated papers; metallic crinkled papers; handmade papers with flowers, seeds, and leaves embedded in them; papers made of tree barks; thin papers with gold threads running through them . . . the selection is dazzling. These papers all make wonderful layering additions to your cards, but generally do not provide a suitable surface for stamping.

5. *Tissue paper*—Tissue paper is available in a variety of colors and patterns. This paper makes a fun stamping surface, although it is somewhat fragile. Dye-based inks work best on this thin paper.

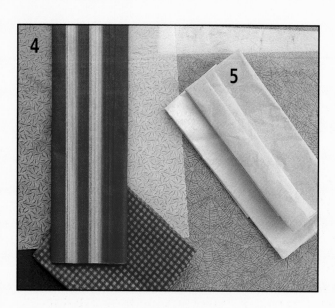

6. *Vellum paper*—Vellum is a very smooth, translucent paper. It comes in both text weight and card stock weight. The text-weight vellum makes an elegant liner inside a card. The card stock weight is fun to heat-emboss and layer over a printed card. Because you can see through it, the play between the two layers can produce interesting effects. Vellum paper, like glossy card stock, is coated so that the ink sits on top of the paper instead of soaking into it. What this means for the stamp artist is that if you use pigment ink on vellum, it must be heat-embossed to become permanent. If not heat-embossed, pigment ink on vellum will smear.

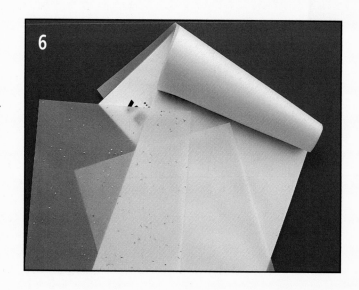

234

7. *Sticker paper*—Sticker paper comes in both matte and glossy formats. It is generally a white paper with an adhesive backing. You will have fun using it to apply stamped images to your artwork. Sticker paper is not a good surface on which to heat-emboss because the heat gun will cause the adhesive on the back of the paper to buckle.

8. *Construction paper*—I do not recommend construction paper (not shown) for rubber stamp projects. It is an inexpensive paper that does not hold up well to stamping, paper layering, or the test of time. It fades quickly and rips easily.

Choosing the right ink

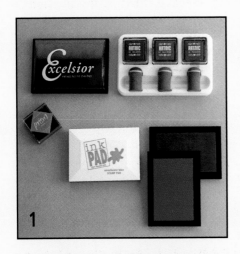

It is important to recognize that one ink or ink pad may not necessarily be the same as another. Different types of ink have been specially formulated for specific surfaces and effects.

1. *Dye-based ink*—Dye-based ink is a thinner ink and works especially well on a detailed stamp. It is available in ink pads and brush art markers. With dye-based ink pads, the ink is saturated onto a felt pad and encased in plastic. They come in different sizes and a wide variety of colors, as well as rainbow pad format. Re-inkers are available for dye-based ink pads when they begin to dry out. The colors will mix with each other if they come into contact on very absorbent paper, which is an effect you may or may not be trying to achieve. This ink dries quickly, is not formulated for heat-embossing, and will fade over time. Because the ink is waterbased, it cleans up easily with water.

2. *Pigment ink*—Pigment inks are a thicker ink, formulated to stay separate on the paper and not mix with other colors. It is also a much slower drying ink than dye-based ink. This makes pigment ink perfect for heat-embossing. Pigment ink will dry on uncoated papers, but can take several minutes or up to several hours. Unless it is heat-embossed, pigment ink will not dry on coated papers, such as glossy card stock. Pigment ink is available in two formats—markers and pads. The pads are available in a variety of sizes and consist of a saturated foam pad encased in plastic. Pigment ink pads are available in a wide variety of colors and metallics, as well as rainbow colors and even clear. Re-inkers are available for pads that have become dry. Pigment ink will resist fading over time.

3. *Permanent ink*—Permanent ink is just that, permanent. It requires a solvent-based cleaner for cleaning. Permanent ink pads come in a limited number of colors. I highly recommend using black permanent ink with detailed stamps and outline stamps. When you color the printed images with water-based markers, you will not drag the black outline into the colored markers as you would if the outlines were stamped with a dye-based ink pad or marker.

4. *Fabric ink*—Fabric inks are formulated to be permanent on fabric, even when washed. The ink is saturated onto foam pads encased in plastic. They are available in a wide variety of colors. Re-inkers are also available.

5. *Crafter's ink*—Crafter's ink is a multipurpose pigment ink, formulated to be permanent when heat set. It is suitable for use on wood, fabric, shrink plastic, and terra-cotta. It is available in rainbow pads in which each individual color is removable from the entire collection of pads, if desired. The ink is saturated onto a foam pad and encased in plastic.

Other surfaces

When you first became interested in rubber stamping, you probably envisioned yourself creating projects on paper. That is the logical place to begin. As you become more familiar with the basic techniques, you will look for other materials on which to stamp and discover that the choices are plentiful! Basically, you can print an image on any surface your heart desires, as long as you use the correct ink. Fabric, plastic, terra-cotta, wood, cork, metal, walls, porcelain . . . the list is seemingly endless. You will soon be stamping on all these surfaces and more and get terrific results, but it is a good idea to start with paper. As the song goes, "let's start at the very beginning . . . ."

How do I ink a stamp with a marker?

What You Need to Get Started:

Brush art marker: magenta
Folded gift tag: glossy white (cut to size to fit your stamp)
Hole punch: 1/8"
Ribbon: satin, 1/8"-wide, magenta (8")
Stamp: girl holding a heart

When you think of inking rubber stamps, you probably think of ink pads. Ink pads are a good choice for doing the job, but did you know that you can also ink a stamp with a colored brush art marker? They work beautifully and give you a tremendous array of color choices for a very small investment. And, it couldn't be easier!

Simple Gift Tag

Here's How:

1. Ink the stamp, using the magenta marker and the following method:

- Hold the stamp, rubber die side up, in one hand.

- Hold the marker in your other hand and brush it against the rubber die, using the side of the marker, not the tip. This helps achieve quick coverage without wearing down the tip of your marker.

- Color the entire image. Remember, the part of the rubber die that makes the impression is the raised part. The recessed part of the image does not print and, therefore, should not be colored.

2. Give a quick puff of your breath on the image to remoisten the ink.

3. Print the image by placing the stamp, rubber die side down, onto the front of the gift tag. Without rocking or twisting the stamp, give it a little pressure. It does not take a lot of muscle.

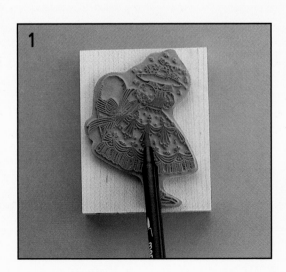

237

4. Lift the stamp straight up and off the gift tag. Admire your work!

5. Using the hole punch, punch a hole in the upper left-hand corner of the gift tag.

6. Thread the ribbon through the hole.

How to Thread a Gift Tag Ribbon:

1. Fold the ribbon in half.

2. Insert the folded end of the ribbon through the punched hole and pull through about 2".

3. Using your fingers, open up the folded end to form a loop.

4. Thread the two loose ends of the ribbon through the loop you are holding.

5. Pull the loose ends gently so that the loop tightens around the card corner.

What are the different methods I can use for coloring a stamped image?

There are many different tools you can use to color a stamped image, each producing a different effect. Dual-tipped brush art markers produce a bold-looking image whereas colored pencils or watercolor paints produce a softer glow. Watercolors and chalks are easy to mix and a natural choice for shading. Different pencil colors can be layered and intermingled, adding depth to your work. Take some time to play with these coloring tools and discover the effects you can achieve. Experimentation will produce exciting results!

Angel Ornaments

Here's How:
1. Ink the stamp, using the black ink pad. Print the image four times onto white card stock.

2. Using scissors, cut out each stamped image, leaving ¼" of white card stock all around the edge.

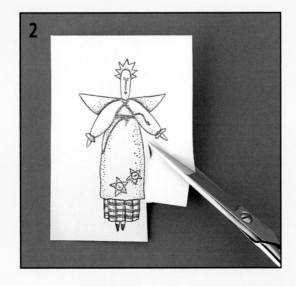

3. Apply adhesive to the back of each stamped image and adhere them onto dark green card stock.

4. Using the scissors, cut the dark green card stock around each image, leaving a ¼" border all the way around, except at the top of the angel's crown, leaving enough paper to punch a hole for the cord.

5. Refer to pages 240–241. Color the stamped image with either chalks, colored pencils, markers, or watercolor paints, following the specific instructions for each coloring technique.

6. Using the hole punch, punch a hole in the dark green card stock at the top of the angel's crown. Thread a 5" piece of paper cord through the hole and twist it closed.

5a. Chalks:

Much like watercolor paints, chalks are easy to blend and have a light and lovely look.

1. Apply the chalk color to the image in small circles. If desired, you may apply the chalk colors using the makeup applicator. You will not have great control applying color in tiny areas, but don't let that frustrate you. Chalks look best when they are smudged and soft looking. If you wish, chalk erasers can be used to eliminate unwanted color.

2. Once you have finished applying the color, spray the image with the matte-finish sealer to permanently set the chalk.

5b. Colored Pencils:

1. It is natural to see pencil marks when you use colored pencils. Rather than fight this, use the marks to add texture to the stamped image. Crosshatching, coloring in one direction and then coloring over it in the opposite direction, produces interesting results, as does coloring an area with two coordinating colors.

2. Colored pencils should be sharpened by hand with a good pencil sharpener. You will find that sharp points and dull points produce different results. Sharp points are handy for coloring small areas. Dull points produce broader strokes of color that look softer and are easier to blend.

5c. Markers:

1. Color larger areas, using the broad tip of the marker, and smaller areas, such as the belt on the angel's gown, using the fine tip.

2. In addition to the bold color you can achieve with markers, you will enjoy the control you have in putting the color where you want it. As you color the printed image, proceed in order from the lightest color first to the darkest color last. That way, you are less likely to drag darker colors into the lighter colors.

3. Do not go over a spot with a marker too many times. The color will become very dark, and you will see the marker's brush strokes.

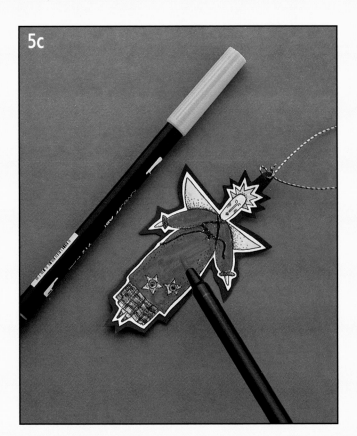

5d. Watercolor Paints:

Translucency and ease of blending are the two hallmarks of watercolor paints. It is easy to achieve a very soft, artistic look for a stamped image when you use watercolor paints.

1. To begin, wet the paintbrush and then make tiny circles in the color, fully loading the brush. Test it out on scrap paper to see if the color is too strong or too weak. You can always add more water or more paint to adjust the effect.

2. When painting the image, experiment with the brush strokes to see what appeals to you. Use a liner brush for getting into very small areas.

Remember, you employ watercolors to create a more unstructured, painterly result. Staying in the lines is not necessarily a goal.

241

How do I use markers to achieve a multicolored effect?

Stamped art is certain to elicit "oohs" and "aahs" when you begin adding several colors to the image. When people ask, "How did you do that?," they will be amazed when you tell them how easy it really is.

Colorful Bookmark

Here's How:

1. Ink the leaf portion of the stamp, using the side of the dark green marker.

2. Ink the berry portion of the stamp, using the side of the purple marker.

3. Give a quick puff of your breath on the image to remoisten the ink.

4. Print the image onto the bookmark.

5. Repeat as desired. You can usually get a second printing without having to reapply more ink color by puffing on the image and printing it again.

6. When you are ready to change the color of the raspberry to magenta and then to red, you will need to clean off the old color before applying the new color.

7. Using the method described for *How to Thread a Gift Tag Ribbon* on page 238, attach the cord of the tassel through the hole.

Troubleshooting:

• Sometimes, even though you have completely inked a bold-faced image, part of the image will not print. This leaves a spot in the middle of the printed image. You can easily fix this problem. Using the brush art marker that coordinates with the unprinted part of the image, fill in the gap with a light dotting motion directly onto the paper.

• Occasionally, a stamped bold-faced image will leave excess ink on the paper, creating little rivers of ink on the paper. You can fix this by turning the paper over, ink side down, onto a piece of scrap paper. Gently rub the back of the printed paper. All the excess ink will transfer to the scrap paper, leaving your work perfectly dry and clean.

Design Tip:

• Notice how the images are printed off the edge of the bookmark so that some of them appear only in part. This is a fun technique that draws the eye all over the bookmark, creating a more dynamic overall effect.

How do I create a watercolor look with markers?

What You Need to Get Started:

Brush art markers: aqua; magenta; orange; pink; red
Card: folded glossy white, 4¼" x 5½"
Dye-based ink pad: black
Stamps: phrase; star

Beautiful watercolor effects can be achieved by apply-ing several colors of brush art markers on a single bold-faced image. The inks run together and create a palette of colors.

Rainbow Star Card

Here's How:
1. Ink a small portion of the star stamp, using the side of the pink marker.

2. Beginning at the edge of where the first color left off, ink another portion of the stamp, using the orange marker.

3. Continue in this manner, using the red, magenta, and aqua markers, until the entire stamp is inked. Don't worry if the edges seem to be mixing where the marker colors meet. This adds to the watercolor effect.

4. Give a quick puff of your breath on the image to remoisten the ink.

5. Print the image onto the upper right-hand corner of the card.

6. You will probably be able to get a second printing, without having to re-apply the markers, by puffing on the image and printing again.

7. Continue coloring and stamping until the card is covered with images, using the photo opposite for placement.

8. Ink the phrase stamp, using the black ink pad. Print the image onto the lower left-hand corner of the card.

The stars exist that we might know how high our dreams can soar.

Design Tips:

- When applying many colors onto a single stamp, start with the lightest color and then continue with the midtones, saving the darkest color for last. This avoids dragging darker colors into the lighter colors, causing them to muddy.

- When printing images in a random fashion, start in the middle of the paper and work out toward the sides. Print the images at different angles to achieve a nice jumbled effect. Try to keep the spaces between the images uniform. You do not want part of your work to be densely stamped and other parts to be sparsely stamped.

How do I heat-emboss?

What You Need to Get Started:

Dual-tipped brush
  art markers:
  light aqua;
  royal blue;
  pink; red; tan;
  yellow
Embossing
  powder: clear
Heat gun
Journal:
  purchased
Paper adhesive
Paper: glossy
  white (larger
  than the
  stamp)
Pigment ink pad:
  dark blue
Scissors
Stamp: outline of
  a beach scene

Heat-embossing is a process that I still find magical after many years of rubber stamping. By sprinkling embossing powder on wet ink and then applying heat until the powder melts, you create a raised, shiny image. Heat-embossing is the type of technique that will make your friends and family exclaim, "I can't believe you made this!"

Decorative Journal

Here's How:

1. Ink the stamp, using the dark blue ink pad and the following method:

- Hold the stamp with the rubber die facing you, resting it on a piece of paper. Hold the ink pad in your other hand.

- Bring the pad to the stamp and tap it lightly all over the die, making certain to ink it evenly and completely. Do not press the ink onto the die with any force as it will muddy the printed image.

2. Print the image onto the paper, taking care not to rock or twist the stamp. Give it a little muscle and then lift it straight off the paper. Don't touch the stamped image—it will smear!

3. Sprinkle the embossing powder over the stamped image.

4. Pour off the excess embossing powder either back into its container or onto a piece of scrap paper. (Fold the scrap paper in half and use it as a funnel to pour the excess powder back into the container.)

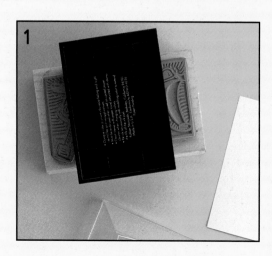

5. Preheat the heat gun for about 10 seconds and then hold it about 4" away from the stamped image. In about 15 seconds you will see the embossing powder melt, become raised and shiny, and adhere to the stamped image. Once the embossing powder is fully melted and smooth, turn off the heat gun and allow the image to cool for 30 seconds.

6. Color the printed image, using the markers and the photo below for color placement. Use the broad tip of the marker for large areas and the fine tip for smaller areas.

7. Cut out the image, using the scissors.

8. Apply adhesive to the back of the stamped image and adhere it to the front of the journal.

Troubleshooting:
- If the image is bumpy after you have heat-embossed it, you need to heat-emboss the image a little longer until all the powder is fully melted.

- If the image changes color after heat-embossing, or you smell something funny during the heat-embossing process, you are embossing the image too long. You may find that you have also scorched the paper.

- Remember, most images will heat-emboss completely after 15 seconds. There is no way to fix an over-embossed image. Start again with a fresh piece of paper.

How do I incorporate color into my work using embossing powders?

What You Need to Get Started:

Embossing ink pad: clear
Embossing powders: claret; cobalt; copper; antique gold
Heat gun
Picture frame with matte: purchased
Stamps: leaf designs (5)

A stamping artist uses color in many ways to bring life to the artwork. Embossing powders are available in a myriad of hues and provide a wonderful way to add color and texture to your projects.

Heat-embossed Picture Matte

Here's How:

1. Ink a stamp, using the clear ink pad. Print one image onto the picture frame matte.

2. Pour one color of embossing powder over a portion of the stamped image. Pour the excess powder back into its container.

3. Pour the second color of embossing powder over a portion of the stamped image adjacent to the one you have just powdered. Pour off the excess powder over the part of the image you powdered first. (Since that part of the image already has the powder affixed to it, the second color powder will not adhere to it.) Continue in this manner until the entire image is covered. You may use as many embossing powders on a single image as you like.

4. Heat-emboss the stamped image, using the heat gun.

5. Continue stamping and heat-embossing until the entire matte is covered.

248

Troubleshooting:

- Occasionally, you will get a stray particle of embossing powder on the piece and heat-emboss it by mistake. Once it has been heat-embossed, you cannot remove it. However, there are tricks to prevent this from happening in the future.

After pouring off the excess powder, but before heat-embossing the image, use a small dry paintbrush to brush off the stray powder or flick your fingers on the back of the stamped piece to tap it off. Also, try wiping the paper with a static-free dryer sheet before you begin stamping.

How do I create backgrounds with a rubber brayer?

A rubber brayer is a soft rubber roller on a handle. Once ink is applied to the brayer, it allows for continuous coverage, making it an excellent tool for producing backgrounds quickly. Since this is an introductory book, I have avoided focusing on tools that have only limited application, but a brayer is so versatile, you will reach for it again and again.

Brayer: rubber,
   6"-wide
Brush art markers:
   aqua; dark
   blue;
   royal blue;
   brown;
   cinnamon;
   cranberry;
   dark green;
   medium green;
   pea green;
   seafoam green;
   dark orange;
   medium
   orange;
   hot pink; red;
   yellow
Cards: glossy
   white, 5½" x
   8½"
Decorative-edged
   scissors
Dye-based ink
   pad: rainbow
Embossing ink
   pad: clear
Glitter
Glue pen
Paper adhesive
Recipes
Ruler
Scissors
Stamps: angel;
   apple; leaf;
   muffin; palm
   tree
Sticker paper:
   glossy white

Recipe Cards

Here's How:

1. Refer to the individual recipe cards on pages 251–253. Ink the brayer and roll it over the card, following the specific instructions for each card. Reink the brayer as necessary.

2. Type or hand-print a recipe on the paper of your choice.

3. Trim the edges of the recipe paper, using the decorative-edged scissors.

4. Apply adhesive to the back of the recipe and adhere it onto the background card.

5. Ink the coordinating stamp, using the markers and the photo on page 252 for color placement. Print the image onto sticker paper. Cut out the image, using the scissors, and press it onto the recipe card.

6. Since you will be using the cards in the kitchen, you may want to laminate them to keep them clean.

Trouble Shooting:
- A brayer should be stored with the metal bar down so that the wheel doesn't rest against anything, which might cause an unwanted impression in the rubber.

Here's How to Make a Recipe Book:
   A handmade recipe book makes a great gift for the bride-to-be, a new neighbor, or a thoughtful friend. There are several ways to turn your stamped recipe cards into a book:

- Purchase a photo album with pocket pages that are the right size to hold the cards.

- Punch a hole in the top left hand corner of the card and insert either a locking ring (available at any hardware store) or a pretty ribbon.

- Look for a sturdy folder at the stationery store to hold the cards.

1a. Baked Apple Card:

1. Ink the apple stamp, using the red marker. Hold the inked stamp on the table with the die side up and roll the brayer across the stamp several times, moving the brayer each time, so that the image appears on different parts of the brayer.

2. Roll the brayer across the length of the card several times until the brayer is too dry to print. Re-ink the stamp and repeat the process.

3. Ink the apple stamp, using the medium green marker. Repeat the brayering process.

4. Ink the apple stamp, using the yellow marker. Repeat the brayering process.

5. Using a ruler as your guide and the medium green marker, draw a border around the card.

See photo on page 252.

1a. Design Tips:

• Using stamps and a brayer together in this manner produces a soft watercolor look. To give your background a focal point, try stamping some apples directly onto the card. They will seem to pop out of the brayered background.

• Remember that when you roll a brayer over an inked stamp and then roll it onto paper, the image reverses. A flower that may lean to the left on the stamp is going to lean to the right once brayered. This can be a lovely effect when brayered

images are combined with stamped images.

1b. Blueberry Muffin Card:

1. Hold the brayer so that the roller spins freely.

2. Draw a tight, squiggly line along one edge of the brayer, using the brown marker. Turn the brayer so that you can continue to draw the line until it becomes an unbroken circle.

3. Draw three more lines evenly spaced along the brayer, using the brown marker.

4. Between the brown lines, continue drawing lines in the same manner, using the dark blue, royal blue, and cranberry markers.

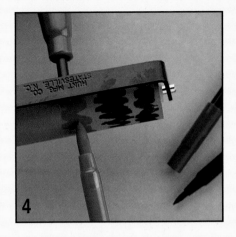

5. Roll the brayer along the length of the card. Once you have covered the card horizontally, turn the card so you can repeat the process vertically.

See photo on page 252.

1b. Design Tip:
• Try inking the brayer with straight lines, a herringbone pattern, or curvy lines. You may want to make the background with just horizontal or vertical lines. Experiment and design your own backgrounds.

Best Blueberry Muffins

1. Preheat oven to 350. butter muffin tins
2. Cream 6 T. butter and 3/4 C. sugar
3. Beat in 2 eggs, one at a time
4. In a separate bowl, whisk 2 C. flour 2 t. baking powder, and 1/2 t. salt
5. Add dry ingredients to the wet ingredients and beat well.
6. Stir in 1/2 C. milk and 2 t. vanilla until smooth.
7. Stir in 2 C. berries.
8. Fill muffin cups half way.
9. Sprinkle muffins tops with 1 T. sugar mixed with 1 t. cinnamon
10. Bake for 30 minutes

Hearty Autumn Soup

ace 1 chopped onion, 2 peeled and diced sweet potatoes and 4
C. of vegetable ... in a saucepan and boil.
educe heat, co ... er for 25 minutes.
Cool slightly a ... until smooth.
Return to sau ... d half.
Season with ... ice to taste. Serve
warm.

Best Baked Apples Ever

Core a tart, firm apple. Place it in a saucepan.
Pour 2 cups of apple cider into the pan.
Place 1 vanilla bean, 1 T. vanilla sugar and
1 T. of butter into the cavity of the apple.
Cover and cook on a medium flame for 30 minutes.
Serve warm with whipped cream or sour cream.

1c. Hearty Autumn Soup Card:

1. Ink the leaf stamp, using the clear ink pad. Print the image all over the card. Do not heat-emboss the leaf images.

2. Ink the brayer, using a rainbow pad with an autumn hue. Roll it over the leaves. The embossing ink resists the brayered ink, causing the leaves to appear with a ghostly shadow.

1c. Design Tip:

- Ink the stamp, using the clear ink pad. Heat-emboss the stamped leaf images with clear embossing powder for a more pronounced leaf image. Proceed with brayering technique.

1d. Heavenly Brickle Bar Card:

1. Holding the brayer with the metal bar resting on the table, draw little clouds all over the brayer, using the aqua and seafoam green markers.

2. Roll the brayer back and forth over the card until it is completely filled.

3. Outline several clouds, using the glue pen. Sprinkle glitter over the glue. Pour the excess glitter back into the container.

1d. Design Tip:

- Instead of clouds, draw squiggles, dots, dashes, or any other design you desire onto the brayer. Roll the brayer over the card as desired to create an instant patterned background.

1e. Tropical Fruit Salsa Card:

1. Roll the brayer across the rainbow ink pad, making certain you are rolling with the stripes of the pad. (Rolling against them will cause the inks to mix and become muddy.) Once you get to the end of the pad, pick up the brayer and begin again, repeating the process at least four more times until the brayer is fully covered.

2. Roll the brayer back and forth across the length of the card, pressing hard, until the card is completely covered.

1e. Design Tips:

- Try printing the card on the diagonal or create a brayered plaid by rolling the brayer both horizontally and vertically.

- If the brayer does not cover the entire width of the card, turn the paper around, re-ink the brayer, and roll the brayer to cover the remaining part of the card.

253

How do I use stamps to create a background?

What You Need to Get Started:

Bone folder
Corner rounder
 punch
Decorative paper:
 navy blue (for
 journal title);
 yellow (for
 journal cover)
Dye-based ink
 pads: black;
 navy blue;
 cranberry;
 green; plum
Foam tape
Heavy cardboard:
 4½" x 5½" (2)
Heavy paper:
 black, 30" x
 4¼"
Paper adhesive
Ruler
Scissors
Stamps: faux
 passport;
 faux postage;
 large photo
 frame; "Bon
 voyage!"
 phrase

An image doesn't always have to have a starring role in a piece of stamped art. By overlapping images, you can create a dynamic background that comes together quickly. As you are choosing images to overlap, don't overlook word stamps—they make very strong statements! Once you have created this background, layer one or two important images on top and your project is complete.

Travel Photo Journal

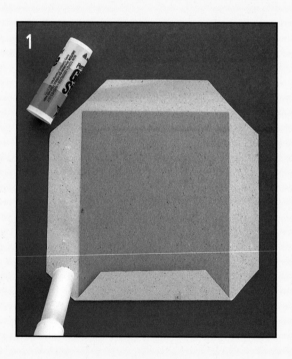

Here's How:
1. To make the front and back journal covers, cut the yellow paper to 1" larger than the cardboard on all sides and center one piece of cardboard on each piece of the yellow paper. Trim off the corners of each piece of the paper. Apply adhesive to each edge of the paper. Fold down the overlapping edges of the paper and adhere them to the cardboard.

2. Using a bone folder and ruler, fold the long black paper accordion-style into six equal sections of 5" x 4¼", making certain to begin and end with valley folds.

3. Apply glue to the back side of one end (the first page) of the folded paper and adhere it to the back of the front cover. Adhere the remaining end to the back of the back cover. The journal is now constructed.

4. Ink the faux-postage and faux-passport stamps, using the ink colors of your choice. Randomly print the images onto the cover, making certain to overlap the images.

5. Ink the phrase stamp, using the black ink pad. Print the image onto a separate piece of the yellow paper for the journal's title. Trim the corners, using a corner rounder punch.

6. Apply glue to the back of the stamped title and adhere it onto the navy blue paper. Trim those corners as well.

7. Attach the title to the front cover with several pieces of foam tape.

8. To create photo mattes, ink the photo frame stamp, using the black ink pad. Print the image six times onto the yellow paper. Cut out the images, using the scissors.

9. Apply adhesive to the back of the photo mattes and adhere them onto each journal page.

10. Apply adhesive to the back of the photographs from a favorite trip and adhere them onto the photo mattes.

Here's How to Ensure a Long Life for Your Paper Creations:

Whenever you are creating something that you want to last a lifetime and particularly when you are working with photographs, it is imperative that you select the right materials and storage options to ensure these fragile papers a long life.

"Archival quality," "pH balanced," and "acid free" are terms that describe the inks, papers, and adhesives you should use in these special projects. These terms will help you identify products that contain little or no acid, an enemy of paper. Keep in mind, however, that no product can guarantee that the papers will last forever. You can take an extra precautionary step by using acid-free, buffered paper (a paper that helps absorb and neutralize acid).

Another enemy of paper and photographs is sunlight. So whenever possible, keep your paper keepsakes out of direct sunlight. Of course, the most dangerous element paper can come into contact with is any moisture, so take care to keep all paper creations dry. By taking these few precautionary steps, you will help your paper art live a long life.

How do I create borders with paper layering?

Bone folder
Card stock: brown corrugated; green polka-dot; sage green dark plum; off-white
Cup of water: small (for cleaning brush)
Decorative-edged scissors: deckle
Folded card: gold; dark green; olive green; lavender; off-white
Hole punch
Paintbrush: small
Paper adhesive
Permanent ink pad: brown
Raffia
Ruler
Scissors
Stamps: daisy cluster; large birdhouse
Watercolor paint set

Paper layering is an easy technique that adds a pro-fessional polish to the simplest piece of stamped art. Just as matting and a picture frame finish off a piece of artwork you might hang on a wall, paper layering completes the art you are creating by adding a paper border. I have used a single image for a greeting card and show it to you without any paper layering. I also offer five different approaches for the same image, incorporating a variety of paper layering techniques, with each technique varying the look of my card.

Birdhouse Greeting Card

Here's How to Make a Basic Card:
1. Ink the birdhouse stamp, using the brown ink pad. Print the image onto an off-white folded card.

2. Using the watercolor paint set, paint the image, taking care to clean the paintbrush when changing to a new color.

   This example shows the stamped image on an off-white card without any paper layering. Compared to the other examples, it is rather plain.

Here's How to Add Layers:

1. Ink the birdhouse stamp, using the brown ink pad. Print the image onto the off-white card stock.

2. Using the watercolor paint set, paint the image, taking care to clean the paintbrush when changing to a new color.

3. Trim the off-white card stock to a rectangle about ½" larger than the image, using the decorative-edged scissors.

4. Apply adhesive to the back of the off-white card stock and adhere it onto a piece of the dark plum card stock.

5. Trim the dark plum card stock, using the decorative-edged scissors, so that it is about ⅛" larger than the off-white card stock.

6. Apply adhesive to the back of the dark plum card stock and adhere these two layers off center onto the front of a lavender folded card.

Here's How to Silhouette:

1. Ink the birdhouse stamp, using the brown ink pad. Print the image onto the off-white card stock.

2. Using the watercolor paint set, paint the image, taking care to clean the paintbrush when changing to a new color.

3. Cut out the image, using the decorative-edged scissors, leaving about ¼" of the off-white card stock all around the edge.

4. Apply adhesive to the back of the off-white card stock and adhere it onto a piece of the green polka-dot card stock.

5. Trim the green polka-dot card stock, using the decorative-edged scissors, so that it is about ½" smaller on each side than the folded card.

6. Apply adhesive to the back of the green polka-dot card stock and adhere these two layers onto the front of a gold folded card.

Here's How to Add Texture:

1. Ink the birdhouse stamp, using the brown ink pad. Print the image onto the off-white card stock.

2. Using the watercolor paint set, paint the image, taking care to clean the paintbrush when changing to a new color.

3. Trim the off-white card stock to a rectangle about ½" larger than the image, using the decorative-edged scissors.

4. Using the scissors, cut a piece of brown corrugated card stock, slightly smaller than the stamped and trimmed off-white card stock. Apply adhesive to the back of each. Place each piece of card stock on opposing diagonals and adhere them onto a dark green folded card.

5. Using a hole punch, punch half of a hole along the folded edge of the card about one-third and two-thirds of the way down. Thread raffia through the holes. Tie it into a bow.

Here's How to Use Multiple Images:

1. Ink the birdhouse stamp, using the brown ink pad. Print the image onto the off-white card stock.

2. Using the watercolor paint set, paint the image, taking care to clean the paintbrush when changing to a new color.

3. Trim the off-white card stock to a rectangle about ½" larger than the image, using the decorative-edged scissors.

4. Ink the daisy cluster stamp, using the brown ink pad. Print the image all around the edge of an off-white folded card. Paint the images, using the watercolor paint set.

5. Apply adhesive to the back of the stamped and trimmed off-white card stock and adhere it to a piece of the sage green card stock. Trim it all around, using the scissors, so it is ½" larger than the off-white card stock. Apply adhesive to the back of the sage green card stock and adhere these two layers onto the stamped folded card.

258

Here's How to Embellish:

1. Ink the birdhouse stamp, using the brown ink pad. Print the image onto the off-white card stock.

2. Using the watercolor paint set, paint the image, taking care to clean the paintbrush when changing to a new color.

3. Trim the off-white card stock to a rectangle about ½" larger than the image, using the decorative-edged scissors.

4. Apply adhesive to the back of the stamped and trimmed off-white card stock and adhere it onto a piece of gold card stock. Using the scissors, trim the gold card stock so it is about ⅛" larger than the off-white card stock. Apply adhesive to the back of the gold card stock and adhere these two layers onto an olive green folded card.

5. Using a hole punch, punch an even number of holes, evenly spaced, along all edges of the olive green card. Starting at the upper left-hand corner, thread several pieces of raffia in and out through the holes. Tie a bow at the corner where the ends meet.

Here's How to Score and Fold a Card:

You can easily make greeting cards by hand in the color and size of your choosing by using a bone folder and a piece of card stock.

Cards that are not properly folded have a jagged, folded edge and may look as though the paper has been slightly frayed and torn. The trick to making a professional-looking card is all in the scoring and folding.

1. Use a piece of card stock that, once folded in half, will be a bit larger than the card you want to make. Mark off the center very lightly, using a pencil.

2. Hold a ruler down on the center of the card, following the marks you have just made.

3. Using a bone folder, make a line on the paper against the edge of the ruler. You have just broken the outside fibers of the papers enough so that it will fold easily.

4. The score line you have just made will be the outside fold, or mountain fold, of the card. Fold the card stock along the score line and use the bone folder to smooth down the fold.

5. Trim the card down to the size you desire, using a paper cutter.

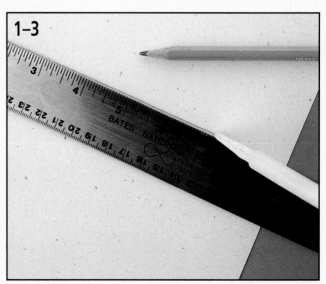

How do I stamp borders?

What You Need to Get Started:

Colored pencils: light blue; green; pink; red; yellow
Permanent ink pad: black
Picture frame card: heart-shaped
Plastic: clear square
Stamp: small posy cluster
Stamp positioner

Stamping borders is a simple and effective way to decorate projects. The tools you need to accomplish the precise placement of the image into a border are a stamp positioner and a clear plastic square. They are often sold together as a set. A stamp positioner is a thick acrylic corner that creates a 90° angle. In addition to creating borders, a stamp positioner is also useful if you want to combine images, such as placing a little girl exactly on a swing or positioning a ball precisely into a clown's hand.

Bordered Picture Frame Card

Here's How:

1. Place the stamp positioner so that the corner is near your left hand and one side of the positioner is horizontal and the other side vertical.

2. Slide the plastic square so that it fits snugly into the 90° angle created by the stamp positioner.

3. Ink the stamp and fit it snugly into the 90° angle of the stamp positioner. Print the image onto the plastic square. (You will wash it off the square when you are finished with your project.)

4. Beginning at the top of the heart-shaped window of the picture frame card, place the plastic square so that the image appears exactly where you want it.

5. Fit the stamp positioner snugly around the corner of the stamped plastic square. Remove the plastic square.

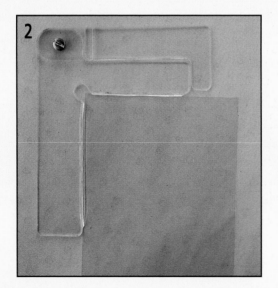

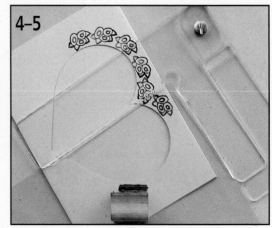

6. Ink the stamp and place it snugly into the 90° corner of the stamp positioner. Print the image.

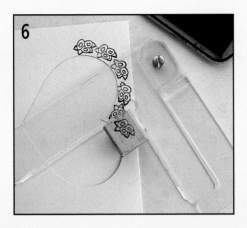

7. Lift off the stamp positioner. The image should be exactly where you wanted it!

8. Continue in this manner, placing the plastic square and the stamp positioner around the window of the frame card. Print the images until the border is complete.

9. Print an additional image in each lower corner of the card.

10. Color the images, using the colored pencils.

Troubleshooting— Here's How to Fix Smudges and Unwanted Lines:

You are nearing the completion of your card and it looks terrific. While printing one of the last images, your hand jumps and you print some unwanted lines. Don't despair. There are a few ways you can correct this:

- A white correction pen can cover small lines and smudges effectively.

- Try sponging on a background color and thereby soften the effect of the unwanted lines.

- Work the lines into a patterned background that you put in by hand.

- Incorporate the unwanted lines into the images, using a coordinating pen.

- Cut the image away from the offending background and use it as a motif.

What are some simple borders that I can create?

What You Need to Get Started:

Brush art markers:
  light blue; dark green; grass green; light green; orange; pink; purple; red; violet; yellow
Card stock: glossy white, 2¾" x 4"; scraps
Craft adhesive
Craft knife
Cutting mat
Dual-tipped markers: black; purple
Embossing markers: clear; green; red
Embossing powder: clear
Foamcore board
Glue pen
Heat gun
Lollipop sticks
Makeup sponge: wedge-shaped
Paper adhesive
Pinking shears
Ruler
Spray acrylic sealer: matte finish
Stamps: daisy; hydrangea; rose; tulip
Ultra-fine glitter: yellow

Nothing gives a more tailored look to a project than a border. Somehow a border focuses your work and completes it at the same time. Creating borders can be as simple or as complex as you wish it to be. Below I show you some fast and easy border ideas. Once you are comfortable with these, try them in variations or combinations and you will be delighted with the beautiful effects you can produce!

Plant Markers

Here's How:
1. Ink the flower stamp, using the brush art markers. Print the image onto the white card stock.

2. Refer to the individual flowers on pages 262–263. Add the border, following the specific instructions for each plant marker.

3. Write the name of the flower, using the black dual-tipped marker.

4. Spray the plant marker with a coat of matte-finish sealer. Allow it to dry.

5. Place the foam core board on a cutting mat and cut a piece slightly smaller than the plant marker, using the craft knife with a fresh blade.

6. Push one end of the lollipop stick into the center of the piece of foam-core board so that it makes a 1"

indentation. Remove the stick, dip one end into the craft adhesive and then re-insert that end into the foamcore board. Allow it to dry for several hours.

7. Apply paper adhesive to the back of each plant marker and adhere them onto the foamcore boards.

2a. Daisy:
1. Position the ruler along the edge of the card and draw a border, using the yellow brush art marker. Go over the lines you have just drawn, using a glue pen. Sprinkle the yellow glitter over the card. Pour the excess glitter back into the container. Allow the card to dry for several minutes.

2b. Hydrangea:
1. Position the ruler ¼" from the border. Using the fine tip of the purple dual-tipped marker, draw a border around the edge of the card, leaving a little space around any leaves or stems that are stamped off the edge of the card.

2c. Rose:

1. Position the ruler along the edge of the card and draw a border, using the red embossing marker. Heat-emboss it with clear embossing powder, using the heat gun. Set the ruler in slightly from the red border and draw in a green border, using the green emboss-ing marker. Heat-emboss it with clear embossing powder, using the heat gun.

2d. Tulip:

1. Trim one edge of a piece of scrap paper, using pinking shears. Gen-erously ink about 1" of one side of a makeup sponge, using the pink marker. Using the scrap paper as a stencil, swipe the sponge over the pinked edge of the paper, creating the zigzag image on the card.

Variations:

1. Ink the makeup sponge, using the embossing ink. Using a pinked edge of scrap paper as a stencil, swipe the sponge over it, creating a zigzag border on the card. Heat-emboss the zigzag border.

2. Cut scrap paper, using any decor-ative-edged scissors. Use the cut edge as a stencil.

3. Draw a border of dots and dashes with the black dual-tipped marker for a "stitched" look.

4. Make a border, using the clear embossing marker. Sprinkle several colors of embossing powder onto the ink and heat-emboss.

5. Make a border with a layer of double-sided tape. Sprinkle tiny beads, flecks of mica, or any one of the many available textured add-ons onto the tape.

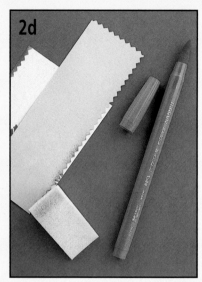

How do I enhance my stamped art with shadows and shading?

**What You
Need to
Get Started:**

Buttons: small
Card stock: white
Colored pencils:
  light blue;
  brown; gray;
  pink; dark
  purple;
  dark yellow
Craft adhesive
Cup of water
Decorative-edged
  scissors: scallop
Decorative papers:
  blue; pink
Fine-line pen:
  brown
Hole punch: ¼"
Paintbrush: small
Paper adhesive
Paper gift bags:
  light blue; pink
Permanent ink
  pad: brown
Ribbon: light blue
Ruler
Scissors
Stamps: baby and
  blanket; baby
  and parachute;
  baby shoes
  (small and
  large); carriage;
  diaper pin;
  heart with
  wings; "Heaven
  sent from up
  above;" "It's a
  Boy;" star;
  word banner;
  "Yippee"
Watercolor
  pencils:
  light blue; light
  brown

To really give your stamped art an artist's finish, there is no technique better than adding shadows or shading. The images will look grounded instead of floating on the page. Don't be intimidated— you do not need an art degree to be able to add just the right touch of visual dimension! Many stamps provide the shading lines within the image and others can be shaded simply with a gray colored pencil.

Gift Bags for New Babies

Here's How to Make the Blue Bag:

1. Using scissors, cut the card stock 1½" smaller than the size of the gift bag (measuring from the handles).

2. Ink the stamps, using the brown ink pad. Print the images onto the white card stock, using the photo opposite for placement.

3. Using the brown pen and a ruler to guide you, draw "stitch" marks around the images. Make certain that all of the horizontal lines and vertical lines are parallel to each other.

4. Color the images, using the colored pencils.

5. Using the gray colored pencil, add shadows to the stamped images.

Generally, if the imagined light source is in the upper left-hand corner, you should add the shadow next to the bottom and lower right side of the image.

6. Apply paper adhesive to the back of the stamped and colored card stock and adhere it

onto a piece of pink decorative paper. Trim the paper, using the decorative-edged scissors, so it is slightly larger than the card stock. Apply paper adhesive to the back of the pink paper and adhere it onto the bag.

7. Apply craft adhesive to the backs of the buttons and adhere them onto the bag.

Design Tips:
• Feel free to experiment with shadows since colored pencils can be erased easily with a white artist's eraser.

• When you want a soft effect for the outline stamps, try using a brown ink pad. It provides a subtle but effective difference. Save the black ink pad for images that require a stronger contrast.

Here's How to Make the Pink Bag:
1. Ink the shoes and phrase stamps, using the brown ink pad. Print the images onto separate pieces of card stock.

2. Color the shaded areas of the printed shoe image, using the light blue watercolor pencil. Color the soles of the shoes, using the light brown water-color pencil.

3. Wet a small paintbrush and sweep it over the watercolor pencil lines so that they soften and begin to flow together. Leave the areas of the shoes with more shading a darker

blue, while pulling some of the color into the unshaded part of the shoe. Make certain that the parts of the shoe that would be highlighted are left white.

4. Trim around each image, using the decorative-edged scissors. Apply paper adhesive to the back of each and adhere them onto layered pink and blue decorative papers that have also been trimmed so each is slightly larger than the other.

5. Using the hole punch, punch two holes in the center of the card stock with the shoe image about ½" apart from each other. Thread a 3" piece of ribbon through the holes from the front to the back. Cross the ribbon ends and feed them back through the holes from the back to the front.

6. Apply paper adhesive to the back of each piece of light blue decorative paper and adhere each onto the front of the bag, using the photo below for placement.

How do I create a scene with rubber stamps?

What You Need to Get Started:

Brush art markers: blue green; grass green; light green
Card stock: white, 7¾" x 10"
Colored pencils: light blue; medium brown; cocoa; dark gray; lime green; orange; pink dark yellow; light yellow
Craft knife
Cutting board
Dye-based ink pads or markers: aqua; black; brown; sage green
Scissors
Self-adhesive notes
Stamps: alphabet; bear; campfire; grass; hot dog on stick; rocks; small clouds; television; trees; water; water-skier
Utility sponge: round (or make-up)
Video tape cover

You can create scenes by combining stamped images. The scenes can range from a simple juxtaposition of several images to an elaborate, realistic work of art. A few techniques will help you make the stamps work towards reproducing the scene you envision. You will learn how to make and use masks, use multiple prints from a single inking, and create the illusion of depth with intensity of color.

Video Tape Cover

Here's How:
1. Ink the bear, campfire, and television stamps, using the black ink pad. Print the images onto the card stock. These are foreground images.

2. Print each of those images onto self-adhesive notes (a separate note for each image), making certain that a portion of the image is printed over the part of the note backed with adhesive. Cut out each image. You have just created masks for these images.

266

3. Place each mask over the corresponding image. (The adhesive part of the mask will hold it in place.) Ink the tree stamp, using the grass green, blue green, and light green markers. Print the image next to and over the masked bear. Don't worry—when you remove the mask, the images will look like they are in the background, behind the masked image. Without re-inking the stamp, print two more sets of trees. They will appear faded and further away than the first set of trees.

4. Remove the bear's mask to reveal a forest with depth.

5. Replace the bear's mask. Ink the rocks and hot dog stamps, using the black ink pad. Print these images onto the card stock.

6. Make a mask for the rocks and adhere them to the corresponding images. Ink the grass stamp, using the light green marker. Randomly print the image. Re-ink the grass stamp, using the grass green marker. Print the image towards the bottom of the card. Because it is darker, this section of the grass will appear closer to the viewer. Ink the grass stamp, using the blue green marker. Print the image a few times to add more dimension to the grass.

7. Ink the sponge, using the brown ink pad. Sponge the grass and campfire area to make the ground look more realistic. Remove all masks.

8. Ink a clean section of the sponge, using the sage green ink pad. Sponge in the sky, making certain to sponge over the trees and right up to the grass so that there is no area of the scene left uncolored. You have created a natural-looking horizon line.

9. Color the images, using color-ed pencils, markers, and the photo on page 269 for placement.

10. Place the television mask on the cutting mat and cut out the screen portion, using the craft knife. Discard the screen. You have just created what is called a "mortise" mask. It will allow you to stamp inside the television screen without overlapping onto the television cabinet.

11. Place the mortise mask over the television. Ink the water-skier stamp, using the black ink pad, and the water stamp, using the aqua ink pad. Print these images within the television screen. Ink the small cloud stamp, using the sage green ink pad. Print the image within the television. Color the sky, using a light blue colored pencil, and the water, using a medium blue colored pencil. Remove the mask.

12. For the video's title, ink the alphabet stamps, using the black ink pad. Print the images onto the cover.

Design Tips:

- Developing a scene takes a bit of forethought and planning. Decide on two or three images which will be the central focus of the scene. These elements will probably be placed in the foreground. Then, choose the images you want to use in producing the background.

- If it is an outdoor scene, remember that you will need to create the ground and sky, the which must meet at the horizon line. Interior scenes also have a horizon line, where the walls and floor meet. This can be drawn or stamped.

- Most scenes you design will require a proper sense of perspective. Smaller and lighter images appear farther away, while larger and darker images appear closer. Choose stamps that support the sense of perspective you are trying to create. Try to balance size, color intensity, and layout so that the primary elements draw the viewer's focus, and the background elements set the stage.

Layout:

A great way to help you arrange the layout for the scene is to first print each image on scrap paper and cut them out. Position them on a test sheet of card stock until you are pleased with the scene. Tape the pieces down and use this test sheet as a guide for your stamped art. Experiment with coloring ideas on this sheet as well.

Remember, when making a stamped scene always start with the foreground and work backwards, layering the background images behind the foreground images.

Masks:

When cutting masks, cut through several layers of self-adhesive notes at one time, creating duplicate masks. When one becomes dirty or torn, you have another one ready to go. Save the clean masks on a clean sheet of card stock.

When cutting masks, cut them out on the inside of the image's outline. They will be slightly smaller than the original. When you use these masks, you will be able to stamp backgrounds that come right to the edge of the foreground image without an undesirable halo effect as shown right.

Masks can be useful if you want only part of an image to print. Cover the part of the paper you don't want printed with the mask. Ink the stamp, and print the image, printing the unwanted part of the image onto the mask. Lift the mask and you have produced a partial image. This technique can work particularly well when you are printing borders and don't want the corners to be printed twice (once from the vertical printing and again from the horizontal printing). Mask the corner after it has been printed once and print the second corner over the mask. Voila! A perfect border.

Multiple Prints from a Single Inking:

This can be an effective technique for showing motion. Ink and print the main image first, then without re-inking the stamp, print two or more impressions behind it and slightly overlapping as shown right. The blurred impression produces the illusion of movement.

269

How can I use one stamp effectively to design an entire project?

Beads: assorted
Bone folder
Card stock: sage green; rust; flecked tan, 5½" x 8½"
Dye-based ink pad: black
Embossing ink pad: clear
Embossing powders: jasper; verdigris
Folded note cards, 4¼" x 3½": sage green; rust
Heat gun
Paper adhesive
Plastic: clear square
Raffia: rust
Ruler
Scissors
Stamp: bear claw
Stamp positioner
Stationery paper: flecked tan with coordinating envelope

Even after you have amassed your stamp collection, you will find that it can be challenging and fun to design an entire project using just one stamp. You will also be pleasantly surprised at the different looks you can achieve with a single image by varying layout, color, and texture.

Bear Claw Stationery Set

Here's How to Make the Greeting Card:

1. Ink the stamp, using the black ink pad. Print the image onto the plastic square, using the stamp positioner.

2. Using the bone folder and ruler, score and fold the flecked tan card stock in half to create a card.

3. Ink the stamp, using the clear embossing ink pad. Print the image along the front of the card, using the stamp positioner and the plastic square. Heat-emboss the images, using the jasper embossing powder for the bottom and top rows and the verdigris embossing powder for the middle row.

4. Using the scissors, trim the triangular shapes from the bottom of the card.

5. Cut a piece of the sage green card stock to fit the inside of the card. Apply adhesive to the back of the card stock and adhere it to the inside of the card. Cut a piece of the rust card stock to fit over the back of the card with a small overhang, forming a border on the bottom. Apply adhesive to the back of the card stock and adhere it onto the back of the card.

Here's How to Make the Small Folded Card:

1. Ink the stamp, using the embossing ink pad. Print the image in the upper left-hand corner of the folded note card.

2. Heat-emboss the image, using the verdigris embossing powder on the rust card and the jasper embossing powder on the sage green card.

Here's How to Make the Stationery:

1. Ink the stamp, using the black ink pad. Print the image onto the plastic square, using the stamp positioner.

2. Ink the stamp, using the embossing ink pad. Print the image along the top and bottom of the stationery paper and on the envelope flap, using the photo opposite for placement. Heat-emboss the images, using the jasper and verdigris embossing powders and the heat gun.

3. Tie the decorated sheets of stationery together with raffia. Tie coordinating beads to the ends of the raffia.

Design Tips:

- As an exercise in creativity, try designing a few other cards, each with a unique look but composed of the same materials. Think about what appeals to you in each card. This will help you develop your own individual style.

- Don't overlook the impact of forming a circle with the stamped image as shown right. Suddenly the single image takes on a whole new dimension.

- As you experiment with the layout of your cards, notice how the negative space (the blank space between the stamped images) becomes as much a part of the design as the image itself. When you are using only one image, the area you don't stamp is as important as the one you do!

How do I incorporate collage elements with stamping?

What You Need to Get Started:

Adhesive foam dots
Angel hair: gold
Card stock: off-white, 5" x 7"
Charms: brass sun; tiny brass star
Craft adhesive
Cup of water
Embossing powder: clear
Handmade papers: different patterns of black and gold (3)
Heat gun
Paintbrush: small
Paper adhesive
Photo album: black, spiral bound
Pigment ink pad: copper
Pigment powder: gold
Scissors
Shaped confetti: large gold star
Stamps: checkerboard star; dotted star; sun

Collage is a French word that literally means "pasting." Collage is a process in which papers and found objects are pasted together to form a pleasing whole. By providing central or background images, stamping can enhance the beauty of a collage.

Celestial Photo Album

Here's How:

1. Tear irregular-shaped pieces from each of the handmade papers, using the following method:

- Place the paper on a clean surface. Load a small paintbrush with water and brush on the line where you want the tear to be.

- Hold the paper in place with a hand on one side of the water line and gently pull the opposite side with the other hand. The paper should tear easily and leave an interesting edge with the fibers fanned out. Allow the paper to dry before you use it in the project.

2. Ink the sun, checkerboard star, and dotted star stamps, using the copper ink pad. Print the images onto the off-white card stock (print the checkerboard star twice). Heat-emboss the images, using the embossing powder and a heat gun. Allow them to cool.

3. Using the scissors, cut out the stars, leaving as little card stock border as possible.

4. Gently tear out the sun, leaving about a ¼" card stock border. To achieve a deckle-edged effect around the sun, hold the paper in your left hand with the image facing you and carefully tear it toward you with your right hand.

5. Dip your pinkie finger into the gold pigment powder and gently rub it over all of the stamped images.

6. Place the three pieces of handmade paper over the photo album cover so that they overlap and form a pleasing, balanced composition. Apply adhesive to the back of each and adhere them in place.

7. Apply adhesive to the center of the back of the sun image and adhere the angel hair.

8. Apply adhesive foam dots to the back of the sun image, one of the checkerboard stars, and the confetti star. Attach them to the album, using the photo below for placement.

9. Apply craft adhesive to the remaining checkerboard star and the dotted star and adhere them onto the album. Apply craft adhesive to the two brass charms and adhere them in place.

10. Using the scissors, trim off any handmade paper that may be overlapping the sides of the album.

How do I create die-cuts with rubber stamps?

What You Need to Get Started:

Bone folder
Brush art markers: black; royal blue; brown; light gray; leaf green; light green; dark orange; light orange; light pink; purple; yellow
Card stock: gold; purple; glossy white
Craft knife
Cutting mat
Embossing powder: clear
Foam tape
Heat gun
Paper adhesive
Pigment ink pad: black
Ruler
Scissors
Stamps: candy corn; ghost; gravestone; pumpkin; spider; "Trick or Treat"; witch face; "You're Invited"
Utility sponge: round

Make your stamped art stand up and really grab attention. By cutting out part of an image and folding the rest of it back, you create a die-cut. You also create quite a sensation at a spooky Halloween party!

Halloween Party Ideas

Here's How to Make Invitations:

1. Ink the gravestone and "Trick or Treat" phrase stamps, using the black ink pad. Print the images onto the white card stock. Heat-emboss the images, using the embossing powder and the heat gun.

2. Make a mask for the gravestone. Ink, print, and heat-emboss the ghost image so it appears to be behind the gravestone.

3. Ink, print, and heat-emboss the spider image next to the gravestone. Draw the spider thread, using the black marker.

4. Color all images, using the markers and the photo opposite for placement.

5. Score the center back side of the card stock (up to the gravestone but not across it), using the bone folder and the ruler. Place the ghost image on the cutting mat and cut around the top of the image to the score line, using the craft knife. Fold along the score line so the ghost's head pops up. Blacken the exposed edges of the ghost's head, using the black marker.

6. Cut off the excess card stock, using the scissors, so that the folded card now measures 3" x 5".

7. Score and fold the gold card stock in half and cut it to 3¼" x 5¼", using the scissors. Apply adhesive to the front of the gold card stock and adhere it to the underside of the stamped card.

8. Score and fold the purple card stock in half and cut it to 3½" x 5½", using the scissors. Apply adhesive to the front of the purple card stock and adhere it to the underside of the gold card stock.

9. Ink, print, and heat-emboss the "You're Invited" phrase under the gravestone.

10. Ink, print, and heat-emboss four candy corn images onto remaining white card stock. Color each candy corn, using markers and the photo opposite for placement. Using the scissors, cut out the images. Adhere them to the card, using the foam tape.

11. Sponge in the background, using the green and brown markers.

Here's How to Make Placecards:

1. Ink, print, and heat-emboss the witch face image onto the white card stock.

Color the image, using the photo for placement.

2. Score the center back side of the card stock (up to the witch face but not across it), using the bone folder and the ruler. Place the witch face image on the cutting mat. Cut around the hat to the score line, using the craft knife. Fold the card stock so the witch's hat pops up. Blacken the exposed edges of the hat, using the black marker.

3. Cut the folded card to 1¾" x 3½", using the scissors.

4. Sponge in the background, using the yellow and orange markers.

5. Score and fold the purple card stock in half and cut it to 2" x 3¾", using the scissors. Apply adhesive to the front of the purple card stock and adhere it to the underside of the stamped card.

6. Write the guest's name on the stamped card, using the black marker.

Here's How to Make Napkin Rings:
1. Ink, print, and heat-emboss the pumpkin image onto the white card stock. Color the images, using markers and the photo for placement.

2. Draw a 1" x 4" tab on each side of the pumpkin head. These tabs will form the ring around the napkin.

3. Cut out the pumpkin with the tabs, using the scissors. Blacken the exposed edges of the pumpkin, using the black marker.

4. Place the pumpkin on the cutting mat and cut a small portion of the pumpkin's sides away from the tab, using the craft knife, making certain that the top and bottom of the tabs are still attached.

5. Sponge in the background, using the purple marker.

6. Apply adhesive to the tabs and adhere them together. Insert a napkin through the ring.

Here's How to Make a Table Decoration:
1. Ink, print, and heat-emboss five pumpkin images in a row, 1" apart, onto the white card

stock. Color the images, using the markers and the photo for placement.

2. Place the pumpkins on the cutting mat and cut out the left-hand side of each pumpkin, using the craft knife. Blacken the exposed edges, using the black marker. Score the right-hand side.

3. Fold the images accordion style.

4. Using the scissors, trim off the top and bottom edges of the paper, slightly above and below the pumpkins.

5. Sponge in the background, using the purple marker.

How can I add dimension to my stamped art?

Dimension is a wonderful element to incorporate into your stamped projects. There are many exciting tools and materials available that will help you add that extra bit of texture you are looking for. Keep your eyes open for yarns and wire, puff paint and flocking, acetate and mica tiles, and all sorts of textural elements that can be used to make your artwork jump off the paper.

Framed Sunflowers

Here's How:

1. Ink the sunflower stamp, using the black ink pad. Print the image onto ivory card stock. Heat-emboss the image, using the embossing powder and the heat gun. Allow the image to cool. Repeat for a second image.

2. Using the make-up applicator, rub the chalk lightly into the background areas of each image, producing a hint of color.

3. Color one image completely, using the embossing markers and the photo opposite for placement. Heat-emboss the image using the embossing powder and heat gun.

4. Color and heat-emboss the second image. Allow it to cool. Then, cut out only the flowers, using the scissors.

5. With the colored side laying in the palm of your hand, rub the bowl of a spoon into the back of the cut-out flowers, causing the flower centers to

push out. Turn the flowers over and curl the petals slightly inward towards the center.

6. Blacken the edges of the cut-out flowers, using the black marker.

7. Apply three layers of the foam tape onto the back of the cut-out flowers, making certain the tape does not show from the front. Attach the cut-out flowers on top of the first image.

8. Using the scissors, cut out the leaf from the second image. Blacken the edges of the leaf, using the black

marker. Apply paper adhesive to the back of the leaf base and adhere it onto the uncut image. Curl the end of the leaf out.

9. Dilute the craft adhesive and spread a bit onto the center of the dimensional flowers, using your finger. Sprinkle the beads onto the adhesive. Allow the adhesive to dry.

10. Using the scissors, cut the corrugated cardboard to 5" x 7". Using pinking shears, cut the gold card stock ½" larger than the sunflower image on all sides.

11. Apply paper adhesive to the back of the first image and adhere it onto the gold card stock. Apply paper adhesive to the back of the gold card stock and adhere it onto the corrugated cardboard, using the photo for placement.

12. Using the makeup applicator, apply blue chalk all over a small scrap piece of ivory card stock.

13. Ink, print, and heat-emboss the phrase image onto the chalked ivory card stock. Using the pinking shears, cut it out. Apply paper adhesive to the back and adhere it onto a piece of gold card stock cut ¼" larger than the phrase. Apply paper adhesive to the back of the gold card stock and adhere it onto the corrugated cardboard.

14. Place your artwork in the frame.

How do I stamp on fabric?

**What You
Need to
Get Started:**

Apron
Cotton swab
Fabric paints:
   blue; light
   brown; medium
   brown; gold;
   red; yellow
Heavy cardboard
   or foamcore
   board
Kitchen towel:
   tan and white
   checked
Markers,
   permanent or
   fabric: blue;
   brown
Oven mitts: white
Paper towels
Sponge brush
Stamps: butter;
   checkerboard
   border; egg;
   measuring cup;
   mixer; mixing
   bowl; single
   check; wooden
   spoon

When I first began rubber stamping, I almost exclusively used paper. Later, someone encouraged me to try printing images onto fabric. I have been hooked ever since! Fabric stamping is fast and fun and opens up a world of exciting possibilities for you to explore. Baby clothes, sweatshirts, linens, sheets, lamp shades, denim jackets—all are waiting to be transformed by your rubber stamps!

Baking Ensemble

Here's How:
Note: All fabric items follow the same instructions.

1. Lay the fabric item over a piece of heavy cardboard or foamcore board to protect the work surface and provide an even surface for stamping.

2. Dip the sponge brush into the blue paint, wiping off the excess. Apply the paint over the checkerboard border stamp so that the raised parts of the image are entirely covered. Let the paint sit on the stamp for one minute to form a base. Reapply the paint, removing any accumulated paint from the recesses of the image, using a cotton swab.

3. Print the image by placing the rubber die directly onto the fabric, applying even pressure without rocking or twisting the stamp. Lift the stamp off the fabric slowly so that any excess paint doesn't splatter.

4. Continue printing the image in this

manner to create the border. When you reach the point where the border meets at a corner or other junction, use at least three layers of paper toweling to mask over the first part of the border so as to avoid overlapping the ends.

5. Using the method described in Steps 2–3, ink the largest image with the desired paint color. Print the image several times, randomly spaced, onto the fabric. Continue in this manner with the next largest image, and so on, finishing with the smallest image.

6. If desired, outline the printed butter image, using the blue marker, and the egg, using the brown marker. Outlining gives paler images more definition, particularly on a "busier" background.

7. Allow the fabric to dry overnight. Then, put the items in a clothes dryer set on medium heat for 30 minutes. The images are now permanently set and the fabric item can be washed and dried, following the manufacturer's instructions.

Design Tips:

- To keep the garment from looking too busy, try not to use more than seven colors. Also, a little black used repeatedly throughout a busy design helps anchor the other colors and give them focus.

- Vary the sizes and shapes of the stamps so that the design has visual interest.

- To stamp on fabric with a detailed image, use fabric ink pads in the same way you would use a dye-based ink pad. Color the image with fabric marking pens.

Troubleshooting:

- Make certain you scrub the stamps well after each use (an old toothbrush works) so dried paint doesn't build up and obscure the image.

- Because fabric paint is permanent, you will not be able to remove little unwanted lines. These lines can actually be considered an enhancement because they add to the hand-stamped look of the piece.

- If a portion of an image doesn't print when you stamp it, dip a cotton swab into the paint and tap it onto the fabric to fill in the area.

279

How do I create faux finishes with stamps?

What You Need to Get Started:

Acrylic paint: gold; ivory
Clock: wooden, arched
Clock face sticker
Clock movement
Paintbrush
Pigment ink pads: dark blue; grass green; mint green
Spray acrylic sealer: matte finish
Stamp set: faux marble (3 pieces)

Faux finishes are painting techniques applied to a particular material which create the "false" impression of another material. They represent a strong trend in decorating today. These effects can be achieved through stamping! Here I have used wood to make a "marble" clock. Look for stamps that will produce these elegant effects or experiment with some more abstract stamps, layering different colors on top of each other, and see what you can create.

Faux-marble Clock

Here's How:

1. Using the paintbrush, apply two coats of ivory paint onto the body of the clock. Apply two coats of gold paint onto the rim and base. Allow it to dry.

2. Ink the first stamp in the faux-marble stamp set, using the mint green ink pad. Randomly print the image onto the body of the clock.

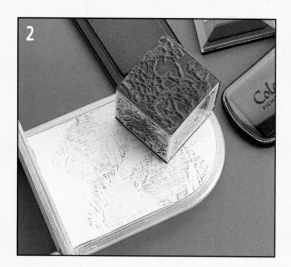

3. Ink the second stamp, using the grass green ink pad. Randomly print the image onto the body of the clock.

4. Ink the third stamp, using the dark blue ink pad. Randomly print the image, although less densely, onto the body of the clock. Allow the ink to dry for 24 hours.

4

5. If desired, repeat the paint and ink applications on the back side of the clock.

6. Spray the entire clock with a coat of matte-finish sealer. Allow it to dry several hours.

7. Apply the clock face sticker and attach the clock movement, following the manufacturer's instructions.

Design Tips:

- There are some wonderful stamps available that simulate the look of wood graining, malachite stone, and leopard, giraffe, and zebra markings, to name a few.

- As you create projects using these stamps, experiment with materials to try simulating the texture of the desired finish as well. For example, a faux-leopard gift bag printed and embossed on suede paper would be a stunning visual and textural treat. A faux-malachite image stamped on slick jade green paper will fool the viewer's eyes and fingers!

How do I use stamps on terra-cotta?

What would make a lovelier gift than a beautiful flowering plant in a flower pot hand-stamped by you? Don't let the curved surface scare you—stamping on a pot is easier than you think!

Rose-covered Flower Pot

Here's How:

1. Using the sponge brush, apply two coats of ivory paint onto the outside of the flower pot. Allow it to dry.

2. Ink the stamp, using the black ink pad. Print the image onto the flower pot. (To stamp onto a curved surface, place one edge of the rubber die on the pot and roll the stamp over the pot until the entire image is printed.)

3. Continue in this manner, printing images around the pot, varying the heights of the rose.

4. Color the roses and leaves, using the paint pens and the photo opposite for placement. Allow the paint to dry.

5. If necessary, trace over the outlines of the roses, using the black paint pen.

6. Spray the entire pot with a coat of glossy-finish sealer. Allow the pot to dry several hours.

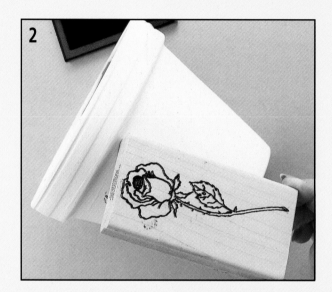

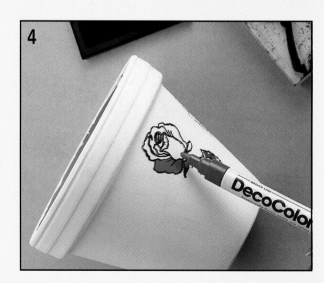

Design Tips:

- You can also stamp on un-painted ceramic pots. The terra-cotta color of the pot lends a wonderful, earthy look when coupled with ethnic or bold image stamps. Use crafter's ink that you heat-set or pigment ink that you heat-emboss. Apply a sealer to protect your work. Try combining stamped images with decorative elements like shells or beads.

- If you want to use a very large stamp to decorate your pot, try this method for getting a clear print of the image. Ink the stamp and place it, rubber die side up, on a flat surface. Holding the pot in both hands, place it on its side onto one end of the image and roll it across the stamp until the entire image has been printed.

How do I use stamps on wood?

What You Need to Get Started:

Crafter's ink pads:
   black; brown;
   dark green;
   purple;
   turquoise
Heat gun
Permanent pen:
   black
Sandpaper: 150-
   grit
Spray acrylic
   sealer: matte
   finish
Stamps: small
   maple leaf;
   small oak leaf;
   small single
   check; small
   spruce leaf;
   small star
Tack cloth
Wooden salad
   bowl: medium
   size

Wood provides a wonderful hard surface for stamping. The interplay of the stamped image and the wood grain is appealing to the eye and the sense of touch. Craft stores carry a large assortment of small wooden pieces to choose from.

Decorative Wooden Bowl

Here's How:

1. Using the sandpaper, sand the bowl smooth. Wipe dust from the bowl, using a tack cloth.

2. Ink the check stamp, using the turquoise ink pad. Print the image in three alternating rows along the inside rim of the bowl.

3. Ink the oak leaf stamp, using the brown ink pad. Print the image repeatedly underneath the checked border.

4. Ink the maple leaf stamp, using the purple ink pad. Ink the star stamp, using the black ink pad. Print the images alternately, underneath the oak leaves.

5. Ink the spruce leaf stamp, using the dark green ink pad. Print the image onto the center of the bowl, overlapping the leaves to form a star pattern, using the photo opposite for placement.

6. Ink the check stamp, using the turquoise ink pad. Print the image in three alternating rows along the outside rim of the bowl.

7. Draw lines along the edge of the bowl, using the black pen.

8. Hold the heat gun about 5" away from a section of the bowl for about 2½ minutes, taking care not to scorch the bowl. Continue until each section has set.

9. Spray the entire bowl with a coat of matte-finish sealer. Allow it to dry several hours.

Note: The bowl is for decorative purposes only.

Design Tips:

*   This project demonstrates stamping on natural, unstained wood. When stamping on darker, stained wood, use bold-faced stamps with pigment ink and heat-emboss the stamped images so that they stand out from the background.

*   If you like the look of a colored bowl with the wood grain showing through, you can easily achieve this effect. Dilute a desired color of acrylic paint with a little water, brush it on with a sponge brush or makeup sponge, and wipe the excess off with a paper towel. Allow the wooden piece to dry and proceed with your stamping.

How do I use foam stamps?

What You Need to Get Started:

Acrylic paints:
   light blue;
   seafoam green;
   peach; yellow
Clothespins
Craft adhesive
Fabric trim:
   peach (1 yd.)
Foam stamp set:
   posy
Lamp base:
   coordinating
Lamp shade kit:
   small
Paper: scraps (to
   test the images)
Permanent fine-
   tipped pen:
   black
Sponge brush
Spray acrylic
   sealer: matte
   finish

Relatively new to the stamp field, foam stamps are an excellent choice for home decorating projects. They are deeply etched, making it easy to achieve a clean printing, and they grip surfaces like walls and furniture very nicely.

Floral Lamp Shade

Here's How:

1. Lay the lamp shade material flat on a clean work surface.

2. Beginning with the large posy stamp, load the sponge brush with the light blue paint, removing any excess paint. Ink the stamp by tapping the sponge brush over the image until it is covered, but not runny with paint.

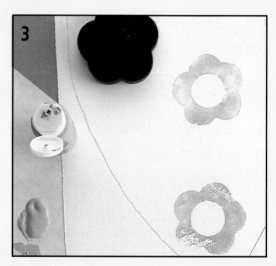

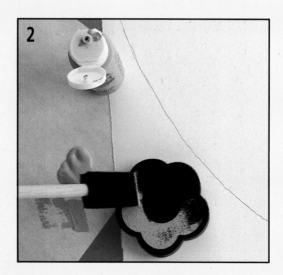

3. Test-print the image by pressing the stamp onto a piece of scrap paper and lifting it straight off. Adjust the amount of paint as needed and print the image onto the lamp shade.

4. Load the sponge brush with the yellow paint in the same manner as in Step 2 and ink the small posy stamp. Print the image onto the lamp shade. Repeat several times so that the small posies loosely circle the large posies.

5. Using the mask provided in the stamp set for the large posy, cover the large printed posy. Load the sponge brush with the seafoam green paint and ink the leaf stamp. Print the image onto the lamp shade to the side of the masked posy. Repeat this process with the smaller printed posy images and smaller leaf stamp.

6. Continue stamping the lamp shade in this manner until the pattern is completed.

7. Load the sponge brush with the peach paint and ink the stamps to be used for the centers of the flowers. Print the images for all the flower centers. Allow all paint to dry several hours.

8. Using the black pen, outline the flowers and leaves with a small "stitch" line.

9. Spray the lamp shade with a coat of matte-finish sealer. Allow it to dry for several hours.

10. Apply adhesive along one side edge of the shade and adhere the two edges of the shade together. Secure the edges, using the clothespins. Allow the adhesive to dry.

11. Apply adhesive along the top and bottom edge of the shade and adhere the fabric trim onto the shade. Allow the adhesive to dry.

12. Assemble the lamp shade, frame, and base, following the manufacturer's instructions.

How do I use stamps to emboss velvet?

What You Need to Get Started:

Iron and ironing board
Satin liner fabric: blue, 46" x 12"
Sewing machine or fabric glue
Silk fringe trim: black (⅓ yd.)
Spray bottle (for misting)
Stamps: clam shell; conch shell; star fish
Velvet fabric: rayon/silk, midnight blue, 46" x 12" (avoid cotton velvet, polyester velvet, or velveteen)

Have you noticed the elegant embossed velvet wearables and home accessories being featured in all of the trendy stores lately? They are so rich looking, but the problem is they are frequently accompanied by a rich price tag! However, you do not need to break the bank to add embossed velvet to your life. Rubber stamps can create distinctive and permanent impressions in velvet. Whether or not you sew, there are all sorts of beautiful things you can create with bold faced stamps and velvet.

Seashell Velvet Scarf

Here's How:
Note: No ink is required for this project. Dry clean all velvet garments.

1. Lay a stamp, rubber die side up, on the ironing board. Beginning at one end of the velvet fabric, place it, nap side down, over the stamp where you want the impression to be made. The wrong side of the fabric should be facing you.

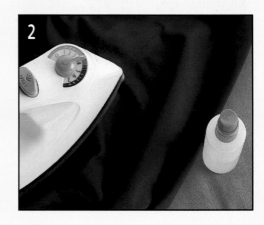

2. Set the iron to "wool" setting with no steam. Lightly mist the back side of the fabric with water so that it is slightly damp. Place the iron onto the fabric and press, without wiggling the iron, for about 20 seconds. Lift the iron, turn it one quarter to the right or left, and press again for five seconds to eliminate any unpressed circles that may have resulted from the iron's steam circles.

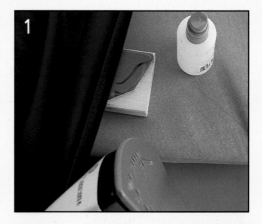

Design Tips:

- Velvet embossing works best with bold-faced stamps. Avoid highly detailed images. The velvet is too thick to be able to pick up fine lines.

- Random placement of images works best with velvet embossing since it is nearly impossible to line up images accurately.

- Not a seamstress? You don't have to be. There are many ways you can use embossed velvet without sewing. Try adding a piece of embossed velvet inside a picture frame card or box. Embossed velvet looks wonderful adhered to a scrapbook cover. Look in stores for plain velvet dresses, shirts, and purses that you can embellish with your own designer touch!

Reposition the fabric over the stamp and repeat this process until the entire piece of velvet is embossed.

3. Sew or glue the velvet to its liner. Sew or glue silk fringe trim onto each short end.

4. Steam seams down so that they lay relatively flat. Do not try to iron the seams as this will leave an unwanted impression in the velvet.

How do I create jewelry with stamps?

What You Need to Get Started:

Charms: small
   star (2)
Colored pencils:
   light blue;
   light green;
   rose; yellow
Crafter's ink pad:
   black
Instant adhesive
Earring backs (2)
Heat gun (or
   toaster oven)
Hole punch: ¼"
Jump rings (2)
Paper: scrap
Permanent pen:
   gold
Sandpaper:
   320-400 grit
Scissors
Shrink plastic:
   opaque
   (2 sheets)
Stamp positioner
Stamp: moon

My favorite material for rubber stamped jewelry is shrink plastic. Stamp on the shrink plastic, cut out the images, and watch them shrink down to make adorable charms. Combine the shrink art you have created with coordinating beads or charms and your friends will wonder which trendy boutique you've been shopping in!

Moon & Stars Earrings

Here's How:
1. Lightly sand the shrink plastic, using the sandpaper, following the manufacturer's instructions.

2. Ink the moon stamp, using the black ink pad. Print the image onto scrap paper. Place the shrink plastic over the image and color the plastic, using the outline from underneath and the photo opposite for placement. Repeat this process for the second earring.

3. Ink the stamp, using the black ink pad. Using the stamp positioner, line up the stamp directly over each scrap paper image. Print the image onto each colored image on the shrink plastic.

4. Using the scissors, cut out the images. Be careful not to smudge the ink as it is not permanent until it is heated.

5. Using the hole punch, punch a hole at the bottom edge of each image.

6. Direct the heat gun at the stamped image until it begins to shrink. It will curl up, contort, and then flatten out.

Once the image is flat and has finished shrinking, turn off the heat gun. (Alternatively, bake the images in a toaster oven at 300° for about three minutes.) It is amazing to see how much your image shrinks. Compare it to the image shown at actual size below.

Image shown actual size.

7. Outline the shrunken images, using the gold pen. Allow the images to dry for about 30 minutes.

8. Insert a jump ring through each hole and thread on a small star charm before closing the jump ring. Apply instant adhesive to two earring backs and adhere one onto the center back of each image to finish the earrings.

Troubleshooting:

- The shrunken images may seem to have changed shape from the original. Horizontally and vertically positioned images shrink slightly differently. If you have laid out an image horizontally and are un-happy with its shrunken form, stamp it vertically and see if you are happier with the results.

- You may be concerned how the finished product will look because the colored pencils do not color evenly on the plastic. You're in luck! As the plastic shrinks, the colors compress and intensify, making this a very forgiving process.

Design Tips:

- Shrink plastic comes in 8½" x 11" sheets in black, clear, opaque, and white. If you use ink to color the image, you must use permanent ink or crafter's ink to perma-nently set the color on shrink plastic. All other inks will smear. Colored pencils or acrylic paints are also excellent choices for color-ing images. Choose large images because they will shrink to half their size.

- You may stamp the image directly onto the shrink plastic with permanent ink. However, make certain the image is completely dry before coloring it. You can also stamp the images you want onto copy paper and then hand-feed the shrink plastic through the copy machine. The images will print nicely onto the shrink plastic. Make certain you have sanded the shrink plastic before you copy the images onto it. Also, only feed shrink plastic through a copy machine that has been turned on recently so that it is not too warm.

- There are many ways to make jewelry using rubber stamps. Heavy paper, poly-mer clay, and paper clay are some other materials that stamp beautifully and can be turned into jewelry.

How do I use stamps with decorative foil?

What you Need to Get Started:

Card stock:
    glossy red
Foil: variegated
    gold
Foil adhesive
Paintbrush or
    sponge brush
Paper adhesive
Scissors
Spray acrylic
    sealer: glossy
    finish
Spray paint:
    glossy black
Stamp: fan
Wooden picture
    frame

Decorative foils add elegance to any project and are easy to use with stamps. Foils come in many colors and in variegated tones and patterns. Instead of using ink on the stamp, you can apply foil adhesive to it. Stamp the image, let the adhesive dry, and apply the foils. It is that easy!

Asian Fan Picture Frame

Here's How:

1. Spray the frame with the black spray paint in a well-ventilated area. Allow it to dry. Apply a second coat if necessary.

2. Spray the frame with a coat of glossy-finish sealer in a well-ventilated area. Allow it to dry.

3. Using the paintbrush or sponge brush, apply a small amount of the foil adhesive all over the stamp. Print the image onto the card stock. Allow it to dry for about 10 minutes (until the adhesive feels tacky). Repeat this process to create four images. Wash the stamp to clean off the adhesive.

4. Take a small amount of foil in your fingers and lay it on top of each printed image. Apply enough foil so that the entire image is covered. Rub off the foil that is not stuck to the adhesive. Using the scissors, cut out the images, leaving a small border of the card stock.

5. Apply paper adhesive to the back of the cut-out images. Adhere one image onto each corner of the frame.

6. Cut out a small piece of card stock for the opening of the frame. Apply adhesive to the back of the art to be framed and adhere it onto the center of the card stock.

Troubleshooting:
- If the details of the image are not pronounced when stamped, try using a thinner coat of the foil adhesive.

How do I use stamps on glass and porcelain?

What You Need to Get Started:

Makeup sponges
Paintbrush
Porcelain dish-
  ware: white
Porcelain paints:
  shimmer
  starter kit
Stamps: polka-
  dot; single
  check

There is no need to settle for ordinary dishes! Decorate your dishware and customize it for any table setting, using rubber stamps and porcelain paint. Go ahead and stamp your glassware to match—it is simple with rubber stamps. All pieces will be dishwasher and microwave safe.

Confetti Dinnerware

* While these paints are completely nontoxic, they are not intended for use on surfaces that come into direct contact with food or drink. For example, avoid painting on the rims of mugs and glasses.

Here's How:

1. Prepare the surface, using the conditioner provided in the paint kit, following the manufacturer's instructions.

2. For both the polka-dot and the single check images, load a makeup sponge, using the first paint color. Apply the paint over the stamp, so the image is lightly covered. Gently print the image onto the rim of the plate.

3. First print the polka-dots, using one paint color, then fill in the balance of the plate rim with polka-dots, using the other three paint colors alternately.

4. Print the checks, using the photo opposite for placement. Allow the porcelain pieces to dry for at least one hour.

5. If desired, apply the glossy sealer provided in the kit, using the paintbrush. Clean the paintbrush with water.

Design Tip:

• Check flea markets, thrift shops, and yard sales for inexpensive, unadorned porcelain pieces. Craft stores also sell a variety of porcelain pieces that work beautifully—including plain white tiles. Several woodenware companies make shelves, tables, trays, trivets, and clocks that are made to encase the tiles—you simply glue them into place. In no time at all you can make an attractive and functional decorated item for your home.

May 19th 1998

→ my cake!

Spencer

Braden

Jake

We had my party in our front yard. It was sooo windy!! I had a dinosaur cake and got a lot of dinosaur toys! It was so much fun!

Abby

← the can was empty!

then there are those who like to watch!

Barb

The campsite

Sophie

Sophie was finding all sorts of treasures!!

Breanna ♥ 2 yrs.
Hannah ♥ 10 mo.

SCRAPBOOKING
for the first time®

Rebecca Carter

Scrapbooking for the first time

Introduction

"Scrapbooking" is a hobby that not only provides a creative outlet for the scrapbook designer, but also promotes a strong sense of self-esteem and belonging for those whose lives and accomplishments are creatively chronicled and compiled into an album or collection of albums.

Great scrapbooks start with great photos. Although professional photos are wonderful additions to a scrapbook, using a professional photographer for all photos is not practical, or necessary. Your own snapshots are going to capture the most memorable moments in life.

The best times and conditions, as far as lighting is concerned, for taking photographs outside are before 10 am and after 4 pm and on a slightly overcast day. The subject should be positioned so the sunlight is hitting them from the side instead of facing directly into the sun.

Add variety to photos by changing the angles at which photos are taken. Try looking through the camera viewfinder at the subject from low, high, and normal camera angles to see which will look best. Children's photos are often better if the photographer kneels down to the child's level before taking the shot. Many older people find photos taken from a slightly higher angle more appealing.

Get closer to the subject when you are taking the photograph. The one comment I hear most often is, "Your pictures are so close-up! In my photos the people are always so far away." At first, it is a little awkward to get so close, but the results are great. The only exception to using this technique is when you are using a flash—especially indoors—as the subject can appear washed out or over-exposed.

Try enlarging your photos. If you have a photo where the image is very small and you would like it to appear larger, either enlarge it on a color copy machine or have the photo printed larger from the negative. Then simply crop the photo so the subject is the main focus.

Good photos come from good photo processing labs. Avoid the temptation to save money by going with a lower-quality lab. Incorrect developing can mean the difference between a photo that lasts and a photo that quickly fades.

Use both black-and-white and colored photos in your scrapbooks. While black-and-white photos last longer, the value of colored photos cannot be denied. Many scrapbook designers recommend taking colored photos for the most part and taking a set of black-and-white photos every six months to one year to preserve family history, in the event that color photos deteriorate.

Keep duplicates of favorite photos and negatives somewhere besides in the home. In the event of a fire, flood, or other natural disaster, at least some photos will survive. Duplicates can be kept with family, friends, or in a bank safe deposit box.

Many photos suggest a theme or represent a special event. For example, a photo of a child blowing out candles on a birthday cake can be used to build a page with a birthday theme. Decide what emotion or mood is reflected by the theme and use it as a guide when choosing paper patterns and accents.

Add color to scrapbook pages by using colored paper products, pens, markers, and more. You may choose to use colors that traditionally represent the theme of the scrapbook page or colors that are complementary to the colors found in the photos. Choose colors that reinforce and enhance the page's theme, not detract from it.

Use a few of the many available scrapbook supplies to accentuate the photos, theme, and colors.

As acid damages photos, it is important to use acid-free supplies when creating scrapbook pages. Scrapbook suppliers and most standard craft stores are great sources for papers, stickers, die-cuts, pens, and other acid-free products.

When you have pages that face each other, try to use complementary or coordinating colors and themes. Your scrapbook will appear neat and organized, not cluttered and hard to follow.

For the person who is scrapbooking for the first time, this section provides a comprehensive guide to products, supplies, and techniques that can be used to creatively compile these treasured histories.

The intent here is to provide a starting point and teach basic skills. The more pages you create, the more comfortable you will feel. Take pride in the talents you are developing and try to resist comparing your pages to any one else's. Everyone has their own style. Remember, the main idea is to get the photos into a photo album—not to have the best looking page in the neighborhood. Happy scrapbooking!

Getting Started

Scrapbooking can be an overwhelming project if it is not broken down into categories. When I first began scrapbooking a few years ago, I bought everything in sight just because it was there, "Oh, that's cute," and "I must need that." From every store I went into, I came out with bags of "stuff" with no plan in mind. The kids and I sat down with boxes of photos and bags of stuff and in no time at all we had a big mess and only one page done. It was not fun.

Being organized has got to be the first priority on the list before beginning.

Organize Your Space

Arrange a place or even designate a "spot" where your supplies and photos are going to be stored. If at all possible, set up a table that can be left up with all of the supplies at hand. This will save time in having to gather the supplies and photos each time you would like to work on a page.

Organize Your Memories

Wash hands thoroughly before handling photos. Natural oils from skin can be harmful to photos, so even clean hands must be washed frequently while working on scrapbooks. When possible, try to handle photos by the edges or wear lightweight gloves.

When you receive the photos back from developing, discard any photos that are out of focus—a blank wall or the back of someone's head. Take a moment to identify the who, what, where, when, how, and why of each photo. Then, later, when you are ready to create the scrapbook page, the memories and thoughts will be fresh in your mind and it will make journaling easier. Write the information on the back or top edges of the photo, using a photo safe labeling pencil.

Many varieties of labeling pencils can be used to safely write on both front or back of a photo and will wipe off with a tissue. Do not use a ballpoint, felt tip, or water-based pen to label photos. These pens may create indentation lines on the photo's face and their inks may eventually bleed through, becoming visible on the face of the photo.

Next, sort these and any other photos and memorabilia that you may already have sitting in that drawer or shoe box. Obtain a box for each member of your family. I suggest a larger box to hold memorabilia, drawings, and special school papers; and another box specifically for photos. These boxes should be acid-free. There are many styles available and they are just the right size to protect the photos. Label the boxes either by the year or by the event.

Employ the knowledge of friends and family members to help identify dates, people, places, and events pictured (a family reunion or gathering is a good place to find such help).

This will take a bit of time, but once they are organized, the photos and momentos will be easily found and the craft of scrapbooking will be a positive experience instead of a headache.

Organize Your Supplies

Here is a list of basic supplies you will need to get started:

Adhesives (acid-free)
Card stock (acid-free)
Photo album
Photo corners
Photo safe pencil
Scissors
Sheet protectors (acid-free) (optional)
Templates
Transparent ruler

Adhesives: There are several different types of adhesives for mounting photos, ground paper, die-cuts, etc. When choosing any adhesive, make certain it is acid-free and photo-safe.

The adhesive a scrapbooker chooses is a personal preference. Some of the different products available are:

Glue stick—This is a basic glue that you may already have at home. It is clean and easy to use. It works well for mounting die-cuts and punch-outs.

Mounting tape—This adhesive is best to use for mounting a photo onto a prefinished photo matte.

Photo sticker squares—Although these double-sided tape squares were developed for adhering a photo, they can be used to adhere just about anything. These are quick and easy.

Wet bond—This is a liquid glue that is available with a jumbo tip for larger coverage or a pencil tip for smaller projects.

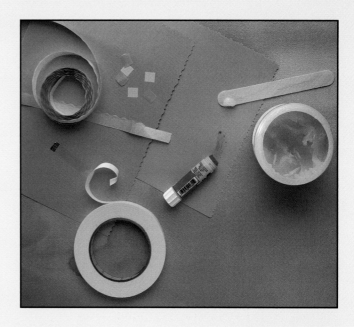

Card Stock: Acid-free colored card stock is one of my favorite items to use on a page because it adds color and dimension without detracting from the photos. It is inexpensive and, by adding the effect of a few different decorative-edged scissors, a thousand layouts can be created. Card stock comes in hundreds of colors, textures, and weights. Be certain to familiarize yourself with the product available.

Card stock is the most widely used paper for scrapbooking and comes in lightweight, medium weight, and heavy weight (sometimes referred to as cover weight). Decide which weight works best for your purposes. Here are a few characteristics to consider:

Lightweight card stock—Choose this weight when you want to use decorative-edged scissors and craft punches, as it leaves a very clean edge. Lightweight card stock is not the best for the ground or background sheet, as it tends to be flimsy once photos are mounted onto it.

Medium-weight card stock—This weight is the most widely used as it is acts well as a ground paper and also is easy to cut with decorative-edged scissors and craft punches.

Heavy-weight card stock—I like to use this weight whenever possible for the ground or background paper, making the page very sturdy. Avoid using this weight when using decorative-edged scissors or punches. The thickness of the paper wears the blades and results in unclean cuts.

Photo Album: Albums and binders are available in all sizes, colors, styles, and formats. The main difference between scrapbooks is in the binding. Album bindings should allow pages to lie flat. Choose from three-ring binders, expandable binders, and bound scrapbooks.

Take some time to decide the size of album you want to use. The 12" x 12" format allows more space to arrange the photos, whereas there may be a larger assortment of stationery and decorative papers available in the 8½" x 11" format.

One approach may be to have at least one album for each family member and another to represent the entire family. Choose a scrapbook album that allows for the greatest amount of flexibility and creativity.

Photo Corners: Photo corners have been used for many years to secure photos on a page without adhering the photo itself. Today, photo corners are available in a variety of styles and colors from transparent to gold and silver.

Decorative photo corners—These photo corners are laser-cut and come flat in a sheet. They need to be folded and assembled and require the use of an adhesive, but they are well worth the time.

Mounting corners—These photo corners are available in a wide range of colors. They are made of heavy paper and must be moistened to adhere onto the page.

Transparent photo corners—These photo corners are self-adhesive. They are designed to hold a photo without detracting from the photo.

302

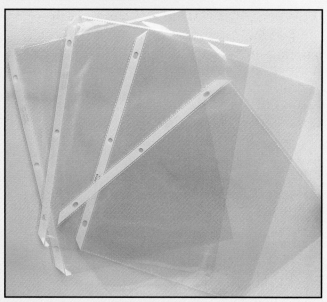

Photo Safe Labeling Pencil: A photo labeling pencil should be used for recording information about the photo and for tracing a stencil or template to a photo.

Scissors: It is important to have a good sharp pair of scissors to ensure clean lines. I prefer to use the type that has a spring in the handle which makes it so your hand does not get tired when cutting for a long time. The spring makes it very easy when cutting around shapes—especially ovals and circles. I use a large pair for general cutting and a small pair for small intricate cuts.

Sheet Protectors: Sheet protectors envelope the scrapbook pages and keep photos on facing pages from rubbing together. They are available in both 12" x 12" and 8½" x 11" formats—for both the three-ring binder and the expandable binder pages. Sheet protectors come in different weights and finishes from nonglare to high-gloss. Choose one that you are comfortable working with and stay consistent from book to book.

Top-loading sheet protectors—These are available in both 12" x 12" and 8½" x 11" formats.

Templates: Templates are used to crop photos and papers into shapes, such as hearts, circles, stars, balloons, etc., to eliminate unnecessary background or to match a theme.

Templates are available in a wide range of shapes and sizes. Transparent templates are useful for exact placement of the design. Cookie cutters also work well as templates

Position templates over item to be trimmed, trace shape, and cut out. Use a photo safe labeling pencil when tracing to a photo as any remnant tracing will wipe off with a tissue.

Transparent Ruler: I use a transparent ruler on almost every page I create. Getting straight lines and making certain the photo is adhered straight are very important on a scrapbook page, and this ruler makes it easy to achieve both.

Beyond the Basic Supplies

As interest grows, so will a collection of fun-to-have supplies. The following is a listing of the many available supplies that I would recommend for quick and easy ways to complete your pages.

Circle Cutter: This tool adjusts to the desired diameter of the circle. It makes a perfectly clean circular cut. The circle cutter is great when a template does not have the exact size of circle you may need.

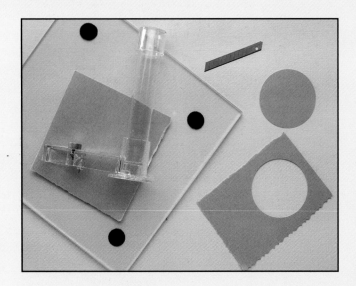

Corner Rounders: These are similar in appearance to craft punches. They trim square corners off photos and papers, leaving curved corners.

Corner Templates: These are used to trim corners on photos and papers into shapes. Position clear acrylic templates over item to be trimmed, trace shape, and cut. Use a photo labeling pencil when tracing to a photo as any remnant tracing will wipe off with a tissue.

Clip-art: Lined art images are available in booklets to copy and cut to accent scrapbook pages. Clip-art is also available in the form of computer software and can be printed to paper and cut out for quick and easy page decorations.

Color Wheel: This tool is a visual representation of the spectrum of colors in the shape of a wheel. When choosing colors, select a primary color and use the wheel to choose complementary colors.

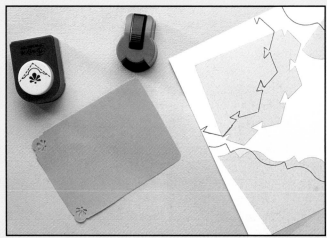

Craft Knife: A knife with a replaceable blade makes cutting straight edges and tight corners clean and easy.

Craft Punches: These are available in several sizes and motifs, from hearts to dinosaurs, stars to palm trees, and more. These are used to punch colored paper or card stock for small shapes to enhance a page.

Crimper: A crimper corrugates papers and cards, adding dimension and texture to a page.

Decorative-edged Scissors: Use these fun scissors to cut paper with distinctive edges. There are several different edges to choose from to accent any theme.

Avoid cutting photos with decorative-edged scissors. These scissors are primarily for cutting and trimming card stock.

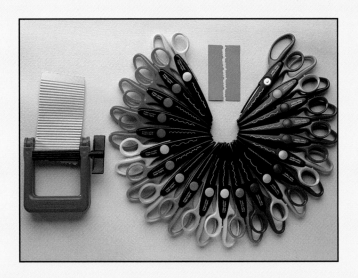

Die-cuts: Die-cuts are available in several colors and sizes. They are cut from varied weights of paper and are a quick way to add thematic shapes and colors to a page. Die-cuts can be purchased individually or in theme packets. Many paper stores have a die-cut machine that patrons can use to cut their own papers, to get both the shape and color they desire.

Embossing Stencils: These brass plates are available in several designs that can be gently pressed into scrapbook papers, creating a raised effect.

Lettering Booklets: Learn creative techniques of writing and decorating the alphabet. These booklets demonstrate how to complete styles, such as dot, outline, and block lettering. Refer to photo on page 306.

Light Box: Available in varied sizes, these boxes have an acrylic top and a light enclosed within. Use them to transfer clip-art or lettering designs directly to the ground paper or paper label. Place the design, right side up, on a light box and the ground paper or paper label on top, right side up. Trace the design to the paper. Note: This technique can be duplicated by holding the design and ground paper or paper label up to a sunlit window. Refer to photo on page 306.

Paper Cutter: A good compact paper cutter is a nice addition to your tools. It will cut the 12" x 12" paper, extend out to 15" for measuring left- or right-handed, and has an inexpensive replaceable blade. I often use this to cut ground paper and trim photos.

Novelty-edged Rulers: These rulers are used to create a continuous pattern along one or more edges of a paper. Patterns include wavy, zigzag, scallop, and more. Position clear acrylic rulers on paper, trace pattern, and cut.

Paper: Add dimension and color to a scrapbook with paper. Card stock (mentioned on page 13) is a heavier weight paper often used as a ground paper or for creating die-cuts. Decorative or novelty papers and stationery are often used for page backgrounds and to create patterns and borders.

Pens, Pencils & Markers: Use these for labeling, highlighting, and journaling. Make certain pens and markers are fade-proof, waterproof, and use pigment ink. Pens and markers are available in all colors and with several different tips, such as .01 tip for creating fine lines, and tiny accents; .05 tip for standard clean lines; and a 45˚ angle for calligraphic effect for titles and special emphasis. Colored pencils that are water-resistant and light-fast can also be used to decorate scrapbook pages.

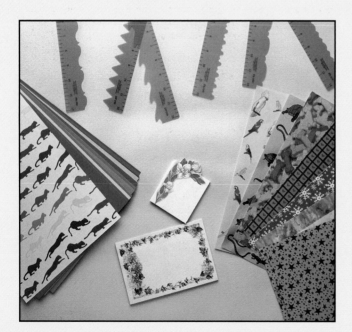

pH Testing Pen: This amazing pen instantly tests acid content of paper.

Premade Photo Mattes: These are available in several colors. Embossed and of card stock thickness, these can be used to matte studio portrait photos.

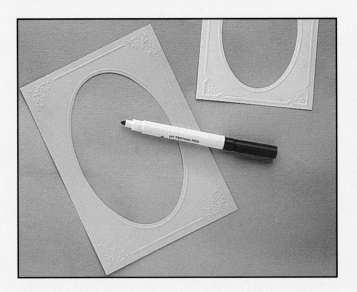

Red Eye Pen: This pen fixes red eyes on photos. It contains a dye that filters out the color red, allowing natural eye features to show through.

Rubber Stamps, Pigment Ink Pads, Embossing Powder & Heat Tool: There are numerous individual rubber stamps, rubber stamp kits, and pigment ink pads available to use to enhance a scrapbook page. After stamping, color in the designs with pigment ink brush markers and/or apply colored embossing powder and heat-set with a heat tool.

Stickers: Stickers are available in all sorts of themes, sizes, and colors. They add instant artistic impact, or color, or humor.

Organize Your Storage

Once you have collected a few basic supplies, store them in a safe place. Shoe boxes with lids work great for storing adhesives, craft punches, and scissors.

Tools such as these can also be stored in clear, plastic, stackable drawers. Portable canvas bags with multiple pockets also prove useful for storing and carrying needed supplies.

Keep items such as stickers, die cut shapes, punch shapes, papers, and scraps either in zipper-type baggies with holes punched along one side of the bags, or in clear 2" x 2" slide size, 3½" x 2" sports card size, 4" x 6" photo size, or 8½" x 11" top-loading protector sheets. Organize them by occasion and color and store them together in a 3-ring binder.

I believe it is important to keep your supplies handy and in a safe place, so the time you spend scrapbooking is time spent creating instead of searching for the lost scissors or glue sticks.

Creating Scrapbook Pages

Once you have gathered and organized your supplies, you are ready to begin creating pages. Here are a few tips for a smooth start.

Sharing Costs

Sharing the expense can really ease the cost of scrapbooking supplies. If a group of friends gets together on the cost of some supplies, such as the decorative-edged scissors and craft punches, you will all have a larger variety of products to create with. Also, there is such a large number of styles of scissors—where do you start? Before you make a large purchase, start with the basics and share the others.

Color-copying Photos

One important tool you may want to consider is a laser or color copier. Copy the photo that seems to be missing its negative or an older photo of parents or grandparents. The laser copier is so advanced that you can make a copy of an old black-and-white photo and mount it onto a page. Black-and-whites are so important to have in photo albums. I have made many laser copies of old photos, framed the copies, and shared them as Christmas presents. What a treat!

Finding a Starting Point

Start where you feel the most comfortable. This may be designing a page for last month's birthday or last year's Christmas celebration. The idea is to just start. Once your first few pages are complete, the rest will become very easy.

Layout

For each page, choose two to four photos. Be selective when choosing and mounting photos. They should be well-focused, interesting, and varied.

The layout of the pages seems to frighten people the most. In 90% of designs, the triangle rule is the easiest to follow. On pages that have more than one photo, place them in a triangle pattern. Refer to examples below.

The placement of stickers, die-cuts, and memorabilia can also follow this same rule.

After practicing this rule on a few pages you will find it easier to do. The pages are more pleasing to the eye because they are balanced.

Finding Balance

Do not feel like every inch of the paper needs to be filled up with stickers or lettering. A very simple rule to follow is, "Less is sometimes better." Remember that the photo is supposed to be the main focus, not the sticker or the printed ground paper. Leave some empty areas, or negative space, and you will find that these are much more appealing pages to look at.

There are some pages that lend themselves to a lot of stuff. Refer to "Life as a Teen" on page 76. This page is purposely filled to capacity because of the intent. However, you should keep these pages few and far between.

Scrapbooking Terms

Sometimes it seems as if scrapbookers speak their own language. The following listing of common terms will help you feel comfortable when you visit the local scrapbook store.

Adhere: Adhering is the actual process of mounting the item or photo, using mounting strips, glue, or photo corners.

Background Paper: Background paper is the paper used as a border onto which the ground paper is adhered or mounted.

Crop: This term is often used to refer to a gathering of friends on a set date at a set time and place to work together on individual scrapbooks and share supplies and ideas for pages. Scrapbookers often plan monthly get-togethers that last for several hours and include potluck-style refreshments. The crop can be held in a scrapbooker's home or in a larger facility, such as a church building. Sometimes a crop is the main event in a getaway weekend with family or friends.

Cropping Photos: Many scrapbook designers will choose to crop, or cut, photos to remove unwanted background, emphasizing the foreground or people, and to create fun shapes. Snapshots, which are often incorrectly framed at the time of photographing the subject, are candidates for cropping. This technique will not affect the stability of a photo. Cropping is completely safe, but it is irreversible. Consider cropping color copies of irreplaceable one-of-a-kind photos.

Cropping studio photos is not recommended, since professional photos are typically framed well, with little unnecessary background. Studio portraits can be framed with decorative paper cutouts or premade photo mattes. NEVER crop an instant photo. Make color copies of instant photos. The color copies can then be cropped as desired and added to pages.

Ground Paper: Ground paper is that onto which the photos are adhered or mounted.

Journaling: Journaling is documenting photos by either hand-writing or lettering names, dates, and events—again, the who, what, where, when, how, and why—on the ground paper. Write personal feelings and humorous captions about the event. Include family stories, poems, and songs that correspond with the photo. For a child's scrapbook, write down first words, favorite phrases, and any grammatical errors and manners of speech to capture the child's development over time.

When adding a journal entry that is quite lengthy, type it or use a computer to avoid making mistakes that would cause you to have to start again.

Lettering: Lettering is the technique of creatively writing and decorating words, phrases, and titles. This technique makes the text an element of page design, drawing attention to the words. There are many different styles to choose from. Write the words in the lettering style on the page in pencil first, then go over pencil with a pen or marker.

Memorabilia: The purpose of creating a scrapbook is to provide a place to keep "scraps!" Tangible reminders of people, places, and events can include any of the following memorabilia.

Announcements
Awards
Birth certificates, hospital bracelets, sonogram
    copies, etc.
Brochures
Certificates
Children's drawings
Greeting cards
Handprints
Letters
Locks of hair
Maps
Marriage licenses
Menus
Newspaper clippings
Obituaries
Post cards
Programs
Report cards
Ribbons
Ticket stubs
Wedding invitations

Make certain to use page protectors to keep these momentos in place.

Pocket Pages: To hold memorabilia separate from a photo page, create a pocket page by gluing two ground papers together along bottom and both sides. Remember to cut a curve into the top edge of the top page for easy access to the contents of the pocket page.

Creating an Archival-quality Scrapbook

Many scrapbookers want their scrapbooks to be archival, or able to stand the test of time. The primary enemy to this goal is acid.

An object that has a pH less than 7.0 is said to have acid, an unstable chemical substance that will weaken paper and photos, leading to yellowing and brittleness. Items kept in a scrapbook or used to decorate the pages should be acid-free or have a pH of 7.0 or more.

When shopping for paper for pages, choose acid-free, lignin-free papers which have had acid removed from the manufacturing process or have been treated to neutralize acids.

Buffered paper, which is not only acid-free, but is also acid-absorbent. Buffered paper has added calcium carbonate that will absorb acid that may come into contact with the paper. Many designers will use buffered paper at the front and back of a scrapbook to protect pages from gasses or acids given off by the binder.

Archival-quality paper may be slightly more expensive, but the expense is worthwhile. Scrapbooks made with low-quality, highly acidic papers will fade and tear over time. Low-quality paper may even irreversibly damage the very photos a scrapbook is intended to protect.

Scrapbook suppliers also sell acid-free stickers, cards, photo corners, and pens to complement acid-free background paper and photos. Permanent pigment pens are the best, since their colors last longer and are less likely to run or smear over time. Read the label on any pen, or call the manufacturer's customer service line if the label does not indicate if the pen is acid-free.

Although a product may start out acid-free, there is no guarantee it will stay that way. Acid can move into the product from other high-acid objects in close contact, from environmental pollutants, or even from contact with oils in human hands. Acid from high-acid products will always migrate to acid-free products.

Do not use crepe paper or construction paper in a scrap book. These papers will fade and tear quickly, and their colors may bleed onto photos.

Remember, never place photos in a "magnetic page" self-adhesive photo album. Self-adhesive albums are covered in polyvinyl chloride (PVC), a plastic that releases hydrochloric acid. Acids will actually eat away at pictures, causing them to become yellow and brittle. To make matters worse, the adhesives in these albums will absorb into photos over time, making them difficult, if not impossible, to remove.

Adhesives used for scrapbooks can also be a source of potential damage. Do not use regular transparent tape, high-acid rubber cement, super glue, or high-acid craft glue in a scrapbook. There are several acid-free adhesives on the market. Carefully read product labels to make certain adhesives are acid-free before using them. If there is a question, call the product customer service line.

Truly archival-quality scrapbooks should be reversible. This means that photos placed in the scrapbook can be taken out again with no resulting damage. To make this possible, a scrapbook designer would need to use either a removable adhesive, or photo corners to secure photos.

Don'ts
The following items and practices should be avoided when compiling scrapbooks:

Ballpoint pen on photos
Construction and crepe paper
Cropping instant photos
Cropping very old or priceless photos
Exposing scrapbooks to water, exhaust, humidity, insects, extreme heat, or direct light
Felt-tip and water-based pens
Fingerprints on photos
Magnetic self-adhesive photo albums and pages
Masking tape
PVC plastic pages
Rubber cement
Storing scrapbooks and photo negatives in the same location
Transparent tape

Important Reminders
Do not forget to "journal" on your pages. The photos are visually interesting, but reading about the story behind the photos is necessary for future generations. Consider inserting actual journal pages into the album every so often. Children's words to a conversation or prayer are always wonderful to read about later—especially for the child as he or she grows older.

Keep in mind the true purpose to putting together a scrapbook—getting the photos into a safe, dry place. If your interest does not include adding stickers, die-cuts, etc., concentrate on mounting and labeling the photos. Protect the memories that can easily fade.

How do I mount a photo onto ground paper?

What You Need to Get Started:

2 photos per page
Adhesive
Card stock: brown for ground paper
Pencil

Start out simple when beginning to scrapbook. The main idea and focus is to get the photos into an album to protect them, instead of being piled into a box "somewhere" in the basement. Some of us prefer this simple style where the photos are nicely displayed on a page without a lot of decoration.

Basic Mounting

Here's How:
1. Arrange the photos on the ground paper as desired.

3. Remove the photos from the ground paper.

4. Beginning with the photos that are closest to the ground paper (if your photos overlap), apply adhesive to the back of each photo. Adhere them onto the ground paper, as marked, one at a time.

2. Using the pencil, lightly mark around the corners of the photos.

Troubleshooting:

Look for adhesives that are acid-free or that are labeled photo safe, meaning that the manufacturer has taken extra steps to ensure that the adhesive is free of materials that might damage the photo.

Avoid adhesives that emit odors or fumes. This is often a sign that the adhesive contains elements which can damage the photo.

Design Tip:

Experiment with different types of adhesives to find those that will make scrapbbooking easy and fun for you. There is such a wide variety to choose from—permanent or temporary, pen or stick, tape or tabs.

How do I create paper frames?

What You Need to Get Started:

2 photos per page
Adhesive
Card stock: brown for ground paper; ivory
Scissors

Placing a paper frame behind a photo gives it a finished look. Hold your photo next to several different colors of card stock to determine which color will best complement the image. Choose a contrasting ground paper so the paper frame stands out against the background.

Paper Frame Mounts

Here's How:
1. Apply adhesive to the back of each photo. Adhere them onto ivory card stock, allowing enough space around the entire photo for a paper "frame."

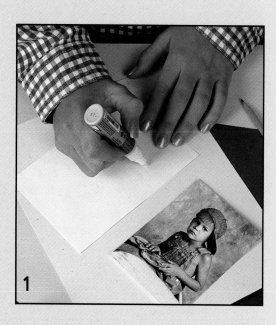

3. Refer to on page 312. Arrange and adhere the photos onto the ground paper.

2. Using scissors, cut the card stock ⅜" larger than the large photos all around and ¼" larger than the smaller photos all around.

1 photo per page
Adhesive
Card stock:
  olive green
  speckled for
  ground paper
Decorative
  border: light
  brown with
  vine design
Decorative paper:
  vine print for
  background
  paper
Decorative photo
  corners: light
  brown with
  vine design
Paper cutter
Pencil
Scissors
Transparent ruler

How do I mount ground paper onto background paper and use photo corners?

Photo corners are mostly for photos that you may not want permanently mounted in the photo album. Photos can be easily removed and used for other purposes. Some photo corners are self-adhesive while others may require the use of an adhesive to adhere them to the scrapbook page.

Decorative Corner Mounts

Here's How:

1. Using the pencil, transparent ruler, and paper cutter, measure, mark, and cut ¾" off of the bottom and one side of the ground paper.

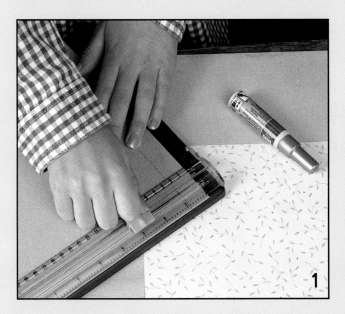

2. Apply adhesive to the back of the ground paper. Adhere it onto the center of the background paper, creating a ⅜" border.

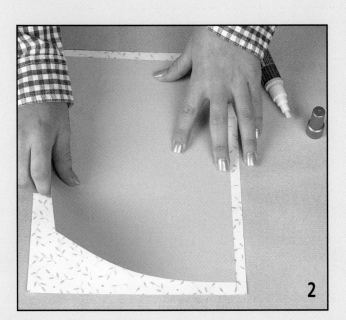

3. Arrange the photo on the ground paper as desired. Apply adhesive to the back of the decorative photo corner. Hold the photo in place with one hand and carefully slide a corner over the photo, adhering it onto the ground paper. Repeat for the opposite corner and then the two remaining corners.

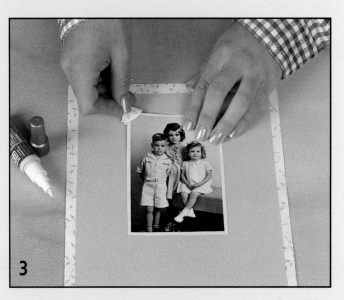

4. Using the scissors, trim the decorative border to fit the width of the ground paper. Apply adhesive to the back of the decorative border. Adhere it onto the ground paper.

Design Tips:

Depending on the type of photo corners you choose, there are a couple of different ways of adhering the corners onto the ground paper. Refer to *Photos Corners* on page 302 for options.

If the decorative photo corners are being used as decorative elements, apply photo sticker squares to the backs of the corners and adhere them onto the sides of the photo instead of at the corners.

How do I use premade photo mattes on a printed ground paper?

What You Need to Get Started:

2 photos per page
Adhesive
Decorative paper: rose print for ground paper
Marker: 0.5 mm black liner
Paper labels
Premade photo mattes to fit photos
Tape

Pre-made photo mattes are prefect for framing professional studio photos. They are cut to a standard size, which makes centering the photos very easy. Most mattes have embossed designs that add texture but do not take away from the image in the photo. Because the mattes are a solid color, they balance out a printed background that may otherwise be too heavy or overpowering.

Pre-made Photo Mattes

Here's How:
1. Place pre-made photo mattes face down on the work surface. Center each photo face down on the matte.

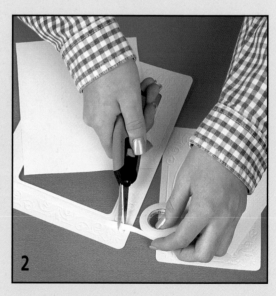

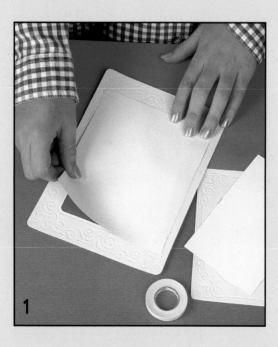

3. Using the marker, add journaling to the paper labels.

4. Refer to page 312. Arrange and adhere the matted photos and paper labels onto the ground paper.

2. Place tape on the sides of the photo matte and adhere the photo.

318

Design Tips:

It is easier to tape the photo behind the frame, and then adhere the frame onto the background. It is much more difficult if you try to adhere the photo and then the frame.

Avoid mistakes by centering the photo correctly before adhering it onto either the matte or the ground paper.

How do I use paper with printed frames?

What You Need to Get Started:

3 photos per page
Adhesive
Card stock: ivory
Craft knife and cutting mat
Decorative paper: print with frames
Marker: 0.5 mm black liner
Scissors
Tape

The page design is already created for you. Simply insert your favorite photos. This process makes completing several pages in one sitting quick and worry-free.

Pre-printed Frames

Here's How:

1. Using the craft knife and cutting mat, cut out openings within printed frames on the decorative paper.

2. Refer to page 318. Treat this piece of paper as a premade photo matte. Place paper face down on the work surface. Center each photo face down on the openings. Tape the sides of each photo to the back of the paper.

3. Apply adhesive to the back of the paper complete with photos. Adhere it to a piece of card stock that is the same size as the decorative paper. The cardstock will protect the back side of the photos.

4. Using the marker, add journaling to the page.

320

How do I use different patterned papers together?

Layering different patterned papers is a great way to make one photo on a page stand out. Do not be afraid to use several papers on one page.

Contrasting Patterns

Here's How:

1. Using the pencil, transparent ruler, and paper cutter, measure, mark, and cut 2" off the top and one side of the ground paper.

2. Apply adhesive to the back of the ground paper. Adhere it onto the center of the background paper.

3. Refer to page 322. Crop the photo as desired.

4. Refer to page 314. Adhere the photo onto the light blue speckled card stock. Cut the light blue card stock ¼" larger than the photo all around.

5. Adhere the light blue speckled card stock onto the dark blue card stock. Cut the dark blue card stock ¼" larger than the light blue speckled card stock all around.

6. Adhere the dark blue card stock onto the ground paper, ⅜" from the top and centered from side to side.

7. To make a paper label, cut a 3½" x 1" piece of tan striped paper. Adhere the tan striped paper onto dark blue card stock. Cut the dark blue card stock ⅛" larger than the tan striped paper all around.

8. Adhere the dark blue card stock onto light blue speckled card stock. Cut the light blue speckled card stock ⅛" larger than the dark blue card stock all around.

9. Using the marker, add journaling to the paper label.

10. Adhere the light blue speckled card stock onto the ground paper, ¼" from the photo and centered from side to side.

What You Need to Get Started:

1 photo per page
Adhesive
Card stock: dark blue; light blue speckled
Decorative-edged scissors: zigzag
Marker: 1.2 mm black liner
Paper: blue plaid for background paper; tan striped; tan striped for ground paper
Paper cutter
Pencil
Scissors
Template: rectangle
Transparent ruler

August 1994

How do I use a template to crop photos?

What You Need to Get Started:

2 photos per page
Adhesive
Card stock: olive green speckled; sage green speckled; ivory; tan parchment for background paper; tan speckled for ground paper
Decorative-edged scissors: stamp
Markers: 0.5 mm black liner; 1.2 mm black liner
Paper cutter
Pencil: soft lead
Scissors
Templates: oval; rectangle
Transparent ruler

Cropping becomes necessary when there is a lot of wasted space around the image on which you are focusing. Crop out the undesirable portions to make the most of your photo.

Cropping with a Template

Here's How:

1. Using the pencil, transparent ruler, and paper cutter, measure, mark, and cut ½" off the top and one side of the ground paper.

2. Using the decorative-edged scissors, trim all sides of the ground paper.

3. Apply adhesive to the back of the ground paper. Adhere it onto the center of the background paper, creating a ⅜" border.

4. To crop each photo, place the template over the photo to the best position. Using the pencil, trace the shape onto the photo.

5. Using scissors, cut around the pencil line on each photo. For a smooth cutting line, follow these steps:

• If you are right-handed, hold the photo in your left hand then, with your right hand, open the scissors all the way. Place the photo to the inside "v" of the scissors.

• Make the cut, using all but ¾" from the tip of the blade before opening the scissors again.

• Use long smooth cuts instead of short choppy ones and turn or guide the photo with your left hand not with the scissors.

• Do not cut all the way to the tip of the scissors in the middle of a shape as the paper tends to split.

6. Refer to page 314. Adhere corresponding photos onto the coordinating card stock. Cut the card stock ⅜" larger than the photo all around.

7. Using the decorative-edged scissors, cut a 6¼" x 1¼" piece of ivory card stock. Adhere the ivory card stock onto the sage green card stock. Using scissors, cut the sage green card stock ½" larger than the ivory card stock all around.

8. Using the 0.5 mm marker, add journaling to the ivory card stock.

9. Apply adhesive to the back of the sage green card stock. Adhere it onto the ground paper, centered from side to side and ¼" from the bottom.

10. Refer to page 312. Arrange and adhere the photos onto the ground paper.

11. Using the 1.2 mm marker, add journaling to the ground paper near the photos.

Design Tips:
The children were the focal point in the upper photo, but the excessive background was detracting. Cropping the image brought the focus back to the children and actually made them appear larger.

In the bottom photo, cropping in tight on the child, and using an oval shape to accentuate the hat, gave me the "close up" effect that I was looking for.

Practice first before tracing a template and cutting original photos. If this is your first time cropping a photo or cutting

around corners and ovals, I suggest making color copies of some photos and using them to practice cropping and cutting.

Ovals are the hardest shape to cut. You want smooth cuts—not jagged edges or straight cuts where the line begins to curve. It is better to have a pile of practice sheets instead of a pile of photos that are cropped and cut not to your liking.

Use different sizes and shapes of cropping templates to add interest to the page.

How do I use corner punches and craft punches?

The corner rounder is perfect for rounding the corners of the photo instead of using scissors. The tool is easy to use and all of the corners will match. One simple way to enhance a page is by punching a motif from corners and edges. Use the punched out images for added design around the page.

Decorative Punch-outs

Here's How:

1. Using the corner rounder punch, insert the corner of the photo into the punch and round each corner.

2. Refer to page 314. Adhere photo onto the dark green card stock. Cut the card stock ⅜" larger than the photo all around.

3. Using the snowflake punch, punch each corner of the of dark green card stock. Note: When you are punching out motifs in the corners, it is hard to see the placement. Turn the punch upside down, slide the card stock in, and punch. The punch is harder to hold this way, but you can see the placement of the motif easier.

4. Apply adhesive to the back of the dark green card stock. Adhere it onto the cream card stock. Cut the cream card stock ¼" larger than the dark green card stock all around.

5. Apply adhesive to the back of the cream card stock. Adhere it onto the ground paper.

6. Refer to page 314 to create a paper label. Using scissors, cut a 3¾" x 1¼" piece of white card stock. Apply adhesive to the back of the white card stock. Adhere it onto the dark green card stock. Cut the dark green card stock ⅛" larger than the white card stock all around. Adhere the dark green card stock onto the cream card stock. Cut the cream card stock ¼" larger than the dark green card stock all around. Using the corner rounder, round the corners of the cream card stock.

7. Using markers, add journaling to the paper label.

8. Apply adhesive to the back of the paper label. Adhere it onto the ground paper.

9. Using the snowflake punch, punch approximately 25 snowflakes from the white card stock.

10. Apply adhesive to the backs of the snowflakes. Randomly adhere them onto the ground paper and photo frame.

Troubleshooting:
The more intricate the craft punch, the more the blades will stick after punching. To release the button, press the dot of the design on the underside where the paper comes up, using a ballpoint pen.

Punch through waxed paper several times to lubricate the blades.

When the cuts from the punch are not very clean, punch through very fine sand paper several times to sharpen the blades.

Design Tip:
Overlap the punch designs onto the photo border. This will add some dimension.

"BEST BUDDIES"
Mason and Cody playing in their snow cave. February 2 '97

How do I use templates to embellish pages?

What You Need to Get Started:

2 photos per page
Adhesive
Card stock: white; yellow floral for ground paper; yellow quilted for ground paper; yellow striped for background paper
Decorative-edged scissors: cloud; scallop
Handwritten words or computerized lettering
Marker: 1.2 mm green liner
Paper: blue plaid
Paper label: coordinating
Pencil
Scissors
Templates: circle; oval; rectangle; scallop-edged
Transparent ruler

Most of the new templates have a decorative-edged border. This is a larger design not found on decorative-edged scissors. I like to use these templates to divide up larger areas of paper—like the 12" x 12" papers. The templates take a little more time to use, but add a bit more variety to the pages.

Embellishing with Templates

Note: If this is your first time working with stencils, begin with a very simple edge and work up to more difficult lines.

Here's How:
1. Using the transparent ruler, pencil, and paper cutter, measure, mark, and cut 1" off one side of the ground paper. (If you are using 8½" x 11" paper, measure from the 8½" width.)

2. Place the scallop-edged template along the cut edge. Trace the design. Some of the decorative-edged templates may not be long enough to accommodate the 12" x 12" scrapbook pages. After tracing the design along the edge of your paper, slide the template up and continue the pattern.

3. Using scissors, carefully cut along traced line. Cut slowly to get nice smooth lines.

4. Cut a 1½" strip of white card stock that is the length of your page. Place the scallop-edged template along one

long edge and trace the design. Carefully cut along traced line.

5. Cut a 3" strip of background paper that is the length of your page.

6. Apply adhesive to the back of the ground paper along the scalloped edge only. Position the scalloped white card stock strip under the ground paper so about ⅛" of white is extending beyond the ground paper. Adhere them together.

7. Apply adhesive to the back of the white card stock strip along the scalloped edge only. Position the 3" strip of background paper under the ground paper and white card stock so the total width is equal to the total width of your page. Adhere them together.

8. Refer to page 322. Using templates, a pencil, and scissors, crop selected photos as desired. Refer to page 324. Round each corner of desired photos.

9. Refer to page 314. Adhere photos onto the white card stock. Cut the card stock ¼" larger than the large photos and ⅛" larger than the smaller photos all around.

10. Using the cloud decorative-edged scissors, trim the edges of the journal entry paper. Adhere the journal entry paper onto the blue plaid paper. Using scissors, cut the blue plaid paper ½" larger than the journal entry paper all around.

11. Using the 1.2 mm liner marker, add journaling to the paper labels.

12. Refer to page 312. Arrange and adhere the photos, journal entry, and paper labels onto the ground paper.

April 1998

Mom and Dad let Rachel and Tyrel decide on the Spring-break vacation. They decided on the Casa Blanca in Mesquite Nevada.

They HAD to buy me all new stuff from my levi hat to my flower sunglasses. I was all set to go.

It was the perfect weekend and we all had a great time especially in the pool which had a waterslide and a beautiful waterfall surrounded by flower gardens and palm trees. I loved to watch the kids come down the slide and splash water at me at the bottom.

I kept the hat on most of the time but the flower sunglasses were better just to chew on. That grass was a bit "prickly" and would rather sit on dad's lap and play with the camera.

How do I use decorative-edged scissors?

Decorative-edged scissors are a wonderful way to dress up any paper frame or paper border. Most of these scissors will cut two different designs depending on how you hold them in your hand. Choose the edge that will best complement the photo or theme. Never use the decorative-edged scissors on the photo, as it detracts from the photo.

Decorative Edges

Here's How:

1. Using the pencil, transparent ruler, and paper cutter, measure, mark, and cut ½" off the top and one side of the ground paper.

2. Position the cloud decorative-edged scissors in your hand so the desired edge will cut. Trim all sides of the ground paper, matching up the edge design with each cut of the scissors.

3. Apply adhesive to the back of the ground paper. Adhere it onto the center of the background paper.

4. Refer to page 316. Arrange and adhere the photos and the decorative photo corners onto the light blue, lavender, and pink card stock, allowing enough space around the photo for creating a paper "frame."

5. Refer to page 314. Using decorative-edged scissors, cut the card stock ¼" larger than the photo all around.

6. Apply adhesive to the back of the paper label. Adhere it onto the light green card stock. Using decorative-edged scissors, cut card stock ⅛" larger than the paper label all around.

7. Using the markers, add journaling to the paper label.

8. Refer to page 312. Arrange and adhere each framed photo and the paper label onto the ground paper.

Easter
1994

How do I create puzzle pages?

What You Need to Get Started:

7 photos per page
Adhesive
Card stock: navy blue for ground paper; kraft for background paper; light kraft
Stencil: oval puzzle
Decorative-edged scissors: cloud
Marker: gold paint
Scissors

Puzzle templates take all the guesswork out of cropping. This technique is easily accomplished and uses several pictures on one page. A puzzle page is a fun addition to any photo album.

Puzzle Gallery

Here's How:

1. Using the transparent ruler, pencil, and decorative-edged scissors, measure, mark, and cut 1½" off two sides of the ground paper.

2. Using scissors, cut two 1½" x 12" strips from the light kraft card stock. Using the decorative-edged scissors, trim one long edge from each strip.

3. Apply adhesive to the back of the ground paper along the scalloped edges. Position the scalloped light kraft card stock strips under the ground paper so about ¼" of light kraft is extending beyond the ground paper and adhere them together.

4. Apply adhesive to the back of the ground paper with the scalloped light kraft strips. Adhere it onto the center of the background paper.

5. Refer to on page 322. Crop selected photos as desired.

6. Using the template as a guide, arrange the photos on the page with even spacing.

7. Apply adhesive to the back of each photo. Adhere them onto the ground paper one at a time.

8. Using the marker, add journaling to the ground paper.

Troubleshooting:

Use a small piece of removable tape to hold photos in place while adhering each photo permanently. It is important to space each photo evenly to achieve the puzzle effect.

Design Tip:

Decide upon a theme and keep to that theme. Use large subjects for each opening to simplify the look of it.

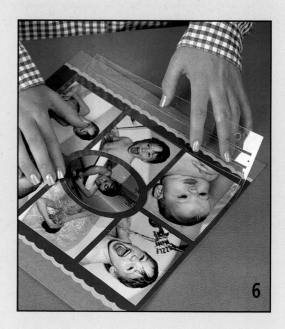

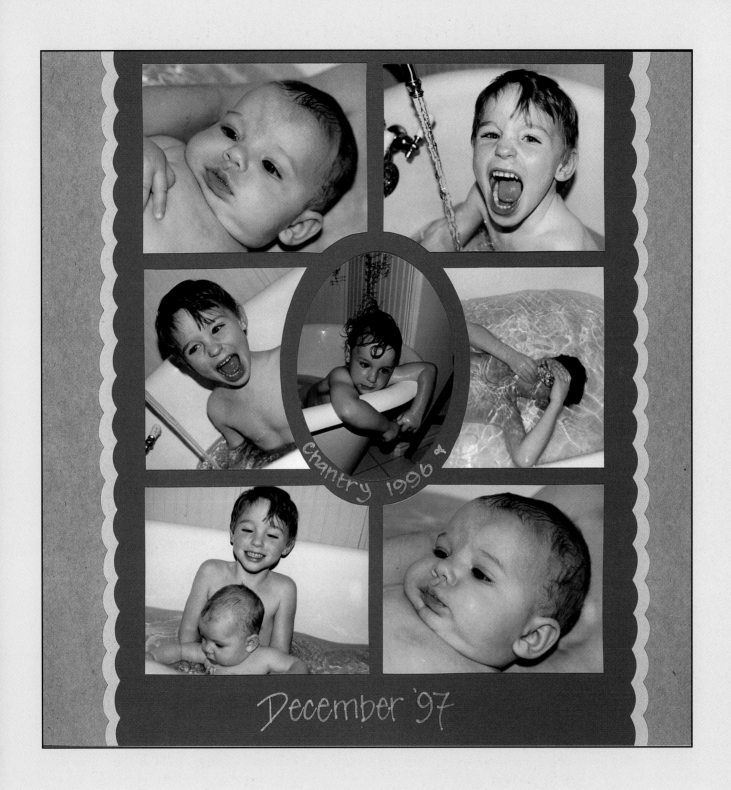

Chantry 1996 &

December '97

How do I silhouette photos?

What You Need to Get Started:

8–10 photos per page
Adhesive
Card stock:
green; red;
white for
ground paper;
Craft knife and
cutting mat
Decorative-edged
scissors: cloud
Die-cuts: birthday
cake; star
Markers: 0.5 mm
black liner;
1.2 mm black
liner
Pencil
Scissors
Templates: oval;
rectangle;
square
Transparent ruler

Silhouetting is perfect if you have a lot of photos of the same event. It is also great if there is a large group of people to show on the same layout.

Silhouetting Figures

Note: Make plenty of color copies for silhouettes so original photos are not ruined.

Here's How:

1. Using the transparent ruler, pencil, and cloud decorative-edged scissors, measure, mark, and cut ½" from the top and one side of the ground paper.

2. Apply adhesive to the back of the ground paper. Adhere it onto the of background paper, lining up the two uncut edges and leaving a colored border on the right and top edges. If you have a facing page, repeat with a second piece of ground paper and background paper, leaving a colored border on the left and top edges.

3. Refer to page 322. Crop photos to be used at the top of the page as desired.

4. Refer to page 314. Adhere one of the cropped photos onto green card stock. Cut the card stock ¼" larger than the photo all around.

5. Using a craft knife or scissors, carefully cut around the photographic or copied images to be used for silhouetting.

5

6. Arrange the blunt-edged silhouetted photos on the ground paper, lining them up along the bottom of the page, and placing them in varying heights, slightly overlapping them if necessary.

7. Arrange the cropped photos on the pages as desired.

8. Place remaining silhouetted photos on the pages as desired.

9. Using the die-cuts as "fillers," carefully slide them into place under and around silhouetted photos.

10. Apply adhesive to the back of each photo and die-cut. Adhere them onto the ground paper one at a time.

11. Using the markers, add journaling to the die-cuts, and ground paper.

areas, use a craft knife, as scissors may bend or tear the photo.

Design Tips:

Not all photos are right for this technique. If you have plenty of photos to use, give it a try. Use this technique sparingly throughout your album.

Choose just a few photos that depict the main event. This will give nice variety to the layout.

Photos with a blunt edge should be used toward the bottom of the page. Photos that can be cut all the way around can stand on their own.

To get into those hard-to-cut

How do I use decorative papers that have borders?

What You Need to Get Started:

1 class photo
1 portrait photo
Adhesive
Card stock: dark red
Decorative paper with border
Die-cuts: assorted
Pencil
Scissors
Template: oval
Transparent ruler

Combine a piece of decorative paper that has a border with a photo or two, a small die-cut, and perhaps a few stickers, and you have an almost instant scrapbook page.

Paper with Decorative Borders

Here's How:

1. Using the transparent ruler, pencil, and scissors, measure, mark, and trim the class photo to fit within the border on the decorative paper.

2. Refer to page 322. Crop the portrait photo as desired.

3. Refer to page 314. Adhere the photo onto card stock. Cut the card stock ¼" larger than the photo all around.

4. Refer to page 312. Arrange and adhere the photos and die-cuts onto the decorative paper.

Troubleshooting:

Avoid layering photos with a heavily printed paper as it becomes very busy and takes emphasis away from the border and more importantly, the photos. Use colored card stock to place behind photos. If your border is really busy, be selective about choosing die-cuts or stickers. Sometimes less is better.

How do I use die-cuts on a page?

What You Need to Get Started:

3 photos per page
Adhesive
Card stock: blue;
   dark sage
   green;
   sage green; tan
   for ground
   paper;
   yellow
Die-cuts: cloud;
   flame; logs;
   mountains;
   tent
Markers: 0.5 mm
   black liner;
   1.2 mm black
   liner
Opaque pens:
   blue;
   white
Pencil
Scissors
Templates: circle;
   oval; rectangle;
   square
Transparent ruler

This is an easy and inexpensive way to add design and color to a page. Die-cuts are ready-made and available in all colors, shapes, and sizes.

Set the Scene with Die-cuts

Here's How:
1. Refer to page 322. Crop selected photos as desired.

2. Refer to page 314. Adhere selected photos onto assorted colors of card stock. Cut the colored card stock ¼" larger than the large photos and ⅛" larger than the smaller photos all around.

3. Refer to page 312. Arrange and adhere the photos and die-cuts onto the ground paper.

4. Using the markers and opaque pens, add journaling to the die-cuts and ground paper.

Design Tip:
Do not be afraid to overlap the die-cuts with each other and also with the photos. Try using them as a background. Layering die-cuts and photos adds dimension to the pages.

How do I use stencils to decorate a page?

What You Need to Get Started:

3 photos per page
Acid-free paint
Adhesive
Adhesive dots: repositionable for stencils
Card stock: blue; brown; ivory for ground paper
Disposable palette
Makeup sponges
Paper towel
Pencil
Scissors
Stencil for memory page
Stickers: letters

Many stencils that were designed for decorative painting techniques easily cross over into the craft of scrapbooking. With just a bit of acid-free paint and a makeup sponge, you can add subtle colored images directly onto the ground paper.

Decorative Stenciling

Here's How:

1. Begin to create the border by centering the stencil along the bottom edge of the ground paper. Secure the stencil to the paper, using the repositionable stencil dots.

2. Pour a small amount of paint onto disposable palette. Dip makeup sponge into paint. Dab sponge on paper towel, removing excess paint.

3. Apply paint from the edge of the stencil onto the ground paper, lightly dabbing to avoid bending the stencil. The paint will be darker around the fish and lighter as it reaches the edge of the paper. Allow the paint to dry.

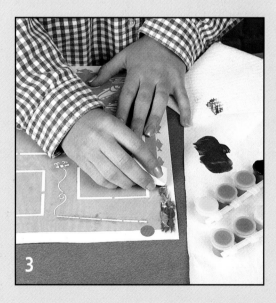

4. Repeat Steps 1–3 for the top edge of the ground paper.

5. Clean the stencil and flip it over. Repeat Steps 1–3 for both sides of the ground paper.

6. Stencil-paint the frames, fish, fishing pole, water, and cattails onto the

ground paper, lightly dabbing to avoid bending the stencil, from the outside toward the center of the motif.

7. Refer to page 322. Crop selected photos as desired.

8. Refer to page 312. Arrange and adhere the photos onto the ground paper within the painted frames.

Troubleshooting:

Begin stenciling slowly. This is a technique which requires patience. Use a small amount of paint to avoid the paint seeping under the stencil.

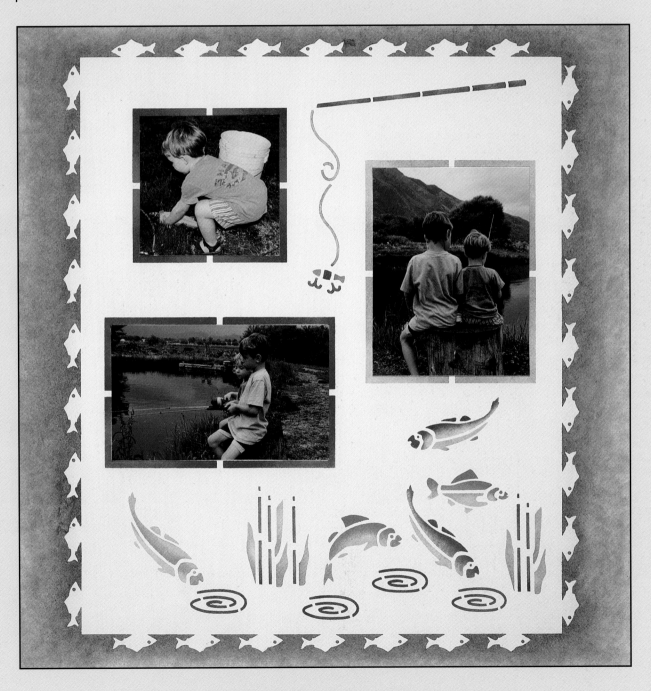

How do I use creative lettering on a page?

What You Need to Get Started:

3 photos per page
Adhesive
Card stock: light blue speckled for ground paper; red; tan speckled; teal; white; yellow
Craft knife and cutting mat
Decorative-edged scissors: cloud; scallop; zigzag
Die-cuts: cloud; sun (2); umbrella
Lettering books
Light box
Markers: 0.5 mm black liner; 1.2 mm black liner; 0.5 mm baby blue liner; 1.2 mm baby blue liner; 1.2 mm red liner
Pencil
Self-adhesive die-cuts: glasses; pail; shovel; starfish (2)
Scissors
Templates: circle; oval; rectangle

A variety of lettering adds personality to any layout. Do not be afraid to experiment with different heights, widths, and colors of lettering on the same page. This technique is fun and very addicting.

Creative Lettering

Here's How:

1. Rip a piece of tan speckled card stock to create the "sand" and position it over the bottom portion of the ground paper.

2. Apply adhesive to the back of the torn paper. Adhere it onto the ground paper. Using scissors, trim tan speckled card stock flush with the ground paper.

3. Refer to page 322. Crop selected photos as desired.

4. Refer to page 314. Adhere photos onto card stock. Cut the card stock ¼" to ⅛" larger than each photo all around.

5. Using scissors, cut two pieces of white card stock for paper labels.

6. Place the selected lettering, right side up, on a light box with the white card stock on top, right side up. Using the pencil, lightly trace the lettering onto the card stock.

7. Using the markers, ink the lettering. Erase any pencil lines once the lettering is inked.

8. Adhere the lettered card stock onto colored card stock. Cut the colored card stock ¼" larger than each piece of lettered card stock all around.

knife to make a small slit in the tan card stock and slide the edge of the die-cut into the slit.

9. Refer to page 312. Arrange and adhere the photos, paper labels, and die-cuts onto the ground paper.

10. Using the markers, add journaling to the ground paper and die-cuts.

Trouble-shooting:
Ink the lettering before adhering the white card stock onto the colored card stock. If a mistake is made, the colored card stock is not wasted.

Design Tip:
To make certain the die-cuts appear as if they are down in the "sand," use the craft

How can I use rubber stamping to decorate a page?

What You Need to Get Started:

2 photos per page
Adhesive
Card stock: blue for ground paper; brown; tan
Colored pencils
Marker: 2.0 mm black calligraphy
Pencil
Permanent ink pad: black
Scissors
Stamp: sunflower
Transparent ruler

Creating borders and backgrounds is simple with stamping. The most appealing aspect of working with rubber stamps is that the images can be used over and over without having to purchase the product every time.

Rubber Stamping Effects

Here's How:

1. Refer to page 314. Adhere photos onto tan card stock. Cut the card stock ⅛" larger than each photo all around.

2. Apply adhesive to the back of each piece of tan card stock. Adhere each piece onto brown card stock. Cut the brown card stock ⅛" larger than each piece of tan card stock all around.

3. Using transparent ruler, pencil, and scissors, measure, mark, and cut a 2¾" x 10½" strip of tan card stock.

4. Ink the sunflower stamp, using the black ink pad.

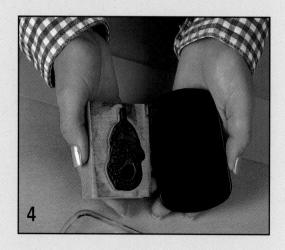

5. Print the image, by placing the stamp, rubber die side down, onto the card stock strip. Without rocking or twisting the stamp, give it a little pressure.

6. Lift the stamp straight up and off the card stock strip. Allow the ink to dry.

7. Randomly print the image over the entire strip of card stock by repeating Steps 4–6.

6–7

11. Refer to page 312. Arrange and adhere the photos onto the ground paper.

12. Using scissors, cut out the single stamped image, leaving ⅛" of card stock all around.

13. Apply adhesive to the back of the single stamped image. Adhere it onto the right side of the ground paper, overlapping the photo if desired.

14. Using the marker, add journaling to the page.

8. Print a single image onto a scrap piece of tan card stock. Allow the ink to dry.

9. Using the colored pencils, color the sunflowers as desired.

9

10. Apply adhesive to the back of the stamped card stock strip. Center and adhere it onto the left side of the ground paper.

Jr. Performance Group '97-'98

How do I use stickers to embellish a page?

3 photos per
  page
Adhesive
Card stock: dark
  blue; burgundy;
  ginger speckled
  for ground
  paper; dark
  green
Corner rounder
Decorative-edged
  scissors:
  scallop; stamp;
  zigzag
Pencil
Scissors
Stickers: animals;
  letters
Transparent ruler

Jazz up any scrapbook page with inexpensive self-adhesive stickers. The variety is endless and the technique is quick and easy. These are also great for children to use when they are designing their own pages.

Sticker Additions

Here's How:

1. Refer to page 324. Round each corner of each photo.

2. Refer to page 314. Adhere photos onto card stock. Cut the card stock ⅜" larger than the large photos all around and ¼" larger than the smaller photos all around.

3. Refer to page 312. Arrange and adhere the photos onto the ground paper.

4. Carefully place stickers as desired to accent the page layout.

5. Add lettering to the page by carefully placing the letter stickers.

Troubleshooting:

When using stickers to add design to a page, try to keep the background very simple. Stickers tend to get "lost" on a heavily printed background; the page becomes very "busy," and the viewer's focus on the photos, the most important element, is diminished.

Remember, stickers are used to add to the story and perhaps a bit of color, not to become the reason you did the page in the first place. Be selective and use just a few stickers per page.

Design Tips:

Take your time placing the stickers. Some sticker brands allow you to remove the stickers and rearrange them before the adhesive becomes permanent, usually before 10–20 minutes.

If you are not certain where to place the sticker, do not peel it from the backing. Cut around the sticker, leaving the backing on, and lay it on the page to see how it looks. When you are satisfied, remove the backing and press the sticker onto the page. One time application is best with stickers, as removing and rearranging them causes the edges of the sticker to turn and sometimes bend.

Hogle Zoo

Spring

1997

How do I use rub-ons to decorate a page?

Rub-ons are like using an oversized sticker—without the silhouette look that comes with a sticker. Rub-ons are great for layering and can be used on almost any surface.

Rub-on Additions

Here's How:

1. Using the transparent ruler, pencil, and paper cutter, measure, mark, and cut ¾" from the top and one side of the ground paper.

2. Refer to page 324. Round each corner of the ground paper.

3. Apply adhesive to the back of the ground paper. Adhere it onto the center of the background paper.

4. Cut out the selected rub-ons, leaving the paper backing attached to the rub-on.

5. Arrange the rub-ons and photos on the ground paper as desired.

6. Rub the design onto the ground paper and background paper.

7. Carefully remove the paper backing by lifting from one corner. Watch for the small black lines to make certain they have adhered onto the paper.

8. Apply adhesive to the back of each photo. Adhere them onto the ground paper one at a time.

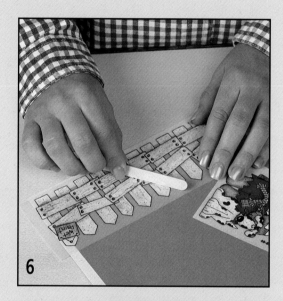

9. Using the markers, add journaling to the ground paper.

Trouble-shooting:

If you are uncertain where you are going to place the rub-on, cut around the motif, leaving the backing on, and lay it on the page to see how it looks.

When you are satisfied, remove the backing and press the rub-on onto the page.

One time application is best, as the back of the rub-on is very sticky and cannot be peeled up to be moved or it will tear apart.

Design Tip:

Do not be afraid to layer the designs—this is a great way to achieve dimension.

Feb.
1996

"a little worn out"

DAVID

2½ yrs old

Wet Paint

How do I use clip-art from pattern books?

What You Need to Get Started:

4 photos per page
Acrylic paints and paintbrushes
Adhesive
Card stock: black for ground paper; blue; olive green; orange; rusty red; white; yellow for background paper
Corner rounder
Craft punch: star
Decorative-edged scissors: scallop; stamp; zigzag
Lettering books
Markers: 0.5 mm black liner; 1.2 mm black liner; 1.2 mm wheat liner
Paper cutter
Pattern book
Pencil
Scissors
Templates: circle; oval; rectangle
Transparent ruler
Watercolor paper: lightweight

This technique allows you to choose clip-art from books without using a computer. The images can be reduced or enlarged to fit the area you want to fill and may or may not be colored.

Clip-art Creations

Here's How:

1. Using the transparent ruler, pencil, and paper cutter, measure, mark, and cut ⁵⁄₁₆" from the top and one side of the ground paper.

2. Refer to page 328. Round each corner of the ground paper.

3. Punch a star in each corner of the ground paper.

4. Apply adhesive to the back of the ground paper. Adhere it onto the center of the background paper.

5. Refer to page 322. Crop selected photos as desired.

6. Refer to page 314. Adhere photos onto card stock. Cut the card stock ¼" to ⅛" larger than each photo all around or large enough to accommodate punching either on each corner or along one edge.

7. Punch stars from each corner of the selected card stock.

8. Select clip-art images from the pattern book. Using a photocopy machine, copy the images onto white card stock or watercolor paper, reducing or enlarging as desired.

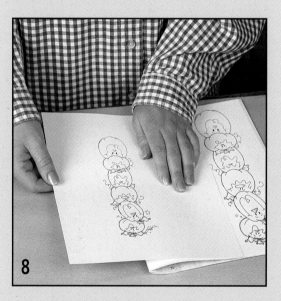

9. Dilute acrylic paints with water to the consistency of a wash for a watercolor effect. Using the paintbrush, color the images as desired, beginning with a light wash and apply darker washes to create the shading. Allow paint to dry.

10. Using scissors, cut out images.

9

Troubleshooting:

Choose designs that are easy to color. Make certain the designs do not overpower the page or compete with the photos.

Lay out your page and make certain the size of the clip-art works before adding color.

Color the image first before cutting it out. You can use colored pencils, markers, acrylic paints and paintbrushes, or watercolor paints and paintbrushes to color patterns. Seal these with an acrylic sealer.

Use scissors with a sharp point to cut around the colored image.

11. Refer to page 338. Cut a piece of white card stock for paper label. Pencil and ink in the lettering.

12. Adhere the lettered card stock onto colored card stock. Cut the colored card stock ¼" larger than each piece of lettered card stock all around.

13. Refer to page 312. Arrange and adhere the photos, clip-art images, punched stars, and paper label onto the ground paper.

Turkey Day
November
1998

How do I use computer clip-art?

In this technological age of computers, software made up of clip-art images is readily available and provides a quick and easy way to decorate a scrapbook page. Most clip-art programs contain both black line art and colored images.

Computer Clip-art Fun

Here's How:

1. Refer to page 322. Crop selected photos as desired.

2. Refer to page 314. Adhere photos to card stock. Cut the card stock ¼" to ⅛" larger than the photos all around.

3. For reference, arrange the photos on a piece of white paper as desired.

4. Select clip-art images from the booklet provided with the computer clip-art. Arrange the images on a page in your document, positioning them to correspond with the layout of your photos, leaving ½" of white along the top and one side of the page.

5. Choose a coordinating font. Add journaling on your page by typing the information on the page within the document.

6. Print the page with the clip-art images and lettering. Using paper cutter, trim ½" from the top and one side of the printed page.

7. Apply adhesive to the back of the printed page. Adhere it onto the center of the red card stock.

8. Apply adhesive to the back of each photo. Adhere them onto the printed page one at a time.

Design Tip:

After choosing your photos for the page, measure the openings where the clip-art images will be placed. Size your image correctly before printing to save time that might otherwise be spent reducing or enlarging on a copy machine.

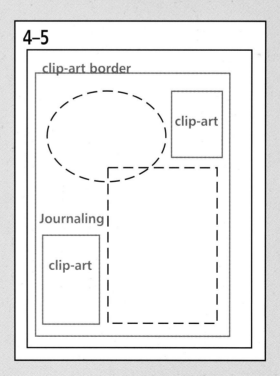

Refer to page 322. Refer to page 314.

What You Need to Get Started:

2 photos per
   page
Adhesive
Cardstock: sage
   green; orange;
   red for back-
   ground paper
Computer clip-art
Decorative-edged
   scissors: zigzag
Paper: white
Paper cutter
Pencil
Scissors
Transparent ruler

How do I use natural papers on a page?

What You Need to Get Started:

1 photo per page
Adhesive
Card stock: olive green; ivory; ivory for ground paper; pink speckled
Corner punch: fan
Corner rounder
Decorative paper: roses print for background paper
Decorative photo corners: black with leaf design
Decorative-edged scissors: deckle
Marker: 0.5 mm black liner
Natural paper
Paper cutter
Pencil
Stickers: green bow; pressed flowers; rose
Transparent ruler

Natural papers made with bits of flowers and leaves seem to lend new life to the photos. Most natural papers are hand-made and have a wonderful texture that stands out against the flatness of "run-of-the-mill" papers.

Natural Paper Embellishment

Here's How:

1. Using the transparent ruler, pencil, and paper cutter, measure, mark, and cut 1½" off the top and one side of the ground paper.

2. Refer to page 324. Round each corner of the ground paper.

3. Apply adhesive to the back of the ground paper. Adhere it onto the center of the printed background paper.

4. Refer to page 314. Adhere the photo onto the ivory card stock. Cut the card stock ¼" larger than the photo all around.

5. Refer to on page 316. Adhere the photo corners with the photo onto the olive green card stock. Cut the olive green card stock ⅜" larger than the ivory card stock all around.

6. Adhere the olive green card stock onto the natural paper. Cut the natural paper ⅜" larger than the olive green card stock all around.

7. Round each corner of the natural paper.

8. Adhere the natural paper onto the pink speckled card stock. Cut the pink speckled card stock ½" larger than the natural paper all around.

9. Punch each corner of the pink speckled card stock.

10. Apply adhesive to the back of the pink speckled card stock. Adhere it onto the ground paper, ½" from the top and centered from side to side.

11. Cut a piece of ivory card stock for a paper label. Punch each corner.

12. Adhere the ivory card stock onto the olive green card stock. Cut the olive green card stock ⅛" larger than the ivory card stock all around.

13. Using the marker, add journaling to the paper label.

14. Apply adhesive to the back of the olive green card stock. Adhere it onto the ground paper, ⅛" from the photo and centered from side to side.

15. Refer to page 342. Carefully place the stickers on the ground paper and paper label as desired.

Troubleshooting:

Make certain you know where the natural stickers are going to be placed. These cannot be removed once they are placed onto the surface. They are extremely delicate, but well worth the extra care.

Design Tip:

If you want to give a photo an old-time look, create a small white border, using deckle decorative-edged scissors and some ivory card stock. This effect finishes a color copy made from an original.

How do I color-tint black-and-white photos?

What You Need to Get Started:

2 photos per page
Adhesive
Card stock: blue speckled; brown speckled ; olive green speckled; olive green speckled for background paper; sage green speckled; ivory; light kraft speckled for ground paper; lavender; plum; yellow
Decorative border: light brown with vine design
Decorative corner punch: fan
Decorative photo corners: light brown with vine design
Decorative-edged scissors: deckle
Marker: 0.5 mm black liner
Natural paper
Paper cutter
Pencil
Pressed flowers
Scissors
Self-adhesive laminate
Spot pens: photo tinting set
Templates: circle; oval; rectangle; square
Transparent ruler

Color-tinting black-and-white photos now is so easy, and spot pens have made it that much easier. This technique is almost like filling in the color in a coloring book.

Tinting Black & White Photos

Note: Carefully read all manufacturer's instructions for the photo tinting pen set.

Here's How:

1. To avoid scratching photos, soften pen tips by rubbing them vigorously on a discarded photo for 20 seconds.

3. Lightly touch the pen tip to the black-and-white photo. Fill in the area, using circular motions and gradually building color.

2. Using a sponge, moisten the area to be colored with water and solution provided in the photo tinting set. Make two or three swipes with the sponge from top to bottom or from side to side so the photo is slightly tacky, but not wet.

Note: If streaking occurs, either the photo has become too dry and needs to be moistened again or you are using too dark a color on a light area.

4. Using a cotton swab, blot excess dye from the photo.

5. Using the transparent ruler, pencil, and paper cutter, measure, mark, and cut 1" off the top and one side of the ground paper.

6. Refer to page 324. Punch each corner of the ground paper.

7. Apply adhesive to the back of the ground paper. Adhere it onto the center of the back-ground paper.

8. Refer to page 322. Crop selected photos as desired.

9. For each photo, refer to page 314. Adhere photos onto coordin-ating pieces of card stock and natural paper. Cut the card stock and natural paper ⅝", ⅜", and ¼" larger than the photo all around.

10. Refer to page 316. For selected photos, adhere photos with photo corners onto the center of the smallest piece of natural paper or card stock.

11. For remaining photos, adhere the photo onto the center of the smallest piece of natural paper or card stock. Repeat the process for the remaining pieces of natural paper or card stock for the desired number of paper layers.

12. Measure, mark, and cut ivory card stock to 2⅜" x 2" for a paper label. Trim off corners.

13. Adhere the ivory card stock onto the lavender card stock. Cut the lavender card stock ⅜" larger than the ivory card stock all around. Punch each corner of the lavender card stock.

14. Using the marker, add journaling to the paper label.

15. Measure, mark, and cut four 1¾" squares, one 2" circle, one 2⅝" oval, and one 2½" x 5" rectangle from ivory card stock.

16. Adhere each piece of ivory card stock onto a coordinating piece of card stock. Cut coordinating pieces of card stock ⅛" larger than each piece of ivory card stock all around.

17. Position pressed flowers on the ivory card stock as desired. Apply adhesive to the back of each flower. Adhere them onto the card stock. Following manufacturer's instructions, apply self-adhesive laminate over the card stock to enclose the pressed flowers.

18. Apply adhesive to the back of the decorative border. Adhere it onto the ground paper ⅞" from the left or bottom edge.

19. Refer to page 312. Arrange and adhere photos, paper label, and pressed flower cards onto the ground sheet as desired.

Troubleshooting:
Save all the photos you may have otherwise discarded so you can practice the tinting technique on them. This is not only for selecting color place-ment but also for experiment-

ing with the moisture needed on the photo to avoid streaking. It is better to practice on a few disposable photos than on a photo that may be difficult to replace.

Design Tip:
Sometimes less color is better. Some photos may need only one or two colors to be the most dramatic.

November 1998

How should I use bright colors?

Summer time usually means bright and fun colors. Keep the ground paper simple and the photos will pop off the page.

Highlight with Color

Here's How:

1. Using the cloud decorative-edged scissors, trim the ground paper ¼" all around.

2. Apply adhesive to the back of the ground paper. Adhere it onto the center of the background paper.

3. Refer to page 322. Crop selected photos as desired.

4. Refer to page 314. Adhere photos onto card stock. Cut the card stock ¼" to ⅛" larger than each photo all around.

5. Refer to page 312. Arrange and adhere the photos and die-cuts onto the ground paper.

6. Using the markers, add journaling to cloud die-cut.

What You Need to Get Started:

3 photos per page
Adhesive
Card stock: neon green; neon pink; teal for ground paper; white for background paper; bright yellow
Decorative-edged scissors: cloud; scallop; zigzag
Die-cuts: cloud; flower; palm tree; star; sun; swirl
Markers: 0.5 mm black liner; 1.2 mm black liner
Pencil
Templates: oval; rectangle
Scissors

Tessa & Rylee
1998

How do I make a pocket page to hold memorabilia?

What You Need to Get Started:

1 photo per page
Adhesive
Cardstock: sage green; orange; red for ground paper
Computer clip-art
Jute: 2-ply (1½ yards)
Memorabilia
Paper: white
Paper punch
Pencil
Scissors
Transparent ruler

The purpose of creating a scrapbook is to provide a place for keeping "scraps." Pocket pages are a wonderful way to keep special momentos close to the photos of the same event.

Memorabilia Pocket

Here's How:

1. Using transparent ruler, pencil, and scissors, measure, mark, and cut orange card stock to 5½" x 8½" for the pocket.

2. Punch holes along the top 8½" edge of the pocket, ⅜" apart.

3. Align the bottom edge of the pocket with the bottom edge of the ground paper. Using the paper punch, punch holes through both pieces of paper, ¾" apart all around.

4. Tape one end of the jute to avoid fraying. Beginning at the top center hole of the pocket and leaving a 6" tail, weave the jute through the holes. Weave through both pieces of paper around the edges and finish weaving through the holes on the top of the pocket. Tie a bow where ends meet.

5. Using transparent ruler, pencil, and scissors, measure, mark, and cut a 4½" x 7½" piece of sage green card stock.

6. Refer to page 332. Carefully cut around the photographic or copied image to be used for silhouetting.

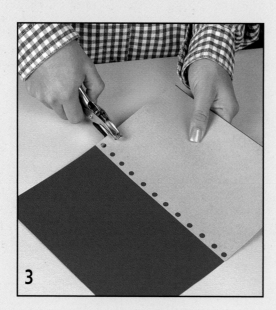

7. Refer to page 63. Prepare print, and cut out clip-art images and journaling.

8. Position the blunt edge of the silhouetted photo along the bottom of the sage green card stock. Arrange the clip-art images and journaling on the card stock as desired.

9. Apply adhesive to the back of each image. Adhere them onto the card stock one at a time.

10. Apply adhesive to the back of the sage green card stock. Adhere it onto the center of the pocket.

11. Place memorabilia into the pocket.

Troubleshooting:

Be aware that memorabilia-filled pocket pages may cause indentations on pages that are place next to them in a binder. Place these and pages with one-of-a-kind photos far apart.

Design Tip:

There are kits available that you can use to create your own pocket pages in no time. The kits are themed and contain stickers, die-cut shapes, colored paper, patterned paper, adhesive strips, and step-by-step directions.

How can I display dimensional items on a page?

What You Need to Get Started:

5 photos per page
Adhesive
Card stock: navy blue; navy blue for background paper; brown; ivory; light kraft for ground paper; dark tan; light tan
Color copies of green leaves
Decorative-edged scissors: deckle; zigzag
Jute: 2-ply (1½ yards per page)
Markers: 0.5 mm black liner; 5.0 mm brown calligraphy
Memorabilia
Memorabilia pockets: self-adhesive
Natural paper
Paper cutter
Paper punch
Scissors
Tape
Templates: circle; oval; rectangle; square

Incorporate purchased memorabilia pockets into your page design to display items that have real or sentimental value. These durable pockets keep small items safe and sound.

Small Pockets on a Page

Note: Before creating the scrapbook page, gather some autumn leaves and place them between two layers of paper toweling. Stack heavy books on top of the toweling. Allow the leaves to dry for approximately two weeks. Take the leaves to a professional copy shop and have them color copied.

If leaves are out of season, they can be purchased already pressed. They are expensive so take good care of them and they can be used over and over.

Here's How:

1. Using the transparent ruler, pencil, and paper cutter, measure, mark, and cut ½" off the top and one side of the ground paper.

2. Using the paper punch, punch holes ½" apart all around the edges of the ground paper.

3. Tape one end of the jute to avoid fraying. Beginning at the top right hole of the ground paper, weave the jute through the holes all around.

4. Apply adhesive to the back of the ground paper. Adhere it onto the center of the background paper.

5. Position the natural paper at an angle on the ground paper. Using the scissors, trim the corners of the natural paper flush with the inside edge of the punched holes.

6. Refer to page 322. Crop selected photos as desired.

7. Refer to page 314. Adhere photos onto card stock. Cut the card stock ¼" to ⅛" larger than each photo all around. If desired, adhere this piece of card stock onto a second piece of card stock. Cut the second piece of card stock ¼" to ⅛" larger than the first piece of card stock all around.

8. To create photo labels and layered paper for memorabilia pockets, cut two pieces of ivory card stock. Adhere each piece of ivory card stock onto a coordinating piece of card stock. Cut the coordinating piece of card stock ¼" larger than the ivory card stock all around.

9. Remove the paper backing from the adhesive on the back of the memorabilia pocket. Adhere the pocket onto

the center of the ivory card stock on the selected layered piece.

10. Refer to page 338. Using the markers, add lettering and journaling to the paper labels.

11. Using scissors, cut out the color copied leaves, making edges wavy for a realistic look.

12. Refer to page 312. Arrange and adhere the photos, memorabilia pockets, photo labels, and leaves onto the ground paper.

13. Fill the pockets with memorabilia.

How do I create calendar pages?

4 photos per
   page
12-month
   calendar: blank
Adhesive
Card stock: blue;
   green; red; teal;
   yellow
Craft punch: star
Decorative-edged
   scissors: cloud;
   scallop; zigzag
Markers: 0.5 mm
   black liner
Pencil
Scissors
Stickers: assorted
Templates: oval;
   rectangle

Making a scrapbook from a calendar is a wonderful way to keep a record of the special events that happen every day. Later, because you took the time to write it down on your calendar, you will be able to remember when and what happened and make certain that it is also recorded in your journal or scrapbook. Combined with favorite photos, it becomes a mini scrapbook to look at from year to year.

Create a Calendar

Here's How to Create September:

1. Refer to page 322. Crop selected photos as desired.

2. Refer to page 314. Adhere photos onto coordinating card stock. Using scissors, cut the card stock ¼" larger than the photo on the sides and bottom and ⅞" larger on the top. Cut the card stock ⅜" larger than the oval photo on four sides, creating a rectangle. Using the decorative-edged scissors, cut the card stock ¼" larger than two remaining rectangle photos all around.

3. Refer to page 324. Punch a star in each corner of the oval photo's card stock frame. Punch stars along the wide edge of the rectangle photo's card stock frame.

4. Refer to page 312. Arrange and adhere photos onto the blank page.

5. Refer to page 342. Carefully place the stickers onto the photo page as desired. Carefully place stickers onto the calendar page that coordinate with the recorded events.

6. Using the marker, add journaling to the photo page.

Here's How to Create May:

1. Refer to page 322. Crop selected photos as desired.

2. Refer to page 314. Adhere photos onto coordinating card stock. Cut the card stock ¼" larger than the photos all around.

3. Refer to page 312. Arrange and adhere photos onto the blank page.

4. Refer to page 342. Carefully place the stickers onto the photo page as desired. Carefully place stickers onto the calendar page that coordinate with the recorded events.

5. Using the marker, add journaling to the photo page.

Design Tip:

Use the calendar to record the small day-to-day events, such as your child's first word, the day you collected flowers, dance recitals, etc.

HAPPY BIRTHDAY

★ ★ ★ ★ ★

to me ! ! ! !

First day of school

AaBbCc

Chantry's
Pre-school Graduation
May 27th

Happy Birthday!

Sophies first time on the grass!

Rachel and Chantry

School Daze

September

cat 123

Sunday	Monday	Tuesday	Wednesday	Thursday	Friday	Saturday
		1 First Day of School	2	3 Chantry chose his school box & pencils	4	5
6	7 ordered Seasame Street Cake	8 First Day of Kindergarten Chantry was ready @ 7a.m.	9 Sophie's 1st Birthday	10	11 Chantry brings home his first homework	12
13 Chantry's First Prayer	14	15	16 Chantry's First Dentist Appt. *Good Job!*	17	18 Sophie takes her first step	19
20 Primary Program	21	22 Sophies First Word "Dad"	23	24 Tyrels Fall Program	25	26
27	28 Tyrel Student of the week	29	30 Rachels Dance Recital			

©Pebbles in my Pocket

May

Sunday	Monday	Tuesday	Wednesday	Thursday	Friday	Saturday
					1	2 Sophie climbs up the stairs
3	4	5	6	7	8 Sophies first time on the grass	9 Tyrel picks flowers for me.
10 Mother's Day Program	11	12	13	14 Chantry picks out his favorite flower to plant	15 Planted Flowers	16
17	18 Rachel's Birthday Family Party 7pm.	19 Chantrys Birthday	20	21	22	23
24	25	26	27 Chantrys Pre-school Program	28	29 Last Day of school	30 Went to the park
31						

©Pebbles in my Pocket

How do I create theme pages?

What You Need to Get Started:

3 photos per page
Adhesive
Card stock: blue; green; red; yellow plaid for ground paper
Decorative paper: theme print for background paper
Marker: 0.5 mm black liner
Memorabilia
Paper cutter
Punch-outs: theme motifs
Scissors
Stickers: numbers
Templates: circle; oval; rectangle
Transparent ruler

Because there are so many products available, a theme page is easy to assemble. Add a few momentos and some stickers and the page quickly comes together.

Mickey & Friends Theme

Here's How:

1. Using the transparent ruler, pencil, and paper cutter, measure, mark, and cut 1" off the top and 2" off one side of the ground paper.

2. Apply adhesive to the back of the ground paper. Adhere it onto the background paper, ½" from the left side and centered top to bottom.

3. Refer to page 322. Crop the selected photos as desired.

4. Refer to page 314. Adhere the photos onto the blue, green, and red card stock. Cut the card stock ¼" larger than each photo all around.

5. Refer to page 312. Arrange and adhere the memorabilia, photos, and punch-outs onto the ground paper.

6. Using the markers, add journaling to the ground paper.

7. Refer to page 342. Carefully place the stickers on the ground paper as desired.

How do I create a "teen" Theme page?

These types of pages are great because "anything goes." The more the better. This technique fits the personality of the theme and is exciting to look at.

What You Need to Get Started:

3 photos per page
Adhesive
Card stock: lime green; hot pink; teal; white for ground paper; bright yellow
Decorative-edged scissors: cloud; scallop; zigzag
Die-cuts: assorted
Lettering book
Markers: 1.2 mm black liner; 1.2 mm green liner
Paper label
Pencil
Scissors
Stickers
Templates: circle; rectangle; square

Life as a Teen Theme

Here's How:

1. Using the transparent ruler, pencil, and zigzag decorative-edged scissors, measure, mark, and cut ¾" from the top and one side of the ground paper.

2. Apply adhesive to the back of ground paper. Adhere it onto background paper, lining up the two uncut edges and leaving a colored border on the left and top edges. If you have a facing page, repeat with another piece of ground paper and background paper, leaving a colored border on the right and top edges.

3. Refer to page 322. Crop selected photos as desired.

4. Refer to page 314. Adhere photos onto card stock. Cut the card stock ¼" to ⅛" larger than each photo all around.

5. Refer to page 338. Pencil and ink in the lettering on the paper label.

6. Refer to page 312. Arrange and adhere photos, paper label, and die-cuts onto the ground paper.

7. Refer to page 342. Carefully place the stickers on the ground paper as desired.

How can I use stationery cut-outs to create a theme page?

What You Need to Get Started:

5 photos per page
Adhesive
Card stock: blue; green; kraft for ground paper; red; white; yellow
Craft knife and cutting mat
Decorative-edged scissors: scallop; stamp; zigzag
Markers: 0.5 mm black liner; 1.2 mm black liner
Scissors
Stationery: patterned 8½" x 11"
Templates: circle; oval; rectangle
Transparent ruler

Stationery is so versatile. Cut out individual images from one sheet of stationery to decorate one scrapbook page. You can use a full sheet of stationery on facing scrapbook page to complement the first with journaling or additional photos.

Boys & Bugs Theme

Here's How:

1. Using the craft knife or scissors, carefully cut out the images from the patterned stationery.

2. Refer to page 322. Crop selected photos as desired.

3. Refer to page 314. Adhere photos to card stock. Cut the card stock ¼" to ⅛" larger than each photo all around.

4. Arrange the cut-out images on the page to create a border. Arrange the photos on the page as desired. Fill in any large gaps with cut-out images.

5. Adhere the cut-out images and photos onto the ground paper one at a time.

6. Using the markers, add journaling to the ground paper.

How can I create 12" x 12" theme pages using 8½" x 11" stationery?

This is one of the funnest techniques to use. The variety of 8½" x 11" stationery is endless and converting these papers to 12" x 12" is so simple. Create your own borders, corner designs, and individual images from one piece of paper.

Pooh Theme

Note: Refer to photos on page 296 for coordinating page layouts. I cut up stationery and placed motifs at the corners of the pages.

Here's How:

1. Using the transparent ruler, pencil, and paper cutter, measure, mark, and cut ¾" off the top and 1¾" off one side of light peach ground paper.

2. Apply adhesive to the back of the ground paper. Adhere it onto the light kraft background paper, ⅜" from the left side.

3. Apply adhesive to the back of the stationery. Adhere it onto the ground paper, ⅛" from the left side.

4. Refer to page 342. Carefully place stickers at different angles down the right side of the background paper.

5. Refer to page 314. Adhere the photo onto the sage green card stock. Cut the card stock ⅜" larger than the photo all around. Adhere the sage green card stock onto the ivory speckled card stock. Cut the ivory speckled card stock ⅛" larger than the

sage green all around. Adhere the ivory speckled card stock onto the rose card stock. Cut the rose card stock ⅛" larger than the ivory speckled card all around.

6. Apply adhesive to the back of the rose card stock. Adhere it onto the stationery, 1" from the top and centered from side to side.

7. Cut the light yellow card stock to 3½" x 1" to create a paper label. Cut the olive green speckled card stock to 5" x 1¼".

8. Apply adhesive to the back of the yellow card stock. Adhere it onto the center of the olive green speckled card stock.

9. Refer to page 314. Punch a heart from each side of olive green card stock on the paper label.

10. Using the markers, add journaling to the paper label.

11. Apply adhesive to the back of the paper label. Adhere it onto the stationery ¼" below the photo and centered from side to side on the stationery.

What You Need to Get Started:

1 photo per page
Adhesive
Card stock: olive green speckled; sage green; ivory speckled; light kraft for background paper; light peach for ground paper; rose; light yellow
Craft punch: heart
Decorative-edged scissors: deckle
Markers: 0.5 mm lavender liner; 1.2 mm lavender liner
Paper cutter
Pencil
Scissors
Stationery: Classic Pooh
Stickers: Classic Pooh
Transparent ruler

BIG HUGS

Breanna and Hannah '98

How do I use a full kit to design several pages?

This is a simple way of assembling many pages at once without having to buy many components. Depending on the company that compiled it, a kit contains a variety of materials from the background paper and framed corners to separate frames and labels, to decorative pieces.

What You Need to Get Started:

4 photos per page
Adhesive
Card stock: olive green speckled; plum; tan speckled
Color copies of leaves
Colored pencils
Marker: 0.5 mm black liner
Pencil
Scissors
Scrapbook kit
Tape

Pre-made Kits

Here's How:

1. Divide the kit into separate pages. Carefully punch out the die-cut borders and images.

2. Coordinate the pre-made photo mattes with the photos. Using scissors, trim selected photos as necessary.

3. Refer to page 318. Place pre-made photo mattes face down on the work surface. Center each photo face down on the matte. Place tape on the sides of each photo matte and adhere each photo.

4. Using the colored pencils, lightly color the embossed areas to tint the images.

5. Refer to page 358. Using scissors, cut out the color copied leaves.

6. Refer to page 312. Arrange and adhere the matted photos and leaves onto ground paper.

7. Using the marker, add journaling to the pages.

Design Tips:

I loved using this embossed kit. It came with eight pages—two completely ready and four that I could create myself, using the frames and corners that were provided.

I chose the fall packet because I have many pictures from past years' Christmas card photos. I have a pile of photographer's proofs that fit many of the smaller frames. Proofs are a great way to fill several pages because not everyone looks good in every photo. Cropping out someone who may have had their eyes closed or who was looking in another direction places the focus on the person who looks great. This makes the most of your photos.

You do not have to stay with the exact kit unless it fits everything you like. Do not be afraid to replace the ground sheet with a piece of colored card stock.

When using colored pencils to tint the embossed images, do not use a sharp point. Sharp points create lines that are not very attractive. Dull the pencil point by first coloring several strokes on a piece of scratch paper, creating a flat edge. A dull point makes a nice even color on the embossed image. You are highlighting the embossed image and therefore should color only the top surface of the image and avoid coloring down into the engraved areas or around the sides. Do not press hard or you may dent the embossed image. Several light applications will achieve a darker color.

Watercolors or water-based, blendable pens will also work for tinting the embossed images.

Some kits only come in 8½" x 11". If you need something to fit a 12" x 12" album format, you can off-set the 8½" x 11" framed sheet to one side of the 12" x 12" ground sheet.

Adhere a piece of card stock to the back of any embossed frame complete with photos that is the size of a page. The cardstock will protect the back side of the photos.

368

SOAPMAKING
for the first time®

Linda Orton

Soapmaking for the first time

Introduction

In early times, soapwort root was used for cleansing and Sumerian writings were among the first to contain information about the process of soapmaking. However, early soaps were not used for cleansing the body, but to clean animal skins and prepare them for tanning and hair removal.

One of the first soapmaking factories was preserved in the ruins of Pompeii. Soap for use on the body is believed to have come to the Roman public baths via the Gauls. When the Roman Empire declined, so did personal bathing with soap. It would be several centuries later, in the beginning of the 17th century in England, before bathing with soap would become vogue again.

In the late 1700s, a French chemist by the name of Nicolas Leblanc discovered the process of extracting soda from salt. At the same time, the findings of Louis Pasteur would establish a standard for personal hygiene to reduce the spread of disease, which in turn encouraged bathing with soap.

The early American colonists would make their soap from rainwater that was allowed to run through hardwood ashes to leach out the lye. A raw egg was placed in the lye solution to determine its strength. If the egg dropped to the bottom, the solution needed to be more concentrated and would be run through the ashes again. If the egg floated above the solution, the solution was too strong and needed to be diluted. If the egg floated just beneath the surface, then the lye solution was of the correct concentration. Fat was collected and heated to render the fats suitable for soapmaking. At that time, soapmaking was more of an art than the science it is today, where we have charts and lye calculators that can be used to determine the exact amount of lye and water to be combined with the fats. With the advent of mass production, purchased soap became more economical and was a time-saver for most households.

Handmade soap has been increasing in popularity since the mid 1980s and has gained an even larger following in recent years. The resurgence of soapmaking began primarily in the area of cold-process, which involves the combination of fats and lye solution in a process called saponification. More recently, melt-and-pour soap bases have become the trend since the materials for them can be purchased at the local craft store and need only be melted, colored, scented, and poured into molds. Wherever your interest lies, be it melt-and pour, rebatching, or cold-process, this section will take you step-by-step through the processes.

Handmade soaps have many benefits for body and mind. Scented oils and botanicals can be added to soap for softening and soothing skin, along with any aromatherapy benefits derived from essential oils. Customize soap to suit your desires in color, fragrance, and/or design. Handmade soaps make unforgettable and personalized gifts for adult and child alike.

Getting Started

Methods

Glycerin Melt-and-Pour

This method is the least technical of the three, yet allows for the most creativity in design. Glycerin melt-and-pour soap base—transparent or opaque—is grated or cut into small squares. The soap base is then melted over medium heat in a double-boiler fashion. A microwave oven can also be used to melt most brands of soap base, but make certain to follow manufacturer's directions when using the microwave. The melted soap base is then poured directly into the prepared mold(s) and allowed to solidify. If the mold that has been used is a loaf-style, it is released from the mold, then cut into individual bars. If individual soap molds have been used, the soap is simply released from the molds. In either case, the soap is ready to be used immediately. Wrapping the finished bars in plastic wrap will help prevent the soap from becoming too dry, in addition to helping preserve the fragrance.

Rebatching

This method of soapmaking involves mixing freshly grated soap with liquid—either water, infused water, or milk. Grated cold-process soap—homemade or purchased—is used. It is then heated on low until the two are blended. The melted soap mixture is then poured directly into the prepared mold and allowed to solidify. Once the soap has been removed from the mold, it is cut into individual bars and allowed to cure.

Cold-processing

This method is the most time-consuming and technical of the three, but the results are worth the extra effort. In this method, a combination of fats (natural oils) are mixed with a lye solution until saponification begins to take place. The soap mixture is then immediately poured directly into the prepared mold and allowed to solidify. Once the soap has been removed from the mold, it is cut into individual bars and allowed to cure.

Molds for soap

Actual soap molds (shown at left) can be purchased for the purpose of molding soap regardless of the soapmaking method you are using.

In addition, there are many other types of molds available commercially that work great for molding soaps. These include, but are not limited to, candle molds, candy molds, plaster molds, and metal tart shells.

All of the above-mentioned types of molds, which mold individual shapes, work best when using the glycerin melt-and-pour method.

When using an individual mold that has a lot of details and/or intricate designs, you will achieve the best impression if the glycerin melt-and-pour method is used.

Keep in mind that you do not have to purchase any of the previously mentioned types of molds. A number of household items (shown above) can be used as molds for your soap and render wonderful results. Some suggestions include loaf pans, plastic containers, shoe boxes, and plastic PVC® pipe. All of these household items work well for making loaf-style soap—molded in "loaves," then cut into individual bars.

An ordinary shoe box is an exceptional choice as a mold when making cold-process soap. Wooden soap molds with lids are available, but can be expensive.

Regardless of the type of mold you are using, it will need to be prepared prior to the soap being poured into it. When using the glycerin melt-and-pour and rebatching methods, common cooking oil is sprayed into the mold(s). When using the cold-processing method, the mold is lined with a plastic garbage bag.

When using PVC® pipe as a mold, one end must be sealed to prevent the melted soap base from leaking out. Plastic wrap, secured with rubber bands and masking tape, is recommended for sealing the opening.

Important Note:

When choosing a mold to be used for making cold-process soap, use only glass, plastic, stainless steel, or wood—aluminum must not be used because of the reaction between it and the lye in the soap.

372

Tools and supplies for melt-and-pour method

Cooking oil spray
Disposable chopstick, bamboo
Glycerin melt-and-pour soap base, transparent or opaque
Heat-resistant glass measuring cup
Kitchen knife, sharp unserrated
Kitchen range or microwave oven
Molds
Skillet, deep

If desired, colorant, scents, botanicals, and other additives can be added.

In addition, metallic or iridescent powders, soap curls, preformed soap shapes, and other small objects, such as seashells, dried flowers, dried fruit, old jewelry, and plastic toys can be added as decorative elements to glycerin melt-and-pour transparent soap.

When using such small objects, caution must be taken to prevent abrasions on the skin. Most importantly, children must be in the company of an adult when using soaps that contain such small objects to prevent choking.

Tools and supplies for rebatching method

Cooking oil spray
Cooling rack
Crockpot or
    Covered casserole dish
Cutting board
Grated soap,
    unscented
Kitchen knife,
    sharp unserrated
Liquid—water,
    infused water,
    or milk
Mold
Oven
Plastic spatula
Wooden spoon

*If desired,
colorant, scents,
botanicals, and
other additives
can be added.*

Tools and supplies for cold-processing method

Bath towels
Blanket
Cooling rack
Cutting board
Disposable chopstick,
    bamboo
Distilled water
Fats
Glass juice jar
    with lid
Hammer
Hand blender,
    optional
Kitchen knife,
    sharp unserrated
Kitchen range
Laboratory
    thermometer (with
    stainless steel shaft),
    0° to 180°F
Large nail
Latex gloves
Lye crystals
Measuring cup
    with pouring spout
Mold, plastic or
    wooden container
    with lid
Plastic garbage bag
Protective eyewear
Scale (must be able to
    weigh up to 5 lb.)
Stainless steel
    stockpot
Wooden spoon

If desired,
colorant, scents,
botanicals, and
other additives
can be added.

Tools and supplies for a botanical infusion

Botanical(s)
Distilled water
Glass canning jar
   with lid
Kitchen range
Measuring cup
   with pouring spout
Saucepan
Strainer

Additives with beneficial properties

Aloe Vera Gel

Aloe vera gel has a number of skin-nurturing properties and is commonly used in soap.

Clay

Finely powdered French clay (bentonite) and kaolin are added to soap made for oily skin. This soap may be too drying for other skin types.

Honey

Honey has a number of benefits to the skin since it contains enzymes, carbohydrates, B-complex vitamins, and vitamins C and E along with minerals. It also provides a protective film on the surface of the skin that retains moisture.

Oatmeal

Oatmeal is commonly used as a skin exfoliant and skin softener.

Oils

Small amounts of natural oils containing beneficial properties can be added at the end of the soapmaking process. Cocoa butter, shea butter, almond oil, avocado oil, carrot seed oil, and jojoba oil are all popular choices.

Pumice

Ground pumice is a good hand cleanser. The abrasiveness of the soap helps remove dirt and grime.

Fats for cold-process soap?

When making cold-process soap, any natural oil can be used. The most commonly used fats include coconut oil, olive oil, and palm oil.

Coconut oil and palm oil both render hard bars of soap with a nice lather. The olive oil is popular for its skin-softening qualities.

Other natural oils—to name a few—that can be used include:
- Almond oil
- Apricot kernel oil
- Jojoba oil
- Shea butter
- Sunflower oil
- Vegetable shortening

Saponification

Saponification is a chemical process that takes place when a solution made from water and lye crystals is mixed with melted fats. The lye solution and the fats are stirred together and as they become incorporated, the soap mixture thickens until "trace" is reached. The soap mixture is then immediately poured into the prepared mold. Saponification continues for an additional 24 to 48 hours or until the mixture becomes solidified.

Each fat has a saponification value, which measures the amount of lye necessary to saponify one gram of fat. The amounts of the fats, along with their saponification values, are inserted into a mathematical formula that will give the total amount of lye needed to saponify a batch of soap. Saponification charts are available, along with the formula, in advanced soap-making manuals when you become adventurous enough to try some soap formulas of your own.

Trace

Trace means when the lye solution and fats mixture becomes thick enough that when drizzled from the wooden spoon onto the surface of the remaining mixture in the stockpot, it will leave a visible trail before it disappears.

Adding color

Glycerin melt-and-pour soap base can be purchased clear or in a variety of colors, both transparent and opaque. This is the easiest way to add color to soap, but other options are available.

Soap dyes (shown at left) are available in powder, tablet, grated, and liquid forms. Liquid colorant is the easiest of the dyes to use and for that reason is the most popular. It produces intense color so must be used in moderation. Another factor that will determine the intensity of the color is whether it is being used with transparent or white opaque glycerin melt-and-pour soap bases. Keep in mind that the colors will vary greatly when used with rebatching and cold-process soaps. Liquid colorant is available in a limited number of colors, but these basic colors can be mixed to create a myriad of other colors. Food coloring can also be used, but is not as colorfast as liquid colorant.

Herbs and spices can also produce nice color combinations. Typically, one tablespoon to ¼ cup is added. Some of the most popular herbs and spices that are used include: instant coffee, instant tea, powdered kelp, carotene, liquid chlorophyll, cocoa, cinnamon, curry powder, turmeric, and paprika. Semisweet chocolate can be melted and added for coloration as well.

Natural pigments, also known as inorganic minerals, are available in powder form and render rich hues. These pigments include ochres, iron oxides, ultramarines, and titanium oxides. Make certain you do not breathe in these fine powders when they are being mixed into the soap. Children of any age should not be present when working with pigment powders.

Cosmetic pigments can be used and are typically very highly concentrated colors.

When layering differing colors of glycerin melt-and-pour soap bases, the soap must be thoroughly sprayed with rubbing alchohol (or witch hazel) before each new layer is applied to assure the soap layers bond together and do not separate

Important Notes:

When adding both color and scent to your soap, always add the colorant before adding the scented oil(s).

When using herbs and spices to add color to soap, the scent of the soap may be altered by the natural scent of the herbs and spices.

Adding scent

Scented oils (shown above) are most often used to add scent to soap and fall into two basic categories.

Essential Oils

Essential oils are extracted from plants and are used as a primary scent when making soap. The cost of essential oils varies greatly according to the production costs of extracting the essence—rose one of the most expensive; peppermint one of the least expensive.

Many essential oils have multiple properties and are used for health and aromatherapy benefits. For this reason, only pure essential oils should be used. Make certain they have not been mixed with any base oils.

Fragrance Oils

Fragrance oils are also used as a primary scent when making soap. Fragrance oils are synthetic and imitate popular scents for soaps, lotions, and other body care products.

Fragrance oils are generally less expensive than essential oils and are believed to have less aromatherapy benefits.

Important Notes:

Not all fragrance oils can be used when making cold-process soap.

Potpourri and other oils used for room-scenting should not be used in soapmaking unless stated otherwise by the manufacturer.

Botanicals

Botanicals (shown above) are also used to add scent to soap, but are not ordinarily used as a primary scent. Most often they are used in conjunction with essential or fragrance oils.

Many botanicals are used for the visual appeal they offer and some are used because of the skin-conditioning qualities they possess.

Calendula leaves, chamomile, ground cinnamon, lemon verbena, oatmeal, peppermint, rosebuds, and rosemary are some of the most common botanicals used in soapmaking.

Instant and leaf teas and instant and ground coffees can also be used for scenting soap.

Botanicals may be used whole or ground into smaller particles or powder. The advantage to grinding botanicals is that it allows them to become better incorporated into the soap and to be less irritating to the skin because of a scratchy texture. A coffee grinder, dedicated to grinding spices and botanicals, makes an excellent choice for grinding small amounts of herbs. Food processors and blenders can be used to chop, but usually require a larger amount of herbs than the soap recipe calls for.

How do I mold and scent glycerin melt-and-pour soap base into decorative bars of soap?

When making decorative bars of soap, using the melt-and-pour method is the easiest. Customized soap can literally be made in a matter of minutes. The glycerin soap base is melted, scented oil is added, then it is poured into molds. Unlike other methods for soapmaking, melt-and-pour soaps are ready for use as soon as the soap cools and sets up.

Glycerin melt-and-pour soap bases are available in transparent (clear and colored) and opaque (white and colored).

What You Need To Get Started:

Cooking oil spray
Disposable chopstick, bamboo
Glycerin melt-and-pour soap base:
  Red transparent, 1 lb.
Heat-resistant glass measuring cup
Kitchen knife, sharp unserrated
Molds:
  3 Triangles, 4 oz.
Scented oils:
  Cranberry fragrance, ¼ tsp.
  Orange essential, ⅛ tsp.
Skillet, deep

Step 2

Cranberry/Orange Jewel Soap

Here's How:

1. Prepare molds by spraying the insides with cooking oil. Wipe away excess oil.
2. Using a sharp kitchen knife, cut the soap base into ½" squares and place the squares into a glass measuring cup.
3. Place the glass measuring cup into a deep skillet that has been filled with water.

4. Heat over medium heat until water begins to boil, then immediately reduce heat to low. Using a disposable chopstick, occasionally stir the melting soap base squares.

   Caution: Avoid overstirring to prevent excess bubbles. In addition, overheating will result in a spoiled batch.

Step 4

5. As the melted soap base begins to build-up on the sides of the measuring cup, scrape it back into the measuring cup and allow it to remelt.

6. Remove measuring cup from skillet and allow melted soap base to slightly cool until a "light film" forms on top.

7. Using the chopstick, remove the film and discard.

Step 7

8. Add scented oils to the melted soap base. Using the chopstick, gently stir to evenly distribute the fragrance.

   Caution: Make certain to mix thoroughly to avoid oil pockets from forming on the bottom of the bars of soap, but avoid overstirring or stirring briskly to prevent excess bubbles.

Step 8

382

9. Pour the melted soap base into prepared molds and allow to cool until solidified.

   Note: To reserve for use at a later time, excess soap base can be poured into a plastic storage container that has been sprayed with cooking oil.

Step 9

10. Turn the molds over and release the bars of soap.

   Note: Filled molds may be placed in the refrigerator to speed the cooling process. If the soap does not release from the mold, place mold in the freezer for approximately 10 minutes. Remove mold from freezer and allow to sit until condensation forms. Soap should then easily release from mold.

Step 10

Design Tip: If colored glycerin melt-and-pour soap base is not available, a colorant can be added to the soap base. See the following two pages.

To make opaque bars of soap, refer to the "Here's How" instructions opposite, substituting white opaque glycerin melt-and-pour soap base for the clear transparent.

How do I add color to glycerin melt-and-pour soap base to make colorful bars of soap?

Colorant comes in powder, tablet, grated, and liquid forms. Liquid colorant is the easiest to use and is available in red, yellow, blue, green, and orange. These basic colors are mixed to create other colors. Liquid colorant should be used in moderation as the colors can be intense. In addition, the colorant will vary depending on whether it is used with transparent or white opaque glycerin melt-and-pour soap base.

What You Need To Get Started:

Cooking oil spray
Disposable chopstick, bamboo
Glycerin melt-and-pour soap base:
   Clear transparent, ½ lb.
Heat-resistant glass measuring cup
Kitchen knife, sharp unserrated
Liquid colorants:
   Blue
   Yellow
Molds:
   2 Ovals, 4 oz.
Scented oils:
   Sage fragrance, ⅛ tsp.
   Sweetgrass fragrance, ⅛ tsp.
Skillet, deep

Step 2

Spirit-of-the-Earth Soap

Here's How:

1. Refer back to Steps 1–7 on pages 381–382.
2. Add one drop blue and nine drops yellow liquid colorant to the melted soap base. Using the chopstick, gently stir to evenly distribute the color.
3. Refer back to Steps 8–10 on pages 382–383.

Design Tip: If using powder colorant, use minute amounts to achieve desired colors as this type of colorant renders the most intense colors. If using solid colorant, slivers are cut from the block and added to the soap base during the melting process.

How do I mix two colors of glycerin melt-and-pour soap base to make swirled bars of soap?

What You Need To Get Started:

Butter knife
Cooking oil spray
Disposable chopstick,
  bamboo
Glycerin melt-and-pour
  soap base:
  White opaque, 1½ lb.
2 Heat-resistant glass
  measuring cups
Instant coffee, 2 tbsp.
Kitchen knife,
  sharp unserrated
Mold:
  Small loaf pan,
  6½" long x
  3" wide x 2" deep
Scented oils:
  Almond fragrance,
  ⅜ tsp.
  Coffee bean fragrance,
  ¼ tsp.
Skillet, deep

Swirled soaps are not only attractive to look at, but they also allow for a blending of complementary fragrances. A lovely, swirled soap is created by gently mixing two or more colors of soap together. In this case, the combination of almond and coffee bean fragrances create a lovely amaretto scent.

Swirled Almond/Coffee Bean Soap

Here's How:

1. Refer back to Steps 1–5 on pages 381–382.

2. Pour one-quarter of the melted soap base into a clean glass measuring cup and set to one side in the deep skillet.

3. Refer back to Steps 6–8 on page 382, adding only the almond fragrance scented oil to the melted soap base.

4. Pour the melted soap base (almond) into prepared mold.

5. Add coffee bean fragrance scented oil to the reserved melted soap base. Using the chopstick, gently stir to evenly distribute the fragrance.

6. Add the instant coffee to the melted soap base (coffee bean). Using the chopstick, gently stir to evenly distribute the color.

7. Pour the melted soap base (coffee bean) into prepared mold on top of the almond layer.

8. Using a butter knife, gently "cut through" the two soap mixtures enabling the colors to "swirl" together and allow to cool until solidified.

Caution: Avoid overmixing or soap will not render a swirled effect.

9. Refer back to Step 10 on page 383.

10. Using the sharp kitchen knife, slice the soap into individual bars.

Note: The two soap mixtures can be "swirled" together in individual molds, but care must be taken to avoid overmixing.

Step 8

Design Tips:

Another method of "swirling" two colors of soap base is to simultaneously pour both soap mixtures into the prepared mold(s).

Melt one ounce of semisweet chocolate and mix into reserved soap base in place of coffee bean fragrance and instant coffee in Steps 5 and 6 above.

Substitute vanilla fragrance for the almond fragrance. Then add cinnamon essential oil and one tablespoon cinnamon powder into reserved soap base in place of coffee bean fragrance and instant coffee in Steps 5 and 6 above.

**What You Need
To Get Started:**

Cooking oil spray
Disposable chopstick,
 bamboo
Glycerin melt-and-pour
 soap base:
 Yellow opaque, ¼ lb.
Heat-resistant glass
 measuring cup
Kitchen knife,
 sharp unserrated
Mold:
 Three-dimensional
 rubber duck
Paper towels
Paring knife
Scented oil:
 Sunflower fragrance,
 ⅛ tsp.
Skillet, deep

How do I mold glycerin melt-and-pour soap base into three-dimensional bars of soap?

Three-dimensional rubber duck soap is perfect for a child's bathroom. Dimensional molds are available in other shapes as well, such as seashells. This dimensional soap is prepared in a mold that snaps together and has a pour spout on top.

Rubber Duck Soap Bars

Here's How:

1. Refer back to Steps 1–8 on pages 381–382.

2. Pour the melted soap base into prepared mold through the hole at the top of the mold and allow to cool until solidified.

3. Gently pull the mold apart to release the three-dimensional bar of soap.

4. Using a paring knife, trim away the excess soap that has been molded to the bar.

   Note: After trimming the soap, the ridge can be smoothed further by dampening your finger and rubbing it along the ridge. Gently rub the dampened ridge with a paper towel.

Step 2a

Step 4

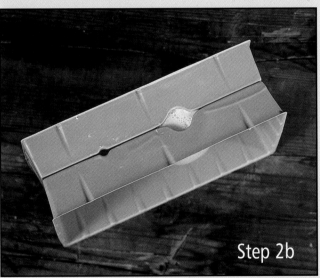

Step 2b

Design Tip: Three-dimensional candle and/or plaster molds also can be used as molds in soapmaking.

What You Need To Get Started:

Cooking oil spray
Disposable chopstick, bamboo
Glycerin melt-and-pour soap base:
  White opaque, ¾ lb.
Gold powder
Heat-resistant glass measuring cup
Molds:
  5 Cherubs, 2 oz.
Paintbrush, small
Scented oil:
  Gardenia fragrance, ⅜ tsp.
Skillet, deep

Gilded Cherub Soap

Here's How:

1. Refer back to Step 1 on page 381.
2. Using a small, dry paintbrush, apply gold powder into the detailed areas of the molds and set aside.
3. Refer back to Steps 2–10 on pages 381–383.

How do I accent the details of a mold with gold powder?

Highlighting detailed areas with gold powder is known as gilding. A small paintbrush—either flat or round—is used to brush the gold powder into the detailed areas, then the powder is allowed to settle into the crevices. In this case, the gilding adds an angelic touch to these heavenly cherub soaps.

**What You Need
To Get Started:**

Cutting board
Rubber mallet or
hammer
Soap bars:
Molded glycerin
melt-and-pour or
freshly cut
cold-process
Soap stamp,
rubber stamp, or
sealing wax stamp

Stamped
Soap Bars

Here's How:

1. Place the bars of
   soap onto a large
   cutting board
   that has been
   dedicated to soap-
   making.
2. Place the stamp on
   the surface of the
   soap as desired.
3. Using a rubber
   mallet, strike the top
   of the stamp four to
   six times. Judge your
   strikes according to
   the hardness of the
   soap bar.

How do I make
stamped impressions
on bars of soap?

*Soap stamps, rubber stamps, and sealing wax stamps with
large details can be used to make stamped impressions on
bars of soap. Generally glycerin melt-and-pour bars of soap
can be stamped any time, but the best impressions are made
after unmolding if the soap is at room temperature. Cold-
process soaps need to be stamped right after being cut into
individual bars.*

How do I emboss bars of soap?

Embossing your soap with a rubber stamp creates a wonderful added accent to your finished bars. The stamp can be re-attached to the mount and used to stamp matching packaging for gift giving.

Embossed Soap Bars
by Marie Browning

Here's How:

1. Prepare the rubber stamp by carefully peeling it from the wooden base.

2. Using rubber cement, glue the rubber stamp, right side up, into the bottom of the mold.

3. Refer back to Steps 1–7 on pages 381–382.

4. Refer back to Step 2 on page 385, adding the liquid colorant of your choice to the melted soap base.

5. Refer back to Step 8 on page 382, adding the scented oil of your choice to the melted soap base.

6. Refer back to Steps 9–10 on page 383.

   Note: The rubber stamp usually comes out of the mold with the soap.

7. Using a corsage pin, carefully pry the rubber stamp from the bar of soap.

Refer back to Steps 1–7 on pages 381–382. Refer back to Step 2 on page 385. Refer back to Step 8 on page 382. Refer back to Steps 9–10 on page 383.

What You Need To Get Started:

Cooking oil spray
Corsage pin
Disposable chopstick, bamboo
Glycerin melt-and-pour soap base: Any color
Heat-resistant glass measuring cup
Kitchen knife, sharp unserrated
Liquid colorant: Any color
Molds
Rubber cement
Rubber stamp
Scented oil: Any fragrance
Skillet, deep

Design Tip: When choosing a rubber stamp, choose a deeply cut stamp with a clean edge.

How do I accent the raised design of a mold with gold leafing?

Soap can be gold-leafed to give it a rich, expensive look. The use of gold leafing adhesive is not necessary to apply the gold leafing because the surface of the soap is sticky enough to allow it to adhere properly. Frankincense and myrrh fragrances add even more richness and elegance to each bar of soap.

Gold-leafed Soap Bars

Here's How:

1. Refer back to Steps 1–7 on pages 381–382.

2. Refer back to Step 2 on page 385, adding three drops green and ten drops orange liquid colorant to the melted soap base.

3. Refer back to Step 8 on page 382.

4. Add the powdered myrrh to the melted soap base. Using the chopstick, gently stir to evenly distribute.

5. Refer back to Steps 9–10 on page 383.

6. Apply gold leafing on top of each bar of soap and gently rub with your finger to adhere. Remove excess gold leafing and set aside.

7. Continue rubbing the gold leafing until it is smooth and thoroughly bonded to the soap.

> *Design Tip: For a different effect, try using copper leafing.*

What You Need To Get Started:

Cooking oil spray
Disposable chopstick, bamboo
2 Gold leafing sheets
Glycerin melt-and-pour soap base:
    White opaque, 1 lb.
Heat-resistant glass measuring cup
Kitchen knife, sharp unserrated
Liquid colorants:
    Green
    Orange
Molds:
    4 Rectangular with raised designs, 5 oz.
Powdered myrrh, 1 tsp.
Scented oil:
    Frankincense/ myrrh fragrance, 3/8 tsp.
Skillet, deep

How do I accent the raised design of a mold with a different color than the actual bar of soap?

When using a mold with a raised design, it is oftentimes important to mold the details of the design in a different color to help them stand out. In this case, the molds have Japanese kanji. Rice flour and green tea are added for an authentic oriental touch.

Japanese Tea Soap Bars

Here's How:

1. Refer back to Steps 1–7 on pages 381–382, using only 2 oz. of the white opaque soap base.

2. Refer back to Step 2 on page 385, adding one drop blue and six drops orange liquid colorant to the melted soap base.

3. Pour the melted soap base into prepared molds, filling only the areas of the raised designs, and allow to cool until solidified.

4. Using the edge of a flat plastic card, carefully scrape and remove the excess soap from the mold.

   Note: A credit card works great for this purpose.

5. Refer back to Steps 1–8 on pages 381–382, using the remaining white opaque soap base.

6. Add the rice flour and the contents from the tea bag to the melted soap base. Using the chopstick, gently stir to evenly distribute.

7. Spray a light mist of rubbing alcohol on top of the soap in the molds.

   Note: Make certain to coat the layer of soap evenly to assure the soap layers bond together and do not separate.

8. Refer back to Step 9 on page 383.

   Note: The majority of the green tea leaves will sink to the bottom of the mold.

9. Refer back to Step 10 on page 383.

What You Need To Get Started:

Cooking oil spray
Disposable chopstick, bamboo
Glycerin melt-and-pour soap base:
   White opaque, 1 lb.
Green tea bag
2 Heat-resistant glass measuring cups
Kitchen knife, sharp unserrated
Liquid colorants:
   Blue
   Orange
Molds:
   3 Japanese with raised designs, 4 oz.
Plastic card, flat
Rice flour, 2 tbsp.
Rubbing alcohol
Scented oil:
   Green tea fragrance, ¼ tsp.
Skillet, deep
Spray bottle

How do I mold glycerin melt-and-pour soap base into layered bars of soap?

Layered bars of soap have more aesthetic value than anything else. However, layering also allows for complementary fragrances to be combined within each individual layer. The inspiration for this soap was a favorite ice cream flavor.

Orange Crème Soap-on-a-Stick

Here's How:

1. Refer back to Steps 1–7 on pages 381–382, using only ½ lb. of the white opaque soap base.

2. Refer back to Step 8 on page 382, adding ⅛ tsp. vanilla fragrance scented oil to the melted soap base.

3. Refer back to Step 9 on page 383, filling the prepared mold no more than one-third full.

4. Refer back to Steps 1–7, on pages 381–382, using the clear transparent soap base.

5. Refer back to Step 2 on page 385, adding two to four drops orange liquid colorant to the melted soap base.

6. Refer back to Step 8 on page 382, adding orange essential scented oil to the melted soap base.

7. Spray a light mist of rubbing alcohol on top of the vanilla layer.

   Note: Make certain to coat the layer of soap evenly to assure the soap layers bond together and do not separate.

8. Refer back to Step 9 on page 382, pouring the orange melted soap base onto the vanilla layer.

   Note: The prepared mold should be no more than two-thirds full.

9. Refer back to Steps 1–7, on pages 381–382, using the remaining ½ lb. of the white opaque soap base.

What You Need To Get Started:

Cooking oil spray
4 Craft sticks
Disposable chopstick, bamboo
Glycerin melt-and-pour soap bases:
 Clear transparent, ½ lb.
 White opaque, 1 lb.
2 Heat-resistant glass measuring cups
Kitchen knife, sharp unserrated
Liquid colorant:
 Orange
Mold:
 Desk organizer, 18" long x 2¾" wide x 2" deep
Rubbing alcohol
Scented oils:
 Orange essential, ⅛ tsp.
 Vanilla fragrance, 1/4 tsp.
Skillet, deep
Spray bottle

10. Refer back to Step 8 on page 382, adding ⅛ tsp. vanilla fragrance scented oil to the melted soap base.

11. Spray a light mist of rubbing alcohol on top of the orange layer.

14. Using the sharp kitchen knife, cut the bar of soap into four equal lengths.

15. Spray a light mist of rubbing alcohol onto each craft stick and gently push into the middle (orange) layer at one end of each bar of soap to resemble an ice cream bar.

Step 11

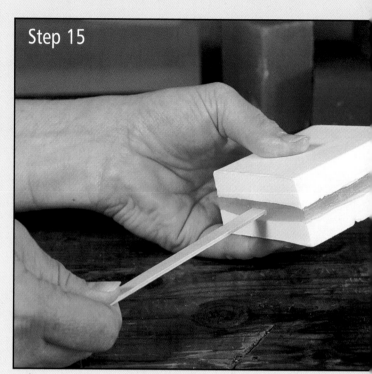

Step 15

12. Refer back to Step 9, on page 382, pouring the vanilla melted soap base onto the orange layer.

   Note: The prepared mold should be full to within ½" from the top.

13. Refer back to Step 10 on page 383.

Design Tip: A blended effect can be achieved by allowing a thick film to form on each layer, then pouring a new layer before the previous layer has set-up.

How do I embed
a preformed soap shape into
a glycerin melt-and-pour
loaf of soap?

What You Need To Get Started:

Cooking oil spray
Disposable chopstick,
 bamboo
Glycerin melt-and-pour
 soap bases:
 Clear transparent, ¼ lb.
 Purple opaque, ½ lb.
 Purple transparent, 1 lb.
Heat-resistant glass
 measuring cup
Kitchen knife,
 sharp unserrated
Masking tape
Molds:
 Plastic container,
  8" long x
  4" wide x ?" deep
 PVC® pipe,
  3" diameter x 8" long
Plastic wrap
Preformed soap shape,
 white "S"
Rubber bands
Rubbing alcohol
Scented oil:
 Plum fragrance, ½ tsp.
Skillet, deep
Spray bottle

Embedding a continuous preformed soap shape into a loaf of soap allows several bars of soap with a similar design to be molded at one time. The basic designs in this soap will vary throughout the loaf, adding interest.

Modern Art Soap Bars

Here's How:

1. Refer back to Steps 1–7 on pages 381–382, using the rectangular container mold and the purple opaque soap base.

2. Refer back to Steps 9–10 on page 383.

3. Using the sharp kitchen knife, slice the soap into three strips. One strip should measure 8" long, 1½" wide, and ⅛" deep. The remaining two strips should measure 8" long, ¼" wide, and ¼" deep.

4. Cut the preformed soap shape in half lengthwise.

   Note: Cutting the soap shape evenly is not important. Any variation in the basic design will add interest to the soap after it has been sliced into individual bars.

5. Prepare the pipe by spraying the inside with cooking oil. Wipe away excess oil.

6. Tear three pieces of plastic wrap large enough to cover one end of the pipe plus approximately 2" to secure it around the sides.

7. Place the pieces of plastic wrap over one end of the pipe and tightly stretch. Hold in place with rubber bands, then secure with masking tape to make certain the plastic wrap is thoroughly attached to the pipe.

8. Place the wrapped end of the pipe on a flat surface so it is standing up.

9. Refer back to Steps 2–8 on pages 381–382, using the clear and purple transparent soap bases.

10. Pour a 1" layer of the melted soap base into prepared pipe mold.

11. Place the three purple opaque soap strips and the preformed soap shape halves into the mold. Hold in place until the soap shapes stand on their own.

    Note: Make certain to leave enough space between the soap shapes so the melted

Step 11

soap base can fill in around the shapes to prevent the soap shapes from falling out when the soap is sliced into individual bars.

12. Spray a light mist of rubbing alcohol into the pipe to cover all soap shapes and the transparent layer.

    Note: Make certain to coat the layer of soap evenly to assure the soap layers bond together and do not separate.

13. Refer back to Step 9 on page 382, pouring the remaining melted soap base into the pipe, covering all of the soap shapes.

14. Remove the plastic wrap from the end of the pipe and gently press the soap out of the mold.

    Note: If the soap does not easily release, a butter knife, gently run around the sealed edges, may help loosen it.

15. Using the sharp kitchen knife, slice the soap into individual bars.

Design Tip: When using PVC® pipe as a soap mold, keep in mind that it will take longer for the soap to cool and solidify than when using a plastic mold.

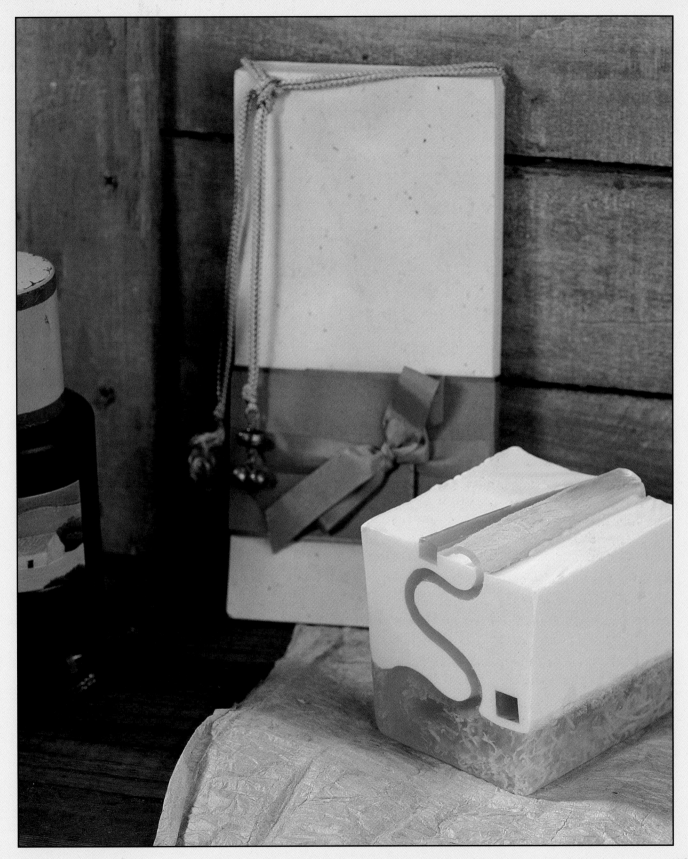

403

How do I embed preformed soap shapes into a layered glycerin melt-and-pour loaf of soap?

What You Need To Get Started:

Cooking oil spray
Disposable chopstick, bamboo
Glycerin melt-and-pour soap bases:
  Clear transparent, ¾ lb.
  Green transparent, scraps
  White opaque, 1½ lb.
  Yellow opaque, scraps
  Yellow transparent, ½ lb.
Grater
Heat-resistant glass measuring cup
Iridescent powder:
  Clear
Kitchen knife, sharp unserrated
Liquid colorants:
  Green
  Yellow
Mold:
  Plastic container, 8" long x 6" wide x 6" deep
Rubbing alcohol
Scented oil:
  Pear fragrance, ¾ tsp.
Skillet, deep
Spray bottle

Embedding a preformed soap shape into a loaf of soap that has been layered with different colors of melt-and-pour soap base makes for a visually appealing loaf. In fact, as a decorative element, slice only a couple bars from the loaf and display the remaining.

Pear-scented Soap Loaf

Here's How:

1. Refer back to Steps 1–7 on pages 381–382, using the yellow transparent soap base.

2. Pour the melted soap base into prepared mold and allow to cool until solidified enough to handle—it should still be slightly warm.

3. Turn the mold over and release the soap. Gently mold the soap into a squiggly shape from the eight-inch side. Set aside and allow to finish cooling and setting up.

4. Using the sharp kitchen knife, cut the green transparent soap base into three 6" strips.

5. Using a grater, finely grate the yellow opaque soap base to make ½ cup.

6. Refer back to Steps 1–7 on pages 381–382, using the clear transparent soap base.

7. Place a pinch of iridescent powder into the melted soap base. Using the chopstick, gently stir to evenly distribute the powder.

8. Quickly stir in the grated yellow soap base.

9. Pour the melted soap base into prepared mold.

10. Place the yellow transparent preformed soap shape and one of the green transparent soap strips into the mold. Hold in place until the preformed soap shape stands on its own. Allow to cool until solidified.

11. Refer back to Steps 1–7 on pages 381–382, using the white opaque soap base.

12. Refer back to Step 2 on page 385, adding four drops green and thirty drops yellow liquid colorant to the melted soap base.

13. Refer back to Step 8 on page 382.

14. Spray a light mist of rubbing alcohol on top of the clear layer with grated yellow soap and to cover all soap shapes.

    Note: Make certain to coat the layer of soap evenly to assure the soap layers bond together and do not separate.

15. Refer back to Step 9 on page 383, placing the remaining two green transparent soap strips as desired.

16. Refer back to Step 10 on page 383.

17. Using the sharp kitchen knife, slice the soap into individual bars. If desired, leave part of the loaf unsliced and display it near the cut bars.

What You Need To Get Started:

Cooking oil spray
Disposable chopstick, bamboo
Glycerin melt-and-pour soap bases:
  Blue transparent
  Green transparent
  Purple transparent
  Red transparent
  Yellow transparent,
    2 oz. each
  White opaque, 1½ lb.
Heat-resistant glass measuring cup
Kitchen knife, sharp unserrated
Mold:
  Half-round loaf,
  7½" long x
  4¼" wide x 2" deep
Scented oils:
  Raspberry fragrance,
    ¼ tsp.
  Vanilla fragrance,
    ⅜ tsp.
Skillet, deep

How do I add chunks of glycerin melt-and-pour soap base into melted soap base to create one-of-a-kind bars of soap?

Adding multicolored bits and pieces of transparent soap base into a melted opaque soap base produces colorful bars of soap. When sliced, each bar of soap is different because of the sizes and colors of soap chunks that were used.

Kaleidoscope Soap Bars

Here's How:

1. Using a sharp kitchen knife, cut all colors of transparent soap base into ½" and 1" irregular-shaped pieces. Set aside.

2. Refer back to Steps 1–8 on pages 381–382, using the white opaque soap base and both scented oils.

3. Pour a ¼" layer of the melted soap base into prepared mold.

Step 5

Step 4

Step 6

4. Randomly place the colored transparent pieces into the mold.

   Note: These soap base pieces should fill the mold ⅓" below the edge.

5. Refer back to Steps 9–10 on page 383, pouring the remaining melted soap bas into prepared mold, covering all colored transparent pieces.

6. Using the sharp kitchen knife, slice the soap into individual bars.

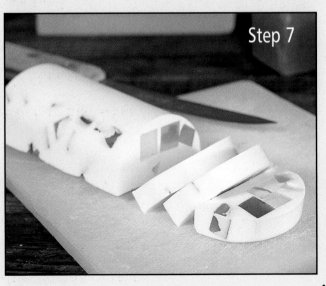

Step 7

How do I mold glycerin melt-and-pour soap base into tiny bars of soap and then embed them into larger bars of soap?

What You Need To Get Started:

Cooking oil spray
Disposable chopstick,
  bamboo
Glycerin melt-and-pour
  soap bases:
Clear transparent, 3/4 lb.
Green opaque, scraps
White opaque, 1/4 lb.
2 Heat-resistant glass
  measuring cups
Iridescent powder:
  Clear
Kitchen knife,
  sharp unserrated
Liquid colorants:
  Blue
  Red
Molds:
  4 Ovals, 3 oz.
  Tiny hearts
Potato peeler
Rubbing alcohol
Scented oils:
  Papaya fragrance,
    1/8 tsp.
  Plum fragrance,
    1/8 tsp.
Skillet, deep
Spray bottle
Toothpick

Tiny bars of soap can be individually molded or cut out with cookie cutters, then placed "inside" larger bars of soap. Opaque shapes can be placed inside transparent bars and vice versa. In addition, soap shavings can also be placed as a decorative element inside bars of soap.

Embedded Tiny Heart Soap Bars

Here's How:

1. Refer back to Steps 1–7 on pages 381–382, using the tiny hearts mold and the white opaque soap base.

2. Refer back to Step 2 on page 385, adding twelve drops blue and four drops red liquid colorant to the melted soap base.

3. Refer back to Steps 9–10 on page 383.

4. Using a potato peeler, shave the green opaque soap base until you have an ample amount of shavings.

5. Refer back to Steps 1–8 on pages 381–382, using the oval molds, the clear transparent soap base, and the scented oils.

6. Place a pinch of iridescent powder into the melted soap base. Using the chopstick, gently stir to evenly distribute the powder.

7. Pour a 1/4" layer of the melted soap base into prepared molds.

8. Place the tiny heart bars of soap, molded side down, and the green soap shavings into the mold. Using a toothpick, push the hearts and the shavings down into the layer of melted soap base and adjust as desired.

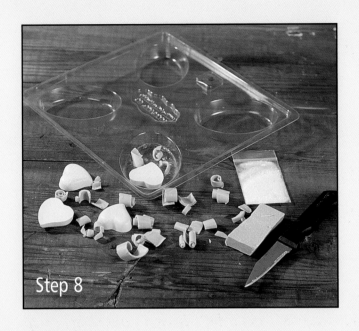

Step 8

9. Spray a light mist of rubbing alcohol on top of the transparent layer, tiny heart bars of soap, and green soap shavings.

   Note: Make certain to coat the layer of soap evenly to assure the soap layers bond together and do not separate.

10. Refer back to Steps 9–10 on page 383, pouring the remaining melted soap base into prepared molds, covering all tiny heart bars of soap and green soap shavings.

How do I embed decorative objects into glycerin melt-and-pour bars of soap?

A decorative effect is achieved when objects are embedded into bars of soap. There are many objects that work well for this purpose. Choose jewelry or seashells, or delight a child by using a small plastic toy. The finished bar of soap will look much like a clear paperweight.

Sea-life Soap Bars

Here's How:

1. Using a potato peeler, shave the green transparent and green opaque soap base until you have an ample amount of shavings. Shape the shavings to resemble sea grass.

2. Refer back to Steps 1–8 on pages 381–382, using the clear transparent soap base and the scented oils.

3. Pour a ¼" layer of the melted soap base into prepared molds.

4. Place the plastic sea-life figures and the green soap shavings into the mold. Using a toothpick, push the plastic figures and the shavings down into the layer of melted soap base and adjust as desired.

5. Using a paring knife, cut one thin piece of green opaque soap base to go along the bottoms of the oval- and rectangular-shaped molds to resemble the bottom of the ocean. Position these pieces in place.

6. Refer back to Steps 1–7 on pages 381–382, using the blue transparent soap base.

7. Spray a light mist of rubbing alcohol on top of the clear transparent layer, plastic figures, green soap shavings, and thin pieces of soap base.

   Note: Make certain to coat the layer of soap evenly to assure the soap layers bond together and do not separate.

8. Refer back to Steps 9–10 on page 383, pouring the blue transparent melted soap base into prepared molds, covering all plastic figures and green soap shavings.

What You Need To Get Started:

Cooking oil spray
Disposable chopstick, bamboo
Glycerin melt-and-pour soap bases:
 Blue transparent, ½ lb.
 Clear transparent, ½ lb.
 Green opaque, scraps
 Green transparent, scraps
2 Heat-resistant glass measuring cups
Kitchen knife, sharp unserrated
Molds:
 Circle
 Oval
 Rectangle
Paring knife
3 Plastic sea-life figures
Potato peeler
Rubbing alcohol
Scented oils:
 Eucalyptus fragrance, ⅛ tsp.
 Lavender essential, ⅛ tsp.
Skillet, deep
Spray bottle
Toothpick

411

How do I fully or partially embed oversized decorative objects into glycerin melt-and-pour bars of soap?

Plastic bath toys can be fully or partially embedded in soap using a common plastic storage container as the mold. A rubber duck can be completely immersed in the soap and emerge as the soap is used. A rubber dolphin—partially embedded—appears to be coming up out of the ocean.

Embedded Duck/Dolphin Soap Bars

Here's How:

1. Refer back to Steps 1–8 on pages 381–382, using the round container mold, the clear transparent soap base, and the rain fragrance scented oil.

2. Pour a ¾" layer of the melted soap base into prepared mold.

3. Place the rubber duck into the mold. Gently push it down into the layer of melted soap base and adjust as desired.

4. Spray a light mist of rubbing alcohol on top of the clear transparent layer and rubber duck.

   Note: Make certain to coat the layer of soap evenly to assure the soap layers bond together and do not separate.

5. Refer back to Steps 9–10 on page 383, pouring the remaining clear transparent melted soap base into prepared mold, completely covering the rubber duck.

6. Refer back to Steps 1–8 on pages 381–382, using the square container mold, the blue transparent soap base, and the ocean fragrance scented oil.

7. Pour a 1½"-2" layer of the melted soap base into prepared mold.

8. Place the rubber dolphin into the mold. Gently push it down into the layer of melted soap base and adjust as desired.

9. Refer back to Step 10 on page 383.

Design Tip: The depth of the mold will depend on the size of the object being fully or partially embedded.

What You Need To Get Started:

Cooking oil spray
Disposable chopstick, bamboo
Glycerin melt-and-pour soap bases:
  Blue transparent, ¾ lb.
  Clear transparent, 1 lb.
2 Heat-resistant glass measuring cups
Kitchen knife, sharp unserrated
Molds:
  Plastic container, 3" diameter x 4" deep
  Plastic container, 4" square x 3" deep
Rubber dolphin
Rubber duck
Rubbing alcohol
Scented oils:
  Ocean fragrance, ¼ tsp.
  Rain fragrance, ⅜ tsp.
Skillet, deep
Spray bottle

How do I mold and create scenes in a glycerin melt-and-pour loaf of soap?

A full-length mold, like a PVC® pipe, needs to be used when creating a continuous scene in a loaf of soap. When the shape is removed from the pipe, it can be cut and placed into the soap to create designs or scenes. In this case, the circular shapes have been cut into halves (the sailboat) and quarters (the sails).

414

Sailboat Soaps

Here's How:

1. Refer back to Steps 5–8 on page 402, preparing both pipe molds.

2. Refer back to Steps 2–7 on pages 381–382, using the ¾"-diameter pipe mold and the white opaque soap base.

3. Refer back to Step 9 on page 383.

4. Refer back to Step 14 on page 402.

5. Refer back to Steps 2–7 on pages 381–382, using the 1¼"-diameter pipe mold and the red transparent soap base.

6. Refer back to Step 9 on page 382.

7. Refer back to Step 14 on page 402.

8. Using the sharp kitchen knife, cut the molded white soap into quarters lengthwise, creating four triangular shapes (for the sails). Cut the molded red soap in half lengthwise (for the sailboat). Cut one thin strip, lengthwise, from one of the halves (for the mast).

   Note: It may be necessary to trim the soap to a 6" length to fit into the rectangular container mold.

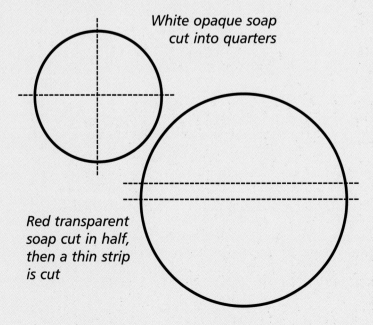

White opaque soap cut into quarters

Red transparent soap cut in half, then a thin strip is cut

9. Refer back to Steps 1–9 on pages 381–382, using the rectangular container mold, the blue transparent soap base, and ¼ tsp. of the scented oil.

10. Before the layer of blue transparent soap has solidified, place the red semicircle in the middle, allowing it to float.

11. Refer back to Steps 2–8 on pages 381–382, using the blue opaque soap base and ½ tsp. of the scented oil.

12. Spray a light mist of rubbing alcohol on top of the transparent blue layer and the sailboat.

    Note: Make certain to coat the layer of soap evenly to assure the soap layers bond together and do not separate.

13. Pour half of the blue opaque soap base into the mold.

14. Place the thin red strip on the sailboat for the mast. Hold in place until the mast stands on its own.

15. Place one of the white quarter-circles against the mast for the lower sail. Hold in place until the sail stands on its own.

16. Spray a light mist of rubbing alcohol on top of the opaque blue layer, the sailboat, mast, and lower sail.

17. Pour the remaining half of the blue opaque soap base into the mold.

18. Place one of the white quarter-circles against the mast for the upper sail. Position this sail on the opposite side from the lower sail. Hold in place until the sail stands on its own.

19. Allow to cool until solidified.

20. Refer to Step 10 on page 383.

21. Using the sharp kitchen knife, slice the soap into individual bars.

How do I mold glycerin melt-and-pour soap base inside a loofah sponge?

What You Need To Get Started:

Botanical:
  Powdered kelp, 1½ tsp.
Disposable chopstick,
  bamboo
Duct tape
Glycerin melt-and-pour
  soap base:
  White opaque, 1 lb.
Heat-resistant glass
  measuring cup
Kitchen knife,
  sharp serrated
Kitchen knife,
  sharp unserrated
Loofah sponge
Plastic wrap
Rubber bands
Scented oil:
  Rain fragrance, ¾ tsp.
Skillet, deep

Soap molded inside a loofah sponge combines the benefits of using a natural sponge and a gentle soap made with kelp to add soothing and healing qualities for healthier skin.

Soap-in-a-Loofah Sponge

Here's How:

1. Using a sharp serrated kitchen knife, slice the loofah sponge into three 1½" slices.

2. Tear two pieces of plastic wrap large enough to cover one end of each loofah sponge slice plus approximately 1½" to secure it around the sides.

3. Place the pieces of plastic wrap over one end of each loofah sponge slice and tightly stretch. Hold in place with rubber bands, then secure with duct tape to make certain the plastic wrap is thoroughly attached to the loofah.

4. Refer back to Steps 2–8 on pages 381–382.

5. Add the powdered kelp to the melted soap base. Using the chopstick, gently stir to evenly distribute the color.

6. Pour the melted soap base into the holes in the loofah sponge slices and allow to cool until solidified.

7. Remove the plastic wrap from the ends of the loofah sponge slices.

8. If necessary, scrape excess soap from the sides of the loofah sponge slices.

Design Tip: Peppermint, eucalyptus, and rosemary essential oils are pleasant as alternative fragrances. They can be used alone or in any combination.

How do I make small bars of soap and frost them to resemble petit fours?

Frosting soap is fun and easy! The results are simply beautiful and surprisingly real. Here is a recipe from Soapsations/Yaley Enterprises. These small bars of soap make wonderful bath and kitchen soap displays when placed in a small antique-type dish or bowl.

Frosted Petit Four Soap

Here's How:

1. Refer back to Steps 1–7 on pages 381–382, using the white opaque soap base.

2. Refer back to Step 2 on page 385, adding just enough liquid colorant to the melted soap base to render the desired shade of pastel.

   Note: You will want to make blue, green, pink, and yellow bars of soap.

3. Refer back to Step 8 on page 382, adding just enough scented oil to the melted soap base to render the desired fragrance.

4. Refer back to Steps 9–10 on page 383. Place the soap bars on a sheet of waxed paper and set aside.

5. Refer back to Steps 2–7 on pages 381–382, using half of the frosting soap bar.

Step 5

Note: The melted soap mixture should have a milky appearance.

6. Pour the melted frosting soap into a large mixing bowl.

   Note: One-quarter cup will more than triple in size when it is whipped.

7. Quickly add 2½ tablespoons of cool water to the melted frosting soap before the soap begins to set-up.

What You Need To Get Started:

Butter knife
Cake decorating book
Cooking oil spray
Cool water
Decorating tips
Disposable chopstick, bamboo
Electric mixer
Eye droppers
Frosting bag
Frosting soap bar
Glycerin melt-and-pour soap base:
    White opaque
Heat-resistant glass measuring cup
Kitchen knife, sharp unserrated
Liquid colorants:
    Blue
    Green
    Red
    Yellow
Measuring spoons
Mold:
    Petit four
Mixing bowl, large
Plastic spatula
Scented oils:
    Fruit-flavored scents
Skillet, deep
Waxed paper

Note: This will help prevent lumps from forming which will clog the decorating tip.

8. Using an electric mixer, immediately begin whipping the frosting soap on low speed. The soap will become bubbly, then creamy, then start to rise. Continue whipping on medium speed until the soap becomes a fluffy, dry texture similar to icing.

Note: The more you whip the soap, the fluffier it becomes and the easier it is to use. Whipping time is approximately three to four minutes before the frosting soap is ready to use.

Step 8

Notes:

If you find that the frosting is too dry and is hard to push out of the frosting bag, just add five to ten more drops of cool water to the whipped frosting and mix well. This will soften the frosting.

The whipped soap can be stored for several months in an air-tight zipper lock bag in the refrigerator.

9. Using an eye dropper, add liquid colorant to the whipped frosting. Using a butter knife, gently stir to evenly distribute the color.

Note: When using two or more colors to render the desired color, use a separate eye dropper for each color of liquid colorant.

Step 9

10. Place the scallop tip on the frosting bag. Using a plastic spatula, fill the frosting bag with the colored frosting.

11. Trim around the edge of several petit four soaps.

12. Using the appropriate tips and colors of frosting, embellish the top of each soap with a flower and a couple leaves.

Note: The instructions for a number of various flowers and leaves can be found in any cake decorating book.

Caution: If children will be using the soap, use a perfume-type fragrance and not a fruit-flavored scent. The soap just might be too tempting to resist!

How do I use the cold-process method to make basic soap?

When making basic soap using the cold-process method, it is a chemical reaction between the lye and the melted fats that makes it possible. Just about any fat or combination of fats may be used when making cold-process soap. Soap qualities—such as the hardness or softness of the bar, whether it is harsh or mild, the size and amount of bubbles it produces— are determined by the types of fats used. The amount of lye used is determined by the saponification value of each fat and the quantity of the fats to be used.

Saponification charts are available in more advanced soapmaking manuals when you become more adventurous and wish to do some experimenting in creating your own soap formulas.

What You Need To Get Started:

Bath towels
Blanket
Cooling rack
Cutting board
Disposable chopstick, bamboo
Distilled water
Fats:
  Coconut oil
  Olive oil
  Vegetable shortening
Glass juice jar with lid, 48 oz.
Hammer
Kitchen knife, sharp unserrated
Laboratory thermometer (with stainless steel shaft), 0° to 180°F
Large nail
Latex gloves
Lye crystals
Masking tape
Measuring cup with pouring spout
Mold:
  Plastic or wooden container with lid
Plastic garbage bag
Protective eyewear
Scale (must be able to weigh up to 5 lb.)
Scented oils:
  Eucalyptus fragrance, 1 tsp.
  Peppermint fragrance, 2 tsp.
Stainless steel stockpot, 12 qt.
Wooden spoon

One Batch of Basic Cold-process Soap Recipe

Distilled water, 33 oz.
Fats:
  Coconut oil, 22 oz.
  Olive oil, 29 oz.
  Shortening, 38 oz.
Lye crystals, 12 oz.
Mold: 11" long x 9" wide x 3" deep

Note: When using lye, use only glass, plastic, stainless steel, or wood—aluminum must not be used. In addition, do not substitute liquid lye for lye crystals.

Eucalyptus/Peppermint Soap

Here's How:

1. Prepare mold by lining with a plastic garbage bag. Using masking tape, secure the garbage bag in place.

   Caution: Make certain the garbage bag is as free of wrinkles as possible to prevent creases from forming in the soap.

2. Using a hammer and a large nail, punch two holes in the lid of the glass jar, large enough for the thermometer shaft to pass through.

   Note: When the lid is placed on the jar, these holes will allow the contents to breathe.

3. Place the glass jar in the kitchen sink. Using a measuring cup with a pouring spout, measure and pour 33 oz. of distilled water into the glass jar.

4. Thoroughly dry the measuring cup and place it on the scale. Adjust the scale to zero so it does not weigh the measuring cup. Carefully pour the lye crystals into the measuring cup until it weighs 12 oz.

   Caution: Lye (sodium hydroxide) is a caustic soda and can be fatal if swallowed. Keep lye out of the reach of children. When working with lye, make certain to wear latex gloves and protective eyewear. Be careful not to breathe in any lye crystals as they can cause serious burns to sensitive tissues.

5. Carefully pour the lye crystals into the glass jar of water.

   Caution: Water should never be poured into lye. It should always be the lye that is added to the water. If the skin comes into contact with lye, it will begin to feel slippery, itch, and/or burn. If any of these sensations occur, immediately rinse the area with vinegar and then running water. If the lye splashes into your eyes, immediately follow the manufacturer's directions on the lye container. Lye can also remove paint. If any should splatter onto a painted work surface, wash it off immediately with water and a mild detergent.

6. Using a disposable chopstick, gently stir the water and lye solution until the lye crystals are completely dissolved.

   Caution: If the lye crystals do not dissolve completely, hazardous chunks of lye can be left in the finished soap.

7. Place the lid (with holes) on the glass jar. The lye solution will immediately begin to heat up and the glass jar will become very hot. It will take the solution several hours to cool—making the solution in the evening and allowing it to cool overnight works well.

   Caution: Do not attempt to move the glass jar from the kitchen sink while the jar is hot. Keep out of the reach of children and pets! It is also a good idea to label the jar with a warning so that family members are not in any danger.

8. Once the lye solution has cooled down, place the shaft of the thermometer into one of the holes in the lid and measure the temperature of the solution. You want the solution to be 105°F. If the solution needs to be warmed up, a warm water bath may be necessary. If the solution needs to be cooled down, a cool water bath may be necessary.

   Note: The thermometer that you are using must be extremely accurate as the temperatures of the lye solution and of the melted fats are critical.

9. At the same time you are getting the lye solution to 105°F, the fats need to be prepared. Refer back to recipe on page 421. Place all of the fats into a stainless steel stockpot and heat on low until the fats are barely melted. Measure the temperature of the fats. You want the fats to be 105°F.

   Caution: The temperatures of the fats and the lye solution must be exactly the same.

It may be easier to use two separate ther-mometers—one for the melted fats, the other for the lye solution.

10. When the fully melted fats and the lye solution reach the same temperatures, they are ready to be combined.

    Caution: Turn the burners on the stove off.

11. Remove the stockpot from the stove and slowly pour the lye solution into the fats, stirring constantly with a wooden spoon. When the lye solution and the fats are combined, there will be a noticeable change in the consistency of the mixture.

    Caution: Make certain to wear latex gloves and protective eyewear.

Step 12

Step 11

12. Continue stirring until the mixture begins to "trace." This process can take from 20 to 90 minutes.

    Note: Trace means when the mixture be-comes thick enough that when drizzled from the wooden spoon onto the surface of the remaining mixture in the stockpot, it will leave a visible trail before it dis-appears.

13. Add scented oils to the mixture. Using the wooden spoon, gently stir to evenly distribute the fragrance.

14. Immediately pour the mixture into prepared mold and place the lid on the mold. Do not cover the top of the mixture with the plastic garbage bag—leave the plastic hanging over the edges of the mold.

    Caution: If there is too much time taken between trace and pouring the mixture into the mold, the soap could begin to set up in the stockpot.

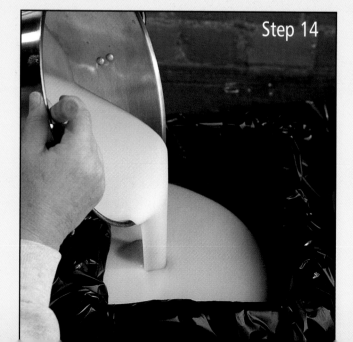
Step 14

15. Cover the mold with bath towels and a blanket to keep the soap at a controlled temperature. Place it out of any drafty areas and allow to cool until solidified (a minimum of 24 hours).

    Caution: If the soap is allowed to cool too quickly it will not set-up properly. Do not get impatient, the soap must be allowed to sit undisturbed for a minimum of 24 hours.

16. After the initial 24 hours, unwrap the mold and remove the lid. Test the soap with your fingers to see if it is firm. If the soap is not set-up, replace the lid and rewrap the mold with the bath towels. Allow to sit for an additional 24 hours.

17. Lift the plastic garbage bag and the soap out of the mold.

Step 17

18. Place the soap onto a large cutting board that has been dedicated to soapmaking. Using a sharp kitchen knife, slice the soap into individual bars.

19. Place the bars of soap on a cooling rack and allow to cure for three to four weeks.

    Note: A thin, powdery surface on top of the soap is common and can be trimmed off. However, if hard, shiny spots appear in the soap, it has not properly saponified and lye

has been left in the soap. In this case, the soap must not be used! It is important to know that though lye is used to make soap, its caustic characteristics are altered during the saponification and curing processes.

Step 18

Step 19

Note: If you are making this soap for rebatching purposes, leave out the scented oils and grate after unmolding.

How do I add botanicals to cold-process soap?

Botanicals added to cold-process soap add color, texture, and/or benefits to the skin. Calendula leaves have healing properties so are great for soaps made for sensitive skin.

Lavender/Mango/Tangerine Soap

Here's How:

1. Refer back to Steps 1–13 on pages 423–424, using the recipe at right, below.

2. Add ground calendula leaves to the traced mixture. Using the wooden spoon, stir until the leaves are well mixed into the mixture.

3. Refer back to Steps 14–19 on pages 424–425.

Design Tips:

*Try using sunflower fragrance scented oil to complement the sunflower oil.
Try substituting ground chamomile for the calendula leaves.*

What You Need To Get Started:

Bath towels
Blanket
Botanical:
 Calendula leaves,
 ½ cup ground
Cooling rack
Cutting board
Disposable chopstick,
 bamboo
Distilled water
Fats:
 Coconut oil
 Olive oil
 Palm oil
 Sunflower oil
Glass juice jar
 with lid, 48 oz.
Hammer
Kitchen knife,
 sharp unserrated
Laboratory
 thermometer (with
 stainless steel shaft),
 0° to 180° F
Large nail
Latex gloves
Lye crystals
Masking tape

Measuring cup
 with pouring spout
Mold:
 Plastic or wooden
 container with lid
Plastic garbage bag
Protective eyewear
Scale (must be able to
 weigh up to 5 lb.)
Scented oils:
 Lavender essential, 1 tsp.
 Mango fragrance, 2 tsp.
 Tangerine essential, 3 tsp.
Stainless steel
 stockpot, 12 qt.
Wooden spoon

One Batch of Cold-process Soap Recipe

Distilled water, 32 oz.
Fats:
 Coconut oil, 30 oz.
 Olive oil, 14 oz.
 Palm oil, 24 oz.
 Sunflower oil, 18 oz.

Lye crystals, 12 oz.
Mold: 11" long x
 9" wide x 3" deep

*Refer to Note
on page 421.*

How do I substitute exotic fats for basic fats when making cold-process soap?

The basic fats used in the cold-process method of making soap include coconut oil, olive oil, palm oil, and/or vegetable shortening. Each of these fats has unique benefits including skin conditioning and good latherability. In addition, a nice hard bar of soap that will last longer than other soaps is produced. In this case, other fats have been included for added skin conditioning benefits.

Rosebud/Sandalwood/Vanilla Cold-process Soap Bars

Here's How:

1. Refer back to Steps 1–19 on pages 423–425, using the recipe at right.

What You Need To Get Started:

Bath towels
Blanket
Cooling rack
Cutting board
Disposable chopstick, bamboo
Distilled water
Fats:
  Almond oil
  Apricot kernel oil
  Coconut oil
  Jojoba oil
  Olive oil
  Palm oil
  Shea butter
Glass juice jar with lid, 48 oz.
Hammer
Kitchen knife, sharp unserrated
Laboratory thermometer (with stainless steel shaft), 0° to 180°F

Large nail
Latex gloves
Lye crystals
Masking tape
Measuring cup with pouring spout
Mold:
  Plastic or wooden container with lid
Plastic garbage bag
Protective eyewear
Scale (must be able to weigh up to 5 lb.)
Scented oils:
  Rosebud fragrance, 2 tsp.
  Sandalwood essential, 1 tsp.
  Vanilla fragrance, 5 tsp.
Stainless steel stockpot, 12 qt.
Wooden spoon

One Batch of Cold-process Soap Recipe

Distilled water, 31 oz.
Fats:
  Almond oil, 5 oz.
  Apricot kernel oil, 5 oz.
  Coconut oil, 36 oz.
  Jojoba oil, 2 oz.
  Olive oil, 14 oz.

Palm oil, 18 oz.
Shea butter, 2 oz.
Lye crystals, 12 oz.
Mold: 11" long x 9" wide x 3" deep

Refer to Note on page 421.

How do I use the rebatching method to make bars of soap?

Soap can be made by using grated cold-process soap that has been mixed with liquid (in this case, goat's milk) and slow-heated until they are combined. Grated cold-process soap which gives the same benefits and aesthetics as homemade cold-process soap can also be purchased.

The advantages to making rebatched soap is that you can make one large batch and divide it up into several smaller batches of soap featuring different colors and/or scents.

Honey/Oatmeal Soap Bars

Here's How:

1. Prepare mold by spraying the inside with cooking oil. Wipe away excess oil.

2. Place grated soap and milk in a crockpot and heat on low for 45 minutes.

3. Using a wooden spoon, stir the grated soap and milk mixture.

   Note: If the milk has been fully absorbed and the mixture is the consistency of oatmeal, it is ready to be molded. If it is not ready, continue to heat, checking at 15-minute intervals. If the mixture appears too dry, a small amount of liquid may be added.

   If the mixture is heated at too high a temperature or for too long, it may turn orange. To help prevent this, make certain the contents in the crockpot fill it at least half way. The "orange color" will only affect the visual appearance of the soap.

   If the mixture is too lumpy, a wire whisk can be used at this point to work out the lumps.

What You Need To Get Started:

Botanical:
  Oatmeal,
  ½ cup finely ground
Cold-process soap:
  Unscented,
  2 lb. grated
Cooking oil spray
Cooling rack
Crockpot, 2 qt.
Cutting board
Goat's milk, 16 oz.
Honey, 2 tbsp.
Kitchen knife,
  sharp unserrated
Mold:
  Plastic container,
  9" long x
  5" wide x 3½" deep
Plastic spatula
Scented oils:
  Chamomile fragrance,
  ½ tsp.
  Vanilla fragrance,
  1 tsp.
Wooden spoon

4. Add scented oils and honey to the melted mixture. Using the wooden spoon, gently stir to evenly distribute the fragrance and the honey.

Step 4

Step 6

5. Add oatmeal to the melted mixture. Using the wooden spoon, stir until the oatmeal is well mixed into the mixture.

6. Pour the melted soap mixture into prepared mold. Using a plastic spatula, gently press the mixture into the mold.

   Caution: Make certain to press thoroughly to avoid air pockets from forming in the mixture.

7. Allow the soap to cool, uncovered, until solidified (approximately 24–48 hours).

8. Turn the mold over and release the soap.

9. Place the soap onto a large cutting board that has been dedicated to soapmaking. Using a sharp kitchen knife, slice the soap into individual bars.

Step 7

10. Place the bars of soap on a cooling rack and allow to cure for three to four weeks.

How do I use the rebatching method to make balls of soap with botanical infusions?

Using the rebatching method is one of the easiest ways to make soap balls. The rebatched soap can be divided, allowing for each division to feature a different color or scent.

In this case, the liquid being added to the grated cold-process soap is an infusion that has been derived from a botanical which has been allowed to steep. This is a good way to get the benefits of an herb, such as antiseptic and astringent, without having the "bulk" in the soap.

Rosemary/Orange/Chamomile Infused Soap Balls

Here's How:

1. Bring the distilled water to a boil in a saucepan.

2. Place the rosemary botanical into a glass jar.

3. Using a measuring cup with a pouring spout, pour the boiling distilled water into the glass jar.

4. Place the lid on the glass jar and allow the rosemary infusion to steep (a minimum of 4 hours). Strain the steeped rosemary infusion to remove the bulk.

Note: Making the rosemary infusion the night before it is to be used is recommended to assure it has been allowed to steep properly.

5. Preheat oven to 180°F. Place grated soap and 3/4 cup rosemary infusion in a covered casserole dish and heat in oven for 45 minutes.

6. Using a wooden spoon, stir the grated soap and rosemary infusion mixture.

What You Need To Get Started:

Botanicals:
   Chamomile, 1 tbsp.
   Rosemary, 1½ tbsp.
Cold-process soap:
   Unscented,
   1 lb. grated
Cookie sheet
Cooking oil spray
Cooling rack
Covered casserole dish
Distilled water, 1 cup
Glass canning jar
   with lid, 1 pint
Liquid colorant:
   Orange
Measuring cup
   with pouring spout
Saucepan
Scented oil:
   Orange essential,
   1½ tsp.
Strainer
Waxed paper
Wooden spoon

Note: If the rosemary infusion has been fully absorbed and the mixture is the consistency of oatmeal, it is ready to be molded. If it is not ready, continue to heat, checking at 5-minute intervals. If the mixture appears too dry, a small amount of liquid may be added.

If the mixture is heated at too high a temperature or for too long, it may turn orange. To help prevent this, make certain the contents in the casserole dish fill it at least half way. The "orange color" will only affect the visual appearance of the soap.

7. Refer back to Step 2 on page 385, adding nine drops (or more, if desired) orange liquid colorant to the melted soap base. Mix with the wooden spoon.

8. Refer back to Step 8 on page 382. Mix with the wooden spoon.

9. Using the wooden spoon, thoroughly stir in the chamomile.

10. Allow to cool until the soap can be handled and will hold its shape.

11. Prepare cookie sheet by covering with waxed paper.

12. Spray your hands with cooking oil and mold the soap into balls. The balls can be any size desired. Place individual balls onto cookie sheet.

13. Over the next 24 hours, periodically rotate the balls to prevent them from getting a flat side. Remold by hand as necessary.

14. Place the balls of soap on a cooling rack and allow to cure for three to four weeks.

To make rosemary/lemon infused balls of soap, substitute four drops of yellow liquid colorant for the orange liquid colorant. In addition, substitute 1 tsp. lemon essential and ¼ tsp. rosemary essential scented oils for the orange essential scented oil and the chamomile botanical.

How do I mold
soap-on-a-rope?

**What You Need
To Get Started:**

Cold-process soap:
 Unscented,
 1 lb. grated
Cookie sheet
Cooking oil spray
Cooling rack
Covered casserole dish
Glass mixing bowl
Measuring cup
Milk, ¾ cup
Waxed paper
Wooden spoon

Using the rebatching method, this novel approach is the basis for making his and hers soaps on a rope. Each one is customized with scented oils and botanicals to complement the characteristics of each gender.

His and Hers Soaps-on-a-Rope

Here's How:

1. Preheat oven to 180°F. Place grated soap and milk in a covered casserole dish and heat in oven for 45 minutes.

2. Refer back to Step 3 on page 431.

3. Divide the soap mixture in half, placing half the mixture into a glass mixing bowl.

4. **To make his soap:** Add five drops green liquid colorant to the melted soap mixture in the casserole dish. Using the wooden spoon, gently stir to evenly distribute the color.

5. Add bay rum fragrance and lime essential scented oils to the melted mixture. Using the wooden spoon, gently stir to evenly distribute the fragrances.

6. Thoroughly stir in the grated lime peel. Set aside to cool.

7. **To make her soap:** Add two drops red liquid colorant to the melted soap mixture in the glass mixing bowl. Using the wooden spoon, gently stir to evenly distribute the color.

8. Add rosebud fragrance and sandalwood essential scented oils to the melted mixture. Using the wooden spoon, gently stir to evenly distribute the fragrances.

9. Thoroughly stir in the dried rose petals. Set aside to cool.

His Soap:	Her Soap:

Botanical:
  Fresh lime peel,
  grated
Cotton cording,
  ⅓ yd.
Liquid colorant:
  Green
Scented oils:
  Bay rum fragrance,
  ½ tsp.
  Lime essential,
  ¼ tsp.
	Botanicals:
	  3 Rose buds, dried
	  Rose petals,
	  1½ tbsp. dried
	Liquid colorant:
	  Red
	Ribbon, 1 yd.
	Scented oils:
	  Rosebud fragrance,
	  ½ tsp.
	  Sandalwood essential,
	  ⅛ tsp.

10. Refer back to Steps 10–12 on page 434. The hanging device must be added while you are molding the soap into balls.

11. **For his soap:** Fold a length of cotton cording in half and tie a knot at the ends. When molding the soap, make certain to leave the entire knot showing, allowing the cording to run through the center of the soap, extending out the top of the ball.

12. **For her soap:** Fold a 7" length of ribbon in half and tie a knot at the ends. When molding the soap, leave only the "loop" extending out the top of the ball.

13. Press the dried rose buds into the soap for a decorative effect. Thread the remaining length of ribbon through the loop and tie a knot at the ends.

14. Refer back to Steps 13–14 on page 434.

How do I make bubbling bath oil?

Handmade soap need not be limited to solid forms. Liquid soap bases can be purchased and personalized with favorite scents, as well as Vitamin E, glycerin, and almond or apricot oils for the benefits that they provide the skin. Here's a recipe by Marie Browning.

The liquid soap and scented oils will separate to create an attractive layered look. Shake the bottle well before pouring the bubbling bath oil into your bath.

What You Need To Get Started:

Almond oil, ½ cup
Disposable chopstick, bamboo
Glycerin, 1 tbsp.
Liquid colorants:
   Orange
   Red
Liquid soap base, ½ cup
Measuring cup with pouring spout
Plastic bottle with flip-top cap, 8 oz.
Scented oil:
   Tangerine fragrance, 20 drops

Tangerine Bubbling Bath Oil

Here's How:

1. Combine the liquid soap base, tangerine scented oil, and four drops red liquid colorant in a measuring cup with a pouring spout. Using a disposable chopstick, gently stir to thoroughly mix.

2. Add the glycerin, almond oil, and ten drops orange liquid colorant to the liquid soap mixture. Using the chopstick, gently stir to thoroughly mix.

3. Carefully pour the liquid soap mixture into the plastic bottle.

   Note: The liquid soap and scented oils will separate into two colored layers after approximately 30 minutes.

How do I make other personal care items?

Salt glow, bath salts, and massage oils, scented to match a favorite glycerin melt-and-pour, rebatched, or cold-process soap, complement one another. When placed in carefully selected bottles and jars, the perfect gift set is created.

Salt Glow

Here's How:

1. Place sea salt, grapeseed oil, and scented oils in a wide-mouth jar and mix well. Place a scalloped shell on top of the mixture. This shell will be used to scoop the salt glow out of the jar when ready to use. Place the lid on the jar.

2. To use the salt glow, scoop an appropriate amount out of the jar. Gently rub the salt glow over areas of the body to remove dry skin. Thoroughly rinse salt glow off with running water.

Bath Salts

Here's How:

1. Place epsom, ice cream rock, and sea salts in mixing bowl and mix well.

2. Add glycerin, liquid colorants, and scented oils. Gently stir to evenly distribute the color.

3. Spoon the mixture into a wide-mouth jar and place a scalloped shell on top of the mixture. This shell will be used to scoop the bath salt out of the jar when ready to use. Place the lid on the jar.

4. To use the bath salts, place three to five scoops under running water.

Massage Oil

Here's How:

1. Place oils and liquid Vitamin E in bottle and mix well.

2. Place assorted shells in bottle.

3. To use the massage oil, place a small amount into the palm of your hand and use for massage.

What You Need To Get Started:

Salt Glow:
Grapeseed oil, ¼ cup
Scented oils:
Rosewood essential, ¼ tsp.
  Sandalwood essential,
  ¼ tsp.
  Vanilla fragrance, ½ tsp.
Sea salt, 1 cup
Shell, scalloped
Wide-mouth jar with lid, 32 oz.

Bath Salts:
Epsom salt, ¾ cup
Glycerin, 1 tbsp.
Ice cream rock salt, 1½ cups
Liquid colorants:
  Blue, 2 drops
  Orange, 8 drops
  Red, 1 drop
Mixing bowl
Scented oils:
  Rosewood essential, ¼ tsp.
  Sandalwood essential,
  ¼ tsp. Vanilla fragrance,
  ½ tsp.
Sea salt, ¾ cup
Shell, scalloped
Wide-mouth jar with lid, 48 oz.

Massage Oil:
Almond oil, ¾ cup
Bottle with sealing lid
  or cork, 12 oz.
Grapeseed oil, ¾ cup
Liquid Vitamin E, 6 drops
Scented oils:
  Rosewood essential, ⅜ tsp.
  Sandalwood essential,
  ⅜ tsp. Vanilla fragrance,
  ¾ tsp.
Shells, assorted small

METRIC CONVERSIONS

INCHES TO MILLIMETRES AND CENTIMETRES

MM-Millimetres   CM-Centimetres

INCHES	MM	CM	INCHES	CM	INCHES	CM
1/8	3	0.9	9	22.9	30	76.2
1/4	6	0.6	10	25.4	31	78.7
3/8	10	1.0	11	27.9	32	81.3
1/2	13	1.3	12	30.5	33	83.8
5/8	16	1.6	13	33.0	34	86.4
3/4	19	1.9	14	35.6	35	88.9
7/8	22	2.2	15	38.1	36	91.4
1	25	2.5	16	40.6	37	94.0
1 1/4	32	3.2	17	43.2	38	96.5
1 1/2	38	3.8	18	45.7	39	99.1
1 3/4	44	4.4	19	48.3	40	101.6
2	51	5.1	20	50.8	41	104.1
2 1/2	64	6.4	21	53.3	42	106.7
3	76	7.6	22	55.9	43	109.2
3 1/2	89	8.9	23	58.4	44	111.8
4	102	10.2	24	61.0	45	114.3
4 1/2	114	11.4	25	63.5	46	116.8
5	127	12.7	26	66.0	47	119.4
6	152	15.2	27	68.6	48	121.9
7	178	17.8	28	71.1	49	124.5
8	203	20.3	29	73.7	50	127.0

YARDS TO METRES

YARDS	METRES	YARDS	METRES	YARDS	METRES	YARDS	METRES	YARDS	METRES
1/8	0.11	2 1/8	1.94	4 1/8	3.77	6 1/8	5.60	8 1/8	7.43
1/4	0.23	2 1/4	2.06	4 1/4	3.89	6 1/4	5.72	8 1/4	7.54
3/8	0.34	2 3/8	2.17	4 3/8	4.00	6 3/8	5.83	8 3/8	7.66
1/2	0.46	2 1/2	2.29	4 1/2	4.11	6 1/2	5.94	8 1/2	7.77
5/8	0.57	2 5/8	2.40	4 5/8	4.23	6 5/8	6.06	8 5/8	7.89
3/4	0.69	2 3/4	2.51	4 3/4	4.34	6 3/4	6.17	8 3/4	8.00
7/8	0.80	2 7/8	2.63	4 7/8	4.46	6 7/8	6.29	8 7/8	8.12
1	0.91	3	2.74	5	4.57	7	6.40	9	8.23
1 1/8	1.03	3 1/8	2.86	5 1/8	4.69	7 1/8	6.52	9 1/8	8.34
1 1/4	1.14	3 1/4	2.97	5 1/4	4.80	7 1/4	6.63	9 1/4	8.46
1 3/8	1.26	3 3/8	3.09	5 3/8	4.91	7 3/8	6.74	9 3/8	8.57
1 1/2	1.37	3 1/2	3.20	5 1/2	5.03	7 1/2	6.86	9 1/2	8.69
1 5/8	1.49	3 5/8	3.31	5 5/8	5.14	7 5/8	6.97	9 5/8	8.80
1 3/4	1.60	3 3/4	3.43	5 3/4	5.26	7 3/4	7.09	9 3/4	8.92
1 7/8	1.71	3 7/8	3.54	5 7/8	5.37	7 7/8	7.20	9 7/8	9.03
2	1.83	4	3.66	6	5.49	8	7.32	10	9.14

INDEX

Beading

Candlemaking

Polymer Clay

Rubber Stamping

Scrapbooking

Soapmaking